CLASSIC
SCOTS
COOKERY

CLASSIC
SCOTS
COOKERY

CATHERINE BROWN

ANGELS' SHARE

Published by the Angels' Share
an imprint of
Neil Wilson Publishing
www.nwp.co.uk

ISBN: 978-1-903238-40-0

Ebook ISBN: 978-1-906476-56-4

Typeset in Sabon
Designed by Belstane
Printed and bound in the EU

CONTENTS

4. Meat

5. Grains and Vegetables

6 Fruits and Puddings

7. Baking

8. Sweeties

9. Preserves and Pickles

10. Hogmanay Halloween and Christmas

INTRODUCTION

MARMALADE, porridge, grouse, whisky and haggis are just a few Scottish food classics that have travelled the globe. They owe their fame, largely, to the millions of expatriate Scots who have taken these eating and drinking habits with them. What Scot in deepest Africa could survive Burns Night without haggis and a bottle of whisky?

But Scottish classics have made it on their own reputation too. Seafood from cool, unpolluted waters is undisputed for quality. There are sweetly succulent soft fruits that mature best in the long, mild Scottish summers. Excellent beef and lamb come from rich grasslands. And there is the unique distillation of whisky, the water of life.

Whisky and smoked salmon have been the trailblazers, successfully exported to every corner of the globe. Now other seafoods – oysters, mussels, langoustines, crabs and lobsters – are catching up. Marmalade has made it up Mount Everest and grouse is flown to top restaurants in London, Paris and New York.

In the meantime, at home, a growing band of enlightened Scottish chefs have taken up the prime quality, locally-produced tag on their menus. They promote Scottish foods in season, support local producers and provide visitors with a unique eating experience.

Though Scotland is a small country its landscape varies dramatically. Fertile agricultural lands in the East and wild mountains in the North, together with seas and islands, shape the nature of the produce and the cooking of the people.

In early times, pastoral Celts herded animals and followed the grazing seasons making milk, butter and cheese throughout the spring and summer. The seafaring Norse salted and smoked fish, to save them for winter supplies. Both traditions survive in a variety of local cheeses and many fish delicacies from 'smokies' to 'finnans'.

The eating traditions have also been shaped by sources of heat and cooking equipment. Slow-burning peat, rather than coal, created cooking heat for much of the population in early times, which resulted in a tradition of slow simmering and stewing in a large pot over a gentle peat fire. Scotch Broth, haggis and Clootie Dumpling are just a few of the classics that depend on the long slow simmer.

On the baking front, few Scots had ovens and baked mostly on a flat metal plate – a girdle – with a handle that was hooked over the peat fire. It was on this that oatcakes were first made, followed by lighter bannocks, soda scones, pancakes and crumpets. Not every home today has a girdle, but every commercial baker still has a hot plate. (English supermarkets in Scotland have had to equip their in-house bakeries with hot plates for the popular girdle-baked scones, pancakes and crumpets.)

Though oatmeal only began to take over from barley as the staple grain around the end of the 17th century, it is now *the* Scottish grain. More versatile than barley, which is now mostly used for distilling whisky, the advantage of oatmeal is that it can be ground into so many different 'cuts': 'pinhead' for haggis, 'coarse' for mealie puddings, 'medium' for oatcakes and 'fine' for bannocks.

Oatmeal, in porridge and brose taken with milk, became the backbone of the Scottish diet for most of the 18th and 19th centuries and is reputed to have given Scots of previous generations their sturdy health. In the 1980s, an American professor discovered from his researches that one of the reasons for this was a gummy soluble fibre in oats, which helped to prevent heart disease in his patients. The news popularised oat-eating throughout the world. But you need look no further than classic Scottish cooking for the most original and frequent use, today, of healthy oatmeal.

Catherine Brown

BROTH CLASSICS

Scotch Broth

'This is the comfortable *pot-au-feu* of Scotland – the pot luck of homely and hearty old-world hospitality,' says Meg Dods in *The Cook and Housewife's Manual* (1826).

For kitchen routines of her day, the attraction of Scotch Broth is its convenience. Made with a large piece of beef or mutton, preferably salted for a week, it provides soup and meat for several days. It is also versatile, in that it changes with the seasons – roots in winter, greens in summer – but always with barley and dried peas. The old style 'pot' barley, without the bran removed, is preferred to polished 'pearly-white', which cooks too quickly and releases too much thick starch into the broth.

Scots can thank their early historical connection with France, during the period of Auld Alliance, for the comfortable *pot-au-feu* broths, as well as the frugal habit of cooking in a pot rather than roasting on a spit. Scotch Broth, however, also becomes popular in England around the late-eighteenth century, though according to Meg Dods it is not always served up in an approved Scottish style.

'English books of cookery, order a sauce for meat boiled in Scotch Broth, of red wine, mushroom-catsup, and gravy with cut pickles – a piece of absurd extravagance, completely at variance with the character and properties of the better part of the dish – namely with the bland, balsamic barley-broth of Scotland.'

An early Scottish recipe in Elizabeth Cleland's *A New and Easy Method of Cookery* (Edinburgh, 1759) includes: a chopped leg of beef, a fowl, carrots, barley, celery, sweet herbs, onions, parsley and a few marigolds. The eighteenth-century traveller, Faujas de Saint-Fond, while on a trip round Mull is served with:

'a large dish of Scots soup, composed of broth of beef, mutton and sometimes fowl, mixed with a little oatmeal, onions, parsley and a considerable quantity of peas. Instead of bread, as in France, small slices of mutton and giblets of fowl are thrown into this soup'.

But it is the influential, and outspoken critic of the Scots, the English lexicographer, Dr Samuel Johnson, who first spreads the word about the merits of Scotch Broth. In August 22, 1773 when Johnson is dining with his travelling friend, James Boswell, at the New Inn on Castle Street, Aberdeen dinner begins with a tureen of Scotch Broth with barley and peas in it. Johnson eats several

platefuls. He seems very fond of the dish, remarks Boswell in his journal.
'You never ate it before?' asks Boswell.
'No, sir; but I don't care how soon I eat it again.'
When writing later to an English friend, Johnson remarks:
'Barley broth is a constant dish and is made well in every house.'

Cock-a-Leekie

'Cocky-leeky: so thick that the ladle stauns o' itsel,' is how James Hogg the Ettrick Shepherd describes the version that he enjoys with his cronies, Christopher North and Timothy Tickler, in their favourite Edinburgh tavern. The racy column about their ambrosial nights (*Noctes Ambrosiana*) which appears in *Blackwoods Magazine* from 1822 to 1835 also refers to hotch potch, which, along with cocky-leeky, they think the two best soups ever created.

Ageing cockerels and mature hens are just the thing to give this broth 'body' and flavour. And as tasty hens and cockerels range freely in everyone's backyard, so sturdy leeks – king of the soup onions – grow in family vegetable gardens. Along the Lothian coastline to the east of Edinburgh market gardeners become so famous for their leeks that their variety of the Common Winter Leek is known as the Musselburgh leek. It is the perfect partner for an old bird.

Distinguished from other leeks by its long leaf, (or 'green flag') and short white, it is described by William Robinson in *The Vegetable Garden* (1885) as a '*poireau du Musselburgh*'.

'The fine qualities of this leek are much better known to the Welsh, Scotch and French than to the English or Irish,' he says.

Its fine qualities are to do with the flavour, from its long green flag, as well as its winter hardiness. When it is not available in summer, cabbage, spinach and/or parsley are used instead.

According to the *Scottish National Dictionary*, the first literary mention of cocky-leeky is in the *Ochtertyre House Book* of 1737, when dinner frequently includes 'cockie leekie'. However it is Meg Dods who gives the first recipe for the dish in her *Cook and Housewife's Manual* (1826):

'Boil from four to six pounds of good shin-beef, well broken, till the liquor is very good. Strain it, and put to it a capon or large fowl, trussed for boiling, and when it boils, half the quantity of blanched leeks intended to be used, well cleaned, and cut in inch lengths or longer. Skim this carefully. In half an hour add the remaining part of the leeks and a seasoning of pepper and salt. The soup must be very thick of leeks, and the first part of them must be boiled down into the soup till it becomes a green lubricous compound. Sometimes the capon is served in the tureen with the cock-a-leekie. Some people thicken it with the fine part of oatmeal.'

Cullen Skink

Fishwives wait on the beach for their husbands, who are returning with the day's catch. The men have been out fishing since dawn in their three-man sailing yawls, hauling in fish on baited lines until the boat is full. It's a good catch for these East Coast fisher folk of the 1850s. The sea is teeming with fish.

The men lay out the day's catch on the beach – haddock, whiting, cuddies, skate and dogfish – and begin to divide it into three equal shares. Their wives pack it into long wicker creels. Then each fishwife heaves the creel onto her back and, in her stout black leather boots, her thick navy worsted skirt, and warm woollen shawl round her shoulders, sets off to walk from village to village with her heavy load.

Her regular customers are delighted to see her and get some of the fresh catch. At farms, she barters her fish for their cheese, eggs and butter. She is always happy to gut and clean the fish. There are many offers of cups of tea and a rest.

Tuesdays, Wednesdays, Fridays and Saturdays are 'country' days. On Mondays and Thursdays she stays at home to gut, salt and smoke surplus fish in her bothan – a wooden smoking shed on the strip of land between her fisher-house and the sea. It has no chimney, but a pile of hardwood sawdust on an earth floor mixed with a few fir cones for extra flavour.

She lights the fire, then damps it down so it will just smoulder, and fill the shed with smoke. Today, some large haddock have been gutted, split open and beheaded. After a soaking in salt, she hangs them on speets (spits with hooks) which rest on runners at the sides of the shed. It's windy, so she must watch the fire does not get too hot and 'cook' the fish.

At home, she cooks her smoked haddock simply in milk and mixes it with potatoes to make a thick soup-stew. It's this dish which the folk historian, F M McNeill, names a Cullen Skink in her book, *The Scots Kitchen* (1929), when she comes across the fishwife's soup/stew (skink) in the fisher town in Cullen. By this time the fish has been named a Finnan haddock after the fishing village of Findon just south of Aberdeen, though, of course, it has been common in other East Coast fishing villages too. As the culinary anthropologist, Peter Lund Simmonds, notes in his book, *The Curiosities of Food* (1859):

'The Finnan, Buckie and Bervie smoked haddock is largely vended in London and other large towns, being esteemed an excellent relish. They are split, cleaned and steeped in strong pickle about three hours, and smoked for 15 or 16 hours.'

BROTHS:

Cock-a-Leekie

(CHICKEN AND LEEK BROTH)

Cook's Tip: If it's impossible to find a chicken with flavour, two well-hung pheasants will make a very good substitute.

Yield: 6-8

1 boiling chicken or a roast chicken carcass
3L (5pt) cold water
Several sprigs of parsley and thyme, plus 3 bay leaves tied in a bundle
    with celery stalk or leek leaves
1 onion stuck with 3-4 cloves
2-3 tablespoons dripping or oil
3-4 onions, finely sliced
1kg (2lb) leeks, finely chopped
50g (2oz) long-grain brown rice or small pasta (pastini)
8 soaked prunes (optional)
2-3 tablespoons chopped parsley
Salt and pepper

COOKING THE CHICKEN: Put the chicken into the water and bring slowly to a simmer. Skim. Add the herbs and clove-studded onion. Cook for about one to two hours. Strain, reserving the liquid.

COOKING THE VEGETABLES AND RICE: Heat the dripping or oil in the pot and add the onions. Cook slowly till transparent. Add the white of leek and cook for another few minutes. Add the rice or pastini and the strained stock. Season and simmer till the rice or pastini is tender, about half an hour. Meanwhile, when the chicken is cool, remove all the meat and chop finely.

FINISHING AND SERVING: Add the green of leek and the parsley to the vegetables and rice (or pastini). Adjust seasoning to taste. Add the chopped chicken and prunes and serve with bannocks or oatcakes in deep soup plates.

Scotch Broth

(STRONG BEEF STOCK WITH BARLEY AND PEAS)

Cook's Tip: For the best flavour, make up the stock the day before and leave to cool overnight. This allows the fat to solidify on the surface so that any excess may be removed.

Yield: 6-8

1.5kg (3lb) brisket, hough (beef shin), nine holes (beef flank) or other meat suitable for long cooking
1 marrow bone
3L (5pt) cold water
50g (2oz) pearl barley, washed
50g (2oz) dried peas
1 whole onion stuck with 4 or 5 cloves
Several sprigs of parsley and thyme, plus 3 bay leaves tied in a bundle with celery stalk or leek leaves
2-3 tablespoons dripping or oil
1 large onion, finely chopped
3 medium carrots, finely diced
Half a medium turnip, finely chopped
4 stalks of celery, finely chopped
2 leeks, finely chopped
1 teaspoon sugar
Salt and pepper
2-3 tablespoons finely chopped parsley or kail (English spelling: kale)

COOKING THE BEEF: Put the meat and bone into a large pot and add the water, barley, peas and clove-studded onion. Bring slowly to the boil and skim. Turn down the heat and add the herbs. Season. Cook at a gentle simmer until the meat is tender. Remove meat and set aside. Discard marrow bone.

COOKING THE VEGETABLES: Meanwhile, heat the dripping or oil in a pot and add the onion, carrots, turnip, celery, white of leek and sugar and cook slowly, stirring occasionally till the vegetables are beginning to soften – about 10 minutes.

FINISHING AND SERVING: Add vegetables to the stock with barley and peas and simmer gently for about 15-20 minutes till they are fully cooked. Remove the bundle of herbs and just before serving, add the green of leek and parsley or kail. Taste and adjust seasonings. Slice some of the meat thinly into bite-sized pieces and put into the centre of heated deep soup plates (or serve separately), pour over broth and serve with bannocks or oatcakes.

Ham and Lentil Broth

(RED LENTILS WITH ROOT VEGETABLES AND TOMATO)

Cook's Tip: Deepen the flavour of this broth by balancing its sour/sweetness with treacle and lemon juice.

Yield: 6-8

1 knuckle of smoked ham
3L (5pt) cold water
Several sprigs of parsley and thyme, plus 3 bay leaves
    tied in a bundle with celery stalk or leek leaves
3 tablespoons dripping or oil, for frying
2 carrots, finely diced
Half a medium turnip (swede) finely diced
3 large potatoes, peeled and thinly sliced
2 medium onions, finely chopped
250g (9oz) red lentils
2 teaspoons tomato puree
1 tablespoon black treacle
2 tablespoons lemon juice or wine vinegar
2 tablespoons dry red wine (optional)
Salt and pepper
2-3 tablespoons chopped parsley

COOKING HAM BONE: Put the ham bone, water and herbs into a pot and bring slowly to the boil. Skim. Simmer slowly for about an hour. Strain.

SWEATING THE VEGETABLES: Meanwhile, heat the dripping or oil in a large soup pot. When hot, add the vegetables and lentils. Stir well. Cover, reduce the heat to low and leave to sweat for a few minutes. Remove lid and stir. Continue stirring occasionally to prevent sticking and burning. After about six to eight minutes, add tomato puree, treacle, lemon juice and wine. Stir well, and add strained stock.

FINISHING AND SERVING: Leave ham bone to cool and then remove meat. Chop finely and return to soup once vegetables are cooked. Adjust seasoning to taste. Add parsley and serve with bannocks or oatcakes in deep soup plates.

Hotch Potch

(LAMB WITH SPRING VEGETABLES)

Though the Scots have few classic vegetable dishes, it's in broths like this that they excel in the subtle combination of fresh vegetables and herbs.

Yield: 6-8

1.5g (3lb 5oz) neck, shoulder, shank or flank of lamb
1 marrow bone
3L (5pt) water
Several sprigs of parsley and thyme, plus 3 bay leaves tied
    in a bundle with celery stalk or leek leaves
2 young carrots, grated
2-3 young white turnips, grated
1 teaspoon sugar
500g (1lb 2oz) fresh or frozen peas
1 oak leaf lettuce, finely shredded
2-3 tablespoons chopped chervil
Salt and pepper

COOKING THE MEAT: Put the meat and bones into a large soup pot and add the water. Bring to a simmer and skim. Add the herbs and cook till the meat is tender and falling off the bones (one to two hours). Strain and leave the meat to cool. Cut off the meat and slice into bite-sized pieces.

COOKING THE VEGETABLES AND SERVING: Add the carrots, turnip and sugar to the stock and simmer for about 10 minutes. Then add the peas, lettuce and chervil. Adjust seasoning to taste. Serve immediately with some of the sliced lamb in the centre of deep soup plates, along with bannocks or oatcakes.

Spring Nettle Broth

(WITH LAMB AND POTATOES)

In the days before fridges, three platefuls of this broth was considered the best pick-me-up after a long, cold winter devoid of fresh greens. Though cooks operated on instinctive wisdom which was handed down from one generation to the next, we now know that nettles are one of the richest sources of iron and increase red blood cells, making us feel better.

Cook's Tip: Wearing rubber gloves, gather fresh new shoots avoiding older leaves which are too bitter. Avoid roadside nettles, or any that might have been sprayed by pesticides.

1.5kg (3lb 5oz) neck, shoulder, shank or flank of lamb
3L (5pt) water
Several sprigs of parsley and thyme, plus 3 bay leaves tied in a
    bundle with celery stalk or leek leaves
2 tablespoons dripping or oil
2 medium onions, finely chopped
4 medium potatoes, thinly sliced
250g (9oz) young nettle tops, very finely chopped
Salt and pepper

COOKING THE MEAT: Put the meat into a large soup pot and add the water. Bring to simmering point. Skim, then add the herbs and cook till the meat is tender and falling off the bones (one to two hours). Strain and leave the meat to cool. Cut off the meat and slice into bite-sized pieces.

COOKING THE VEGETABLES AND SERVING: Heat the dripping or oil in the pan and add the onions. Cook gently till transparent and soft. Add the potatoes, toss in the oil, cover and leave on a low heat for a few minutes. Stir regularly. Add the broth liquid and bring to the boil. Simmer for about 15 minutes till the potatoes are soft. Add the nettles. Adjust seasoning to taste. Serve immediately with some of the sliced lamb in the centre of deep soup plates, along with bannocks or oatcakes.

Wild Mushroom Soup

Cook's Tip: Blending to a smooth texture will give the most intense mushroom flavour.

Yield: 6-8

50g (2oz) butter
2 medium onions, chopped
1 teaspoon salt
2 stalks celery, chopped
3 medium potatoes, peeled and chopped roughly
700g (1lb 7oz) wild field mushrooms (or commercial
    chestnut or other mushrooms), sliced
600ml (1pt) chicken stock or water
    or use 1 tablespoon Japanese miso dissolved in water
750ml (1pt 5fl oz) milk
300ml (10fl oz) double cream
Ground black pepper

MAKING: Melt the butter in a large pot and add the onion. Add the salt and cook slowly until the onion becomes transparent. Add the celery and potatoes and continue to cook over a low heat for another five minutes. Add the mushrooms and continue to toss in the butter for another few minutes. Add the stock or water, bring to the boil and simmer for about 15 minutes or until the potatoes are soft. Remove from the heat and leave to cool.

FINISHING AND SERVING: Put the soup into a blender and blend until smooth. Return to the pan and heat gently. Whisk in the milk and cream gradually. Bring to simmering point but do not boil. Serve immediately with freshly ground pepper, bannocks or oatcakes.

Orcadian Oatmeal Soup

(MEATLESS WITH CARROTS AND TURNIPS/SWEDES)

The oatmeal and milk provide a creamy background in this easy-to-make soup.

Yield: 4

50g (2oz) butter
2 leeks, finely chopped
4 medium carrots, grated
Half a medium turnip (swede), grated
50g (2oz) fine or medium oatmeal
1L (1pt 15fl oz) water
1L (1pt 15fl oz) milk
Salt and pepper
2-3 tablespoons chopped parsley

PREPARING THE VEGETABLES: Melt the butter in a large pot and add just the white of the leeks, the carrot and turnip. Cook over the heat, stirring all the time for about five minutes without colouring. Add the oatmeal and mix through. Cook for another few minutes. Season.

COOKING THE SOUP: Add the water and bring slowly to a gentle simmer. Cook for five to ten minutes till the vegetables are just cooked. Add milk and heat through. Taste to adjust seasoning.

SERVING: Add the green leek and parsley and heat through. Serve with bannocks or oatcakes.

Shetland Reestit Mutton Broth

(WITH POTATOES AND ONIONS)

Reestit mutton (available from Shetland butchers) is made by salting and drying lamb. All cuts are preserved, but the leg is reserved for celebrations at Up Helly Aa in January.

Yield: 6-8

500g (1lb 2oz) reestit mutton
3L (5pt) cold water
50g (2oz) pearl barley, washed
50g (2oz) dried peas
1 whole onion stuck with 4 or 5 cloves
Several sprigs of parsley and thyme, plus 3 bay leaves tied in
    a bundle with celery stalk or leek leaves
2-3 tablespoons dripping or oil
2-3 leeks, finely sliced
1 large onion, finely chopped
4 medium potatoes, finely sliced
Salt and pepper
2-3 tablespoons finely chopped parsley or kail (English spelling: kale)

COOKING MEAT: Put the mutton into a large pot and add the water, barley, peas and clove-studded onion. Bring slowly to the boil. Skim and turn down the heat and add the herbs. Season. Cook at a gentle simmer until the meat is tender. Remove the meat and clove-studded onion.

COOKING THE VEGETABLES: Meanwhile, heat the dripping or oil in a pan and add the white of the leek, onion and potatoes. Cook slowly, stirring occasionally for about five minutes, and add to the broth. Bring to a slow simmer and cook till the vegetables are just tender.

FINISHING AND SERVING: Remove the bundle of herbs and just before serving, add the green of leek and parsley or kail. Taste and adjust seasonings. Slice some of the meat thinly into bite-sized pieces and put into the centre of deep soup plates (or serve separately). Pour over broth and serve as a main meal with bannocks or oatcakes.

Venison Broth

Cook's Tip: This is one of the best ways of dealing with less than tender venison joints which require a long, slow, moist cook.

Yield: 6-8

3 tablespoons oil
1 onion, finely chopped
2 rashers streaky bacon, chopped
1.5g (3lb) venison bones, neck or shank
3L (5pt) cold water
Several sprigs of parsley and thyme, plus 3 bay leaves tied
    in a bundle with celery stalk or leek leaves
12-15 juniper berries
50g (2oz) butter
250g (9oz) haunch of venison and/or other meat from game birds, hare or rabbit
2 carrots, finely chopped
4-5 stalks celery, finely chopped
1 lemon, juice of
125g (4oz) fresh spinach or sorrel, finely chopped
Salt and pepper

BROWNING THE MEAT AND COOKING THE BROTH: Heat the oil in a large pot and cook the onion and bacon till lightly coloured. Add the venison bones, neck and/or shank and brown well. Add the water and bring slowly to a simmer. Skim. Add the herbs and juniper berries, season and simmer gently for three to four hours. Strain.

COOKING THE MEAT AND VEGETABLES: Melt the butter in a pan and toss the meat till cooked but still pinkish in the middle. Keep warm. Add the carrots and celery to the pan and toss till lightly browned. Add the lemon juice and put the vegetables into the broth, bring to a simmer and cook the vegetables till tender. Taste to adjust seasoning.

FINISHING AND SERVING: Place the meat in deep soup plates, and pour the broth round. Add spinach or sorrel. Serve with bannocks or oatcakes.

Grouse Soup

'But, oh! my dear North, what grouse-soup at Dalnacardoch,' says one of the cronies in *Blackwoods* magazine column, *Noctes Ambrosia* (1822-35). 'You smell it on the homeward hill, as if it were exhaling from the heather.... As you enter the inn the divine afflatus penetrates your soul. When upstairs, perhaps in the garret, adorning for dinner, it rises like a cloud of rich distilled perfumes through every chink on the floor, every cranny of the wall.'

Yield: 6-8

3 mature grouse (or the bones and legs from 4-6) or other game birds
2L (3pt 10fl oz) water or poultry stock
6 crushed juniper berries
Bundle of fresh herbs including parsley
2 sticks of celery
50g (2oz) solidified fat from the stock or 2 tablespoons oil
25g (1oz) butter
2 medium onions, finely chopped
2 rashers of bacon, finely chopped
4 stalks celery, finely diced
4 shallots, finely chopped
2 tablespoons long grain polished rice, washed and drained
Salt and pepper
Garnish: chopped parsley

MAKING THE STOCK: Remove the breast meat from the grouse if using whole birds. Put the remainder of the carcasses into a pan, cover with water/stock and add juniper berries, herbs and celery. Bring to the boil, cover and simmer gently for one to two hours. Strain, leave to cool and skim off any excess fat. Remove any edible meat from the carcasses and chop finely for adding to the broth at the end. Discard the carcasses.

FINISHING THE SOUP: Melt the fat/oil and butter and begin by tossing the onions and bacon. When the onions are soft and yellow and the bacon just crisp, add the other vegetables and the rice. The grouse breast meat, chopped finely, may be added at this point or it may be kept for a separate dish. Cover and sweat over a very low heat for ten minutes, checking that it is not burning. Add the strained stock, bring to the boil and simmer until the vegetables are just tender and the rice cooked. If there is any other edible grouse meat from the carcasses, chop finely and add at this point. Taste for seasoning and add parsley. Serve in deep soup plates with boiled potatoes.

Cullen Skink

(FINNAN HADDOCK WITH POTATO BROTH)

Cook's Tip: If finnan haddock on the bone is not available, it's best to use haddock which has been smoked with its skin on. This is usually known as an Aberdeen fillet. It will have a better flavour than smaller fillets which have been smoked without their skin. Dyed 'yellow' fillets are not suitable.

Yield: 4-6

750g (1lb 10oz) floury potatoes (Golden Wonder, Kerr's Pinks), washed
1 onion, finely chopped
1L (2pt) water
500g (1lb 2oz) finnan haddock (either on the bone or
  Aberdeen fillets on the skin)
Milk
50g (2oz) butter
Salt and pepper

COOKING: Put the potatoes and onion into a large pot with the water and simmer till the potatoes are almost cooked. Lay the finnan haddock on top and simmer for two or three minutes till the fish is cooked. Remove the fish, cool, skin, bone and flake the flesh. Meanwhile remove the potatoes and peel. Return to the pan and mash with the onions.

FINISHING AND SERVING: Return the flaked fish to the pan, mix through and add enough milk and butter to make a thick consistency. Adjust seasoning to taste and serve as a main course meal in deep soup plates with bannocks or oatcakes.

Mussel Broth

(WITH ONIONS)

Cook's Tip: While it has become a habit with chefs to jazz up this broth with hot chillies etc, the point of fresh mussels is their delicate sea taste which is lost with this kind of treatment.

Yield: 3-4

1.5kg (3lb) mussels
600ml (1pt) water or light dry white wine
25g (1oz) butter
1 large onion
1 clove garlic
Salt and pepper
1 tablespoon chopped parsley or coriander

COOKING THE MUSSELS: Scrub the mussels if necessary and remove the beards. Discard any that are open (unless they shut when tapped). Put the water or wine into a wide deep pan and bring quickly to a simmer. Add the mussels, stir them about for a minute, and put on a tight lid. Cook quickly until the shells open. This will happen when they are cooked. Overcooking will toughen them. Strain. Keep warm. Reserve the liquid and leave to settle. Taste for saltiness.

MAKING THE BROTH: Melt the butter in a pan and add the onion. Cook without colouring till soft. Add the garlic and cook for a few minutes. Strain the cooking liquor and add. Taste and adjust with more wine/water if too salty. Season with pepper.

FINISHING AND SERVING: Place the mussels in deep soup plates and pour over the broth. Sprinkle over parsley or coriander and serve with bannocks or oatcakes.

Partan Bree

(CRAB WITH RICE AND CREAM)

Cook's Tip: The aim is to let the crabs, rather than the rice and cream, dominate so that it becomes more of a broth and less of a 'cream of' soup.

For the fish stock:
2 medium-sized live crabs
Water to cover
1kg (2lb 4oz) white fish bones
  (monkfish heads, flat fish, cod heads etc)
1 small onion
1 small leek, washed
2 sticks celery
6-8 peppercorns
2-3 bay leaves
Bunch of parsley stalks
25g (1oz) butter

For the broth:
50g (2oz) butter
1 large carrot, chopped
1 medium onion, finely chopped
3-4 stalks celery, finely chopped
50g (2oz) long grain rice
125ml (4fl oz) double cream
Salt and pepper

MAKING THE STOCK: Put enough water to cover the crabs into a large pot and bring to the boil. Add the crabs, holding them down for a few seconds. Simmer for 15 minutes for medium-sized crabs. Remove crabs. Strain liquid and return to the pot. Add the rest of the ingredients for the stock. Bring to the boil, remove scum and simmer gently for 30 minutes. Strain.

PREPARING THE CRAB: Remove all the meat from the crabs. Reserve some of the best meat from the claws and process the remainder in a food processor till it becomes a fine puree. Crush the shells until well broken up with a rolling pin or in a pestle in a mortar. Heat the butter in a pan and add the shells, sauté for 10-15 minutes to extract the flavour. Season. Add the stock and simmer gently for about an hour. Strain into a bowl.

MAKING THE BROTH: Melt the butter in the soup pot and add the carrot, onion and celery. Sauté for five minutes. Add the rice. Stir in and then add the strained stock. Simmer till vegetables and rice are cooked (about 30 minutes). Add the pureed crab meat and cream, stir in well. Taste and adjust seasoning.

FINISHING AND SERVING: Garnish with remaining crab meat. Serve in deep soup plates, along with bannocks or oatcakes.

Dulse Broth

Seaweed adds its unique tang to this broth.

Cook's Tip: Other seaweeds can be added, though dulse was the Highlander's favourite – children would eat it straight from the sea. For a vegetarian alternative, add 1-2 tablespoons of Japanese miso dissolved in some of the water instead of the meat.

Yield: 6-8

1.5kg (3lb 5oz) neck or shoulder of lamb or mutton or reestit mutton (see p13)
3L (5pt) cold water
1 whole onion stuck with 4 or 5 cloves
Several sprigs of parsley and thyme, plus 3 bay leaves tied in a
    bundle with celery stalk or leek leaves
25g (1oz) dried autumn dulse
50g (2oz) butter or 2 tablespoons oil
2 onions, finely chopped
8 medium potatoes, finely sliced
4 medium carrots, grated
6 stalks celery, diced
Salt and pepper
2-3 tablespoons finely chopped parsley or kail (English spelling: kale)

COOKING MEAT: Put the meat into a large pot and add the water, bring slowly to the boil and skim. Turn down the heat and add the onion and herbs. Cook at a gentle simmer until the meat is tender. Remove meat and set aside.

COOKING VEGETABLES: Soak the dulse in some of the broth liquid. Heat the butter or oil in a pan and add the onions. Cook over a low heat till they are translucent. Add the potatoes, carrots and celery and cook slowly stirring regularly for about five minutes. Strain the dulse from the liquid, chop up roughly and add to the vegetables. Cook for another few minutes. Add vegetables and dulse to the soup and bring to the boil. Simmer until the vegetables are tender.

FINISHING AND SERVING: Remove the bundle of herbs and just before serving, add the parsley or kail. Taste and adjust seasonings. Slice some of the meat thinly into bite-sized pieces and put into the centre of deep soup plates (or serve separately). Pour over broth and serve, along with bannocks or oatcakes.

FISH CLASSICS

Fish 'n' Chips

Chippies in Scotland, fish 'oles in Yorkshire, fish shops in London: there are few food marriages that have produced as many offspring as the union of fish and chip. Its origins, however, begin in London, when cold fried fish was sold in the streets by itinerant sellers. Coated in flour batter, dusted with salt, the fish was a popular filler, with a chunk of bread, in the deprived, gin-drinking London of Dickens' *Oliver Twist*.

The fish catch had been divided by quality and freshness. The best, and freshest, went to the rich and the remainder to the poor. Some inevitably ended up in the 'fish warehouse' where salt and batter disguised its less-than-perfect aspects. Large pans of smoking fat in the warehouse did the rest.

Meanwhile, the square, finger-length plug of potato, also fried in deep fat, began its life in a higher social class when it migrated from France. It was originally a novel potato form, adopted along with many other French dishes and styles of eating, the chip was known as potatoes 'a la mode'. How this classy potato migrated to the streets is not clear, but by the late nineteenth century it had become popular, quickly cooked and served up in a comfortingly warm, hand-held bag.

Though the marriage of fish and chips undoubtedly took place in England, Scotland can claim one of the first poke o' chips street-sellers: a Belgian, Eduard de Gernier, who began selling chips with a saucer of peas (known as a 'buster') from his stall in Dundee's Greenmarket in the late nineteenth century. Trade in the streets flourished. Itinerant Italian ice cream sellers began selling chips in the streets during the winter months and later opened shops with large deep fat fryers, selling both fish and chips. It was the chip, however, which had come first – hence 'chippies' in Scotland, fish 'oles in Yorkshire...

While pickled eggs and onions – to cut the fat – became universally popular accompaniments, an East-West divide grew up on the matter of condiments. The West going for a salt and vinegar dousing, while the East choose a generous dollop of spicy brown sauce.

Oysters and a dram o' Gin

The pair of legal wits - not quite drunk yet not quite sober - make their way down Fish Market Close in Edinburgh's Old Town (Auld Reekie). It is the mid-eighteenth century and several decades before the New Town is built. For the moment, a homogeneous mix of people from all social classes live, work and socialise in the tenement lands between the castle and the Palace of Holyrood.

Autumn nights are closing in. An 'r' is back in the month, so oysters are back on the menu as the two revellers dive into their favourite oyster tavern for a night's entertainment. Besides oysters, there is singing and dancing as night deepens the sociability. The company includes the literati and their publishers, as well as parties of well-bred women, advocates and judges, all happily mixing for a night's 'oyster ploy' with gutsy fishwives and lively street traders.

Fresh from the Forth, the large opened 'natives' are piled – by the hundred – on round wooden boards. It is the essence of simple hospitality: chairs and tables in a plain room with an open coal fire in an iron grate. There is no idle ornament or decoration, but clusters of tallow candles for light, shelves on the walls are for spent bottles and hooks for pewter drinking vessels. Cruets of pepper and vinegar are placed on the table along with plates of buttered bread.

Most of the company drink drams of gin with their oysters, sometimes also ale. In every oyster tavern, several thousand oysters a week slip down Old Edinburgh throats. Tonight, once everyone has had their fill, tables are cleared and the fiddler sets up a tune for some energetic reels. Fishwives sing rhythmic sea songs, while genteel ladies sing popular Lowland love songs. And before everyone leaves for the cold walk home, there are warming cupfuls from the landlord's bowl of hot punch.

It's an Old Edinburgh which has been recorded in many ways by social historians, poets and novelists – Burns and Scott in particular. But it is the poet Robert Fergusson (1750-1774), who Burns described as 'by far my elder brother' who catches the spirit of the eighteenth-century oyster eaters better than anyone in his poem 'Caller Oysters':

Auld Reekie's sons blyth faces wear
September's merry month is near,
That brings in Neptune's caller chere,
New oysters fresh;
The halesomest and nicest gear
Of fish or flesh.

What big as burns the
gutters rin,
Gin ye hae catcht a droukit skin,
To Luckie Middlemist's loup in,
And sit fu' snug
O'er oysters and a dram o' gin
Or haddock lug.

Tatties 'n' Herrin'

The summer shielings in the hills are gone, and with them most of the cattle that provided butter and cheese. Even the game and salmon, which were one of their perks, now belong to the sportsmen-landowners. What limited land these late-nineteenth-century Highland crofters have, is used for growing potatoes and perhaps a field of oats, while there is, of course, always the herring.

Nets are cast as the annual shoals arrive in the loch and everyone has a welcome feed of fresh fish. The remaining fish are gutted, and placed in layers with salt in a wooden barrel. Each family has its barrel of salt herring in the byre which will see them through the winter. Known as 'pickled herring', they are used as a piquant flavouring for bland potatoes, usually soaked in water to remove some of the excess salt before cooking.

Though tatties and salt herring is their favourite warming winter meal, it's the first fresh herrin' of the season which is the special summer treat - with tatties of course. For the family dinner, the huge pot of potatoes is cooked over the open peat fire. Now and again, it is checked. And just when the potatoes soften, it is snatched from the fire. Water is poured off, and the pot returned to the fire. But this time the chain is shortened by a link or two so that the waterless pot is now a little further from the heat. On top of the steaming potatoes are laid, side by side, half a dozen large, plump, silvery-scaled herring, ready gutted.

To keep the steam from escaping, a kitchen towel is placed over the pot and the lid is fitted on tightly so that over the next quarter of an hour or so, the fresh herrings steam gently in the heat from the potatoes. When ready, the pot is lifted onto a low stool in the middle of the room. Then the family gathers round and the lid and cloth are removed.

'And the room was instantly filled with a savoury steam that made one's mouth water merely to inhale it,' says Alexander Stewart in *Nether Lochaber* (1883).

'Occupying each a low chair, we were invited to fall to, to eat without knife, or fork, or trencher, just with our fingers out of the pot as it stood. It was a little startling, but only for a moment. After a word of grace we dipped our hand into the pot and took out a potato, hot and mealy, and with another we took a nip out of the herring nearest us. It was a mouthful for a king!'

Fish and fish processing traditions:

Arbroath Smokies: It was the fisherwomen of Auchmithie who first put whisky barrels into the ground, on flat areas of the cliff face, to smoke and preserve their surplus haddock. Cooking them in the hot smoke from a fire in the barrel, the fish took on a rich dark copper colour while inside, the flesh was creamy white with mellow overtones of salt and smoke.

'With the setting sun,' wrote one villager of the early smoking days, 'the boats come home, and in the back houses the lamps are lit. Up the brae come the creels of fish, and soon every woman and child is gutting, cleaning and salting. Little sticks of wood are stuck into the haddocks' gills. And two by two, tied tail to tail, they are hung on wooden spits.'

As the fishing fleet grew, the families of Norse descent who had invented the cure, moved to nearby Arbroath where there was a larger harbour. And instead of barrels on the cliff, the fisher people built square pits in their back yards continuing to call them 'barrels'. This method is still used, despite the invention of computerised smoking kilns.

Crab: Also known in the Scottish dialect as a 'partan', it has a reddish, pink-brown shell and legs tinted with purple while its claws black. The brownish liver meat is strongly flavoured, but the white meat from the claws is more delicate than a lobster. The crab was a common item of food for coastal communities, eking out a living from a meagre environment. More easily caught under rocks as the tide went out than lobster, it became more integrated into the diet especially as a distinctive flavouring for broths (see Partan Bree p18).

Finnan Haddock: (see also Cullen Skink p16) This is a North-East cure and takes its name from the fishing village of Findon, south of Aberdeen. It first became popular nationwide in the nineteenth century as a breakfast dish. 'A good breakfast, as usual,' says Robert Southey in his *Journal of a Tour of Scotland* in 1819, 'with Findon Haddocks, eggs, sweetmeats and honey.' A whole haddock has its head removed but the bone left in. It is split open, brined and smoked to a pale straw colour with no artificial colouring. The Aberdeen fillet, a relative of the finnan, is also undyed but has its bone removed. 'Painted ladies' or 'yellow fillets' are dyed, lightly brined, lightly smoked, skinless small haddocks or whitings and should not be used as a substitute for finnans.

Kipper (Scottish cure): Though the 'kippered' herring was first developed in Northumberland in the 1840s, the Scots have been kippering salmon since the fifteenth century. Kippering herring in Scotland is mainly concentrated around the West-coast fishing grounds where plump herring from the Minch and Loch Fyne have had a long history. Mallaig, and Loch Fyne, kippers have become established among the best cures. It was during World War I that smoking times were reduced and the kippers coloured with a coal-tar dye known as Brown FK (for kippers). Many independent smokers, in recent years, meet the growing demand for undyed kippers supporting the move against needless use of possibly harmful chemicals.

Lobster: While crab was eaten frequently by the fishing communities, lobster became a more valuable export as fishermen recognised its status as a gourmet item. Creel fishing for lobsters began in the late nineteenth century as special boats were constructed to hold the live lobsters during their journey to the lucrative

London market. Because of its high market value, lobster was not eaten widely in Scotland. Today, however, as the move to use more local produce in its local setting gathers momentum, more Scottish lobsters are finding their way onto Scottish tables. Carapace length can be up to 45cm; but it's illegal to land lobsters with a carapace length of under 85mm.

Mussel: As part of the general foraging for food, the dark blue-black common mussel was widely eaten, either as a broth, or as street food sold by itinerant fishwives selling shelled mussels in saucers with condiments. Today, those on sale are mostly cultivated commercially on ropes.

Oyster: Though they were eaten with great relish during the heyday of the Oyster Cellars of the Georgian and Victorian period (see Oysters and a Dram o' Gin p20), by the mid-twentieth century, pollution and over-fishing caused the almost total decline of the native oyster beds. It is only in the last 30 years or so that the oyster tradition has been revived. Native oysters, 'natives', are fan-shaped, almost circular with one half of the shell flat and the other cupped. Pacific oysters are more deeply cupped, have a rougher shell and are more elongated than round. Their flavour depends on the feeding and varies from loch to loch. All Scottish oysters have a Grade A rating, meaning that they have not required purifying by passing through purifications tanks before sale. Most of today's oysters are of the Pacific species (*Crassostrea gigas*) which can be eaten all year round since they do not retain their eggs. 'Natives' (*Crassostrea edulis*), however, do retain their eggs and should only be eaten during months with an 'r' in them – September to April. Flavour will vary according to different feeding in different lochs.

Salmon: Early catches of salmon on the Tay, Spey, Tweed, Don and Dee produced large quantities that were eaten fresh in summer and kippered (smoked and dried) in winter. So common was the fish, that it became a cheap dinner for the working man. But as it became less plentiful, Scottish salmon became established for its quality as a premier gourmet fish. During the latter part of the twentieth century, however, over-fishing and other factors, possibly connected with pollution from fish farms, led to the decline in wild salmon and the rise of the farmed salmon, not all of which has achieved the quality tag. Over-fed, under-exercised farmed salmon have a flabby, oily flesh but the leaner, better exercised farmed salmon is a more attractive option.

Salt Herring: The first recorded use of the word 'herring' – from the Germanic 'heer' meaning an army – occurs in the eighth century. Giant shoals of herring brought prosperity to coastal communities. Armies of fisherwomen followed the herring from port to port, gutting and salting each year's catch which was packed, by the million, in barrels and sold mostly to Russia and the Baltic countries.

Throughout most of the nineteenth century this was a major Scottish cure. Today, they remain a speciality cure, particularly in coastal districts where there has been a strong fishing tradition. The herring is not filleted but the gut is removed and the head left on. It's cured by layering with salt in tubs or barrels and most popularly eaten with potatoes in 'Tatties an' Salt Herring' (see p28).

Scallop: The Great or King scallop has a flat bottom shell and a concave upper shell with a creamy white muscle and an orange roe. Also caught in Scottish waters is the Queen scallop which is smaller than the King with both shells concave. The Princess scallop is an immature Queen which is about the size of a large mussel. They all have a distinctive and subtle sea-flavour from rich feeding in unpolluted waters. The dredged and dived scallop industry did not develop until the 1950s and 60s when divers began harvesting from native beds. In recent years more and more farmed scallop beds have been developed with some areas protected by a Several Fishery Order giving them legal protection. Their flavour is best when the scallop is newly opened. To buy 'shucked' (removed from the shell) it's important that they have not been steeped in water with any preservation additives, as this will result in their natural flavour being lost quickly.

Smoked Eel: A cure which has made a name for itself in recent years as the abundant supply of common eels in some rivers has been utilised by smokers. On the River Tweed, the Salmon Fishers Association have given the eel fishing rights to a trusted local smoker. The eels are caught in nets in the autumn as they return to the sea after feeding. They are starved in the river for two weeks, then immersed in brine and cold-smoked over oak chips for six to seven hours. They are then finished over hot smoke for a few hours which cooks them through.

Smoked Salmon: A strong tradition of smoking salmon developed over many centuries in Scotland as a means of preserving surplus catches. All those living near salmon rivers were adept at smoking, and developed their own cures, which accounts for the variety of Scottish salmon cures today. The most common method is to lay the salmon fillets on trays, layered in salt where they are left for 12-14 hours. Added flavouring ingredients may include juniper berries, herbs, molasses, rum or whisky. Fillets are then washed and dried overnight before smoking, usually over oak chips, but some curers use other flavourings including peat. Distinction must be made between the best quality wild salmon smoked, without added flavourings, and farmed salmon, of dubious quality, which has had many flavourings added. 'All smoked salmon,' as one food critic in the *New York Times* once said, 'is not created equal. Most aficionados, however, give the nod to smoked Scotch salmon as the best. It is, as a rule, the least oily, the most subtly flavoured, has the firmest and most pleasing texture and the least amount of salt.'

OILY FISH:

Fried Herring, Mackerel or Trout Fillets in Oatmeal

Cook's Tip: For a special occasion a hard butter can be made with 125g (4oz) softened butter mixed with 2 teaspoons lemon juice, 1 tablespoon chopped parsley and 3 tablespoons Drambuie. Wrapped in clingfilm and foil and shaped into a cylinder, it should be left to harden in the fridge before cutting and slicing on top of the fried fish. It can be cut into slices and deep frozen.

Yield: 4

2 tablespoons oil or 25g (1oz) butter
2 heaped tablespoons medium oatmeal, lightly toasted
Salt and pepper
4 fresh herring, filleted

TO FRY FILLETED HERRING or MACKEREL: Heat the oil or butter in a large frying pan. Mix the seasonings into the oatmeal on a large plate and spread out. Press the wet fish into it, coating both sides – it is not necessary to moisten the fish with anything since it should be moist enough. Shake off excess oatmeal. When the oil or butter is hot, place the fish flesh-side down into the pan and cook for two to three minutes depending on the thickness of the fish. Turn and cook on skin side for another two to three minutes. Serve immediately with mustard or hard butter.

Soused Herring

Cook's Tip: This works best with herring in the spring before they spawn, when they are at their fattest.

Yield: 6

6 herring fillets
1 level teaspoon salt
Freshly ground black pepper
12 peppercorns
6 cloves
2 bay leaves
1 cayenne pepper
25g (1oz) butter
300ml (10fl oz) cider vinegar
150ml (5fl oz) water

Preheat the oven to 425°F/220°C/Gas 7.

PREPARING THE FISH: Season the fish with salt and pepper. Roll up from head to tail, skin side out. In a large casserole pack together tightly so they hold their shape with tails sticking up. Cover with spices and seasonings. Add butter in pieces. Pour over vinegar and water so the herring is just covered.

COOKING: Put into the hot oven for about 30 minutes, then reduce to 250°F/130°C/Gas ½ and cook for another hour. Leave in liquor till cold. Serve with a tossed green salad.

Tatties an' Salt Herrin'

Cook's Tip: Though it's possible to cook the fish on top of the potatoes – some say this makes the best tasting potatoes – cooking separately allows better control over fish and potatoes. Especially the fickle floury potatoes, that must be drained as soon as they are soft, or they will burst before you know it and turn to 'soup'.

Yield: 4

4 salt herring
1kg (2lb 4oz) floury potatoes (Golden Wonder or Kerr's Pinks), washed
Salt

PREPARING AND COOKING: Wash fish and soak overnight in cold water. Rinse. Place the potatoes in a large pot. Season with salt and almost cover with water, then bring to the boil. Cover with a tight-fitting lid and simmer gently till the potatoes are just cooked. Put the fish into another pot and simmer till the flesh is just soft.

SERVING: Lift out the fish and place on heated serving plates. Drain the remaining water and dry off the potatoes by returning to the heat for a few minutes. Serve the potatoes whole, in their skins, in a large serving dish with butter. (It's traditional to eat with fingers rather than knives and forks.)

Jugged Kipper

Cook's Tip: 'Jugging' a kipper prevents kipper aromas invading the house. It's also more gentle and preserves fish flavour better.

1 whole undyed kipper
Boiling water
1 lemon

TO 'JUG': Place the kipper in a large baking dish. Pour over boiling water. Cover with foil and leave for ten minutes in a warm place. Pour off water and serve kipper with lemon and hot toast.

Grilled Kipper

1 whole, undyed kipper
1 lemon

TO GRILL: Pre-heat grill. Protect grill pan with foil and place kipper on top, flesh side up. Grill for about five minutes depending on the thickness of the kipper. Test at the thickest part to see that it is cooked. Serve with lemon and hot toast.

Whole Grilled Mackerel, Herring or Trout in Oatmeal

Cook's Tip: For a special occasion a hard butter can be made with 125g (4oz) softened butter mixed with two teaspoons lemon juice, one tablespoon chopped parsley and three tablespoons Drambuie. Wrapped in clingfilm and foil and shaped into a cylinder, it should be left to harden in the fridge before cutting and slicing on top of the fried fish. It can be cut into slices and deep frozen.

Yield: 4

4 x 250g (9oz) whole mackerel, herring or trout
2-3 tablespoons medium oatmeal
Salt and pepper
50g (2oz) butter
Serve with: mustard, or hard butter (see recipe in Cook's Tip) and baked potatoes

PREPARING FISH: Wash and clean the fish. Salt the inside lightly, then slash the skin diagonally at the thickest part: this opens up the flesh and allows it to cook more evenly. Mix the seasonings through the oatmeal and press the fish on both sides into the oatmeal.

GRILLING: Heat the grill. Protect the grill pan with foil and lay the fish on top. Put pats of butter on top of the fish. Cook on each side for five to six minutes depending on thickness. Test by opening with a sharp knife at the thickest part: if the flesh nearest the bone still looks opaque, leave for another few minutes.

SERVING: Serve with baked potatoes, mustard or hard butter. It's traditional to serve mackerel with a gooseberry sauce.

Potted Smoked Mackerel with Lemon

Cook's Tip: This recipe can be used as a basic for other smoked fish such as smokies, smoked salmon and kippers (jugged first).

Yield: 4-6

275g (10oz) smoked mackerel, skinned and boned
150g (5oz) unsalted butter, softened
1 clove garlic, crushed
1 lemon, juice of
Salt and pepper

BLENDING: Put the smoked mackerel, butter and garlic into a food processor (or beat by hand for a coarser texture) and blend till smooth. Taste and season with salt and pepper. Add lemon juice to taste. Pack into an earthenware pot. Serve with hot toast.

Baked Salmon with Dill

Cook's Tip: This works best with a middle cut of even thickness, as with a tail cut, the end will be overcooked when the thicker part is still underdone.

Yield: 4

800g (1lb 12oz) cut of salmon, on the bone
50g (2oz) butter, softened
Salt and pepper
2-3 sprigs dill

Preheat the oven to 300°F/275°C/Gas 2.

PREPARING THE FISH: Place two sheets of foil on a baking tray. The foil should be large enough to wrap the fish with some room to spare. Butter the foil and place the fish on top. Season lightly with salt in the cavity and fill with dill. Spread remaining butter on top and sides of fish. Wrap up in foil, leaving space above the fish. There should be some room for the fish to steam.

BAKING AND SERVING: Place in the oven and bake for 30-40 minutes. Remove from the oven and leave in its foil for 10 minutes if serving hot (leave till cold if serving cold). Open up foil and remove skin from fish. Serve on a heated ashet (preferably blue and white). Strain cooking juices on top and decorate with more dill. Serve with boiled new potatoes tossed with butter and chives.

SERVING COLD: Open up foil and remove skin from the fish. Place on a blue and white ashet, garnish with thinly sliced cucumber, wedges of lemon and chopped dill. Serve with mayonnaise.

Seared Salmon Steaks
with Rocket Salad

Cook's Tip: It is a pity to lose the rich flavouring (and useful vitamins including phosphorous) in the fish skin if it's discarded. This method turns it into a crisp delicacy.

Yield: 4

4 x 150g (5oz) salmon fillets, skin left on

Sea salt

125g (4½ oz) rocket leaves, or mixed with other salad herbs

Extra virgin olive oil

Balsamic vinegar

Freshly ground black pepper

1kg (2lb 4oz) Scottish new potatoes

25g (1oz) butter

1 tablespoon chopped chives

PREPARING and FRYING: Heat a heavy-base frying pan and when fairly hot, but not burning, put in the fillets, skin side down. They will stick at first, but gradually the oil in the skin will release the fish. Cook for two to four minutes on either side depending on the thickness of the fish. Open up with a sharp knife through the thickest part to check if cooked through. If still a little opaque leave for another minute. Do not overcook or the fish will be dry.

SERVING: Place salmon on heated plates, season with freshly ground black pepper and serve with rocket salad or mixed green salad tossed with oil and vinegar and boiled new potatoes tossed in butter and chives.

WHITE FISH:

Fish 'n' Chips

Sit at a Japanese tempura bar and your fish sizzles in the oil while you wait for it to be served the minute it's cooked. The secret of perfect frying is instant serving, so serve chips first when they're ready and follow with the fish. The best chips are made with low moisture, traditional Scottish floury potatoes. East-coasters like to season chips with brown sauce while West-coasters prefer salt and vinegar.

Yield: 4

1kg (2lb 4oz) floury potatoes, peeled and cut into large chips
   (suitable potatoes: Golden Wonder, Kerr's Pinks, Maris Piper or Record)

Light batter:
1 egg yolk
250ml (8fl oz) bottled, carbonated water, chilled
75g (3oz) fine, plain white flour (low gluten if possible)
Pinch of bicarbonate of soda
4 x 175g (6oz) fillets of white fish
Salt and vinegar (West Coast seasoning)
Brown sauce (East Coast seasoning)

Preheat a pan of oil for deep frying to 375°F/190°C. To test for correct temperature, drop in a chip which should sizzle vigorously.

BLANCHING THE CHIPS: Dry the chips well in a tea towel and test oil for correct temperature. Add chips, lowering the basket gradually. Toss for the first few minutes and continue to toss every so often. When they are browned and soft, remove. Drain on kitchen paper and serve immediately. Reheat oil to the original temperature.

MAKING BATTER AND COOKING FISH: Put the egg into a bowl and add about three-quarters of the water. Sift the flour and soda on top and whisk in. The consistency should just coat the back of a wooden spoon. Add more water if it is too thick. As soon as it's mixed, dip in the fish. Coat well. Allow to drain off excess. Drop into hot oil. Fry on both sides for about five minutes until the fish rise to the surface of the oil and are golden brown. They should now be ready. Remove and drain on kitchen paper. Serve.

SERVING: Serve with salt and vinegar – West Coast. Brown Sauce – East Coast. Additional accompaniments include: pickled onions, pickled eggs and tomato ketchup.

Buttered Smokie

A speciality of the But 'n' Ben in Auchmithie (original home of the smokie) where a Buttered Smokie High Tea comes with bread and butter, a pot of tea and a choice of scones, tea breads, cakes and clootie dumpling from the cake stand.

Yield: 4

4 Arbroath smokies
50g (2oz) unsalted butter, softened
Freshly ground black pepper
Serve with: bread and butter for tea

Preheat the oven to 350°F/180°C/Gas 4.

PREPARING AND HEATING SMOKIES: Carefully open up the fish and remove the bone. Lay fish flat, flesh side up and spread evenly with butter. Cover with foil and put in the oven for 10-15 minutes until heated through.

SERVING: Serve with a grinding of black pepper and bread and butter for tea.

Finnan an' Poached Egg

A popular High Tea item in the Glasgow tea-rooms of the early nineteenth century created by Miss Kate Cranston and Charles Rennie Mackintosh. Like Buttered Smokies at the But 'n' Ben, it was served with bread and butter, a pot of tea and, of course, goodies from the cake stand.

Yield: 4

750g (1lb 10oz) finnan haddock fillets*
250ml (8fl oz) single cream
4 lightly poached eggs
Freshly ground black pepper

Preheat the oven to 350°F/180°C/Gas 4.

PREPARING AND COOKING FISH: Cut the fish into portion sizes, place skin side down in a baking dish and add cream. Cover with foil and bake for 20-30 minutes till the fish is cooked. Remove from the oven after ten minutes and shake the dish gently to re-coat the fish with cream.

SERVING: Place the fish on a heated serving dish. Place poached egg on top and pour over cream. Serve with bread and butter for tea or with mashed potatoes for dinner.

*Dyed 'yellow' fillets are not suitable

Smokie Kedgeree

An Anglo-Indian invention that first became popular on Edwardian breakfast tables.

Yield: 4

1 Arbroath smokie (or other smoked, cooked fish)
2 hardboiled eggs
50g (2oz) unsalted butter
125g (4oz) boiled long grain rice
Salt and pepper
1-2 tablespoons chopped parsley

For serving: Hot buttered toast

PREPARING THE FISH AND EGGS: Put the fish in a baking dish and pour over boiling water. Leave for a few minutes, remove and cool. Peel off skin and remove bones. Remove the yolks from the eggs and chop the whites finely.

MIXING AND HEATING: Put the butter into a pan and melt. Add the rice and mix through. Add the fish and hardboiled egg whites and heat through gently. Taste for seasoning and mix in chopped parsley.

FINISHING AND SERVING: When steaming hot, pile into a heated ashet. Sieve over the yolks of egg and serve with hot buttered toast.

Eyemouth Fish Pie

Cook's Tip: For a simpler version, the potatoes in the topping can be omitted and the top finished with the grated cheddar and breadcrumbs.

Yield: 4

350g (12oz) fresh white fish, filleted (cod, haddock whiting, ling, sole)
250ml (8fl oz) milk
1 tablespoon finely chopped shallots
Salt and pepper
2 eggs, hardboiled and sliced
3 large tomatoes, skinned and sliced thinly

For the sauce:
25g (1oz) flour
25g (1oz) butter

For the potato topping:
750g (1lb 10oz) potatoes, skinned, boiled and mashed
50g (2oz) mature cheddar, grated
25g (1oz) butter
2 tablespoons breadcrumbs

1 x 1.4L (2½ pt) pie dish

COOKING FISH: Put the fish into a pan with the milk, shallots and seasoning. Cover and simmer very gently for about five minutes till the fish is cooked. Strain (keeping the liquid). Cool.

MAKING SAUCE: Melt the butter in a pan and add the flour. Stir for a few minutes over a gentle heat without colouring. Then add the strained cooking liquor, gradually, stirring all the time. Taste and adjust seasoning. Add fish and shallots and mix in lightly to flake the fish. Adjust consistency with more milk if it is too thick.

FINISHING AND SERVING: Place a layer of half the fish mixture in the pie dish. Cover with the hard boiled eggs, then the tomatoes and finally cover with the remaining fish mixture. Level the surface. Heat up the potatoes and beat in the butter and cheese. Taste for seasoning. Spread on top of fish and finish with a layer of breadcrumbs. Brown under the grill. May be kept hot in a low oven.

Salt White Fish and Potatoes

This is a version – based on the French *brandade de morue* – of Scots 'hairy tatties'; cooked salt white fish beaten through mashed potatoes.

Yield: 8 as a starter

1kg (2lb) salt fish (cod, ling etc)
Water and milk to cover
2 sprigs thyme
2 bay leaves
4 large baking potatoes
250ml (9fl oz) light olive oil
5 garlic cloves
2 tablespoons chopped parsley
Lemon juice to taste
White pepper

PREPARING FISH: Cut fish into even-sized pieces and soak for 24 hours. Discard the water. Put into a pan with half water, half milk to cover. Add thyme and bay leaves. Cover and simmer until the fish is tender and falling off the bones easily. Time will depend on the size and age of the fish.

BAKING POTATOES: Rub the potatoes with oil and pierce the skins. Bake until soft. Scoop out the insides and mash until smooth. Reserve potato shells.

FINISHING THE DISH: Strain the cooked fish, reserving the liquid. Remove the bones and skin from the fish, flake and mash finely. This may be done in a blender for the finest finished texture. Heat the oil in a pan. Crush the garlic. Pour the hot oil gradually into the fish, beating between each addition – or blending if it is done in a blender. When all the oil has been incorporated, remove from the blender and mix through the garlic and parsley then the mashed potatoes. Add cooking liquid to make a consistency of thick cream. Add lemon juice and pepper. Pile into potato shells and serve, alone or with hot buttered toast.

SHELLFISH:

Crab in its Shell

Cook's Tip: The water that the crab is cooked in must be as salty as the sea which prevents any of the crab's flavour being lost by leaching into the cooking water.

Yield: 4

Water
4 medium-sized live crabs
2 tablespoons salt
25g (1oz) butter softened
Salt and pepper
1 lemon

Serve with bread and butter

BOILING THE CRABS: Fill a large pan with water, add salt, and bring to the boil. Put in live crabs one at a time, allowing the water to return to the boil. Boil each crab for about 15 minutes (allow 15 minutes for first 500g (1lb 2oz) plus five minutes per further 500g). Remove and leave to cool.

EXTRACTING THE CRAB MEAT: Remove the claws and legs close to the body shell. Crack the shell of each claw with a wooden mallet without damaging the flesh. Pick out the flesh with a shellfish pick or a skewer. Crack the legs at the joints and pick out the meat or crack open with a mallet. To open the crab, pull off the tail flap and discard. Hold the crab in both hands with two thumbs hard against the base at the bottom of the tail flap and press hard. The whole central part should come out. If it does not, loosen with a knife round where the legs were attached and press again. Pull the central part free and remove the elongated gills (dead men's fingers) along the edges and discard. Cut down the middle and use a skewer to pick out the flesh from the many crevices on both sides. With a teaspoon, scoop out the meat from inside the shell and reserve it. Remove and discard the small stomach sac which is just behind the crab's mouth. To open out the shell, press round the outer edge where there is a weak line: it should break cleanly. Wash the shell well.

SERVING: Mix the brown body meat with the meat from the legs and centre part of the shell. Beat in butter, season and return to the shell, packing into either side, leaving a space in the middle for the claw meat. Serve with crusty bread, unsalted butter and wedges of lemon.

Fresh Cooked Lobster

Cook's Tip: The water the lobster is cooked in must be as salty as the sea which prevents any of the lobster's flavour being lost by leaching into the cooking water.

Yield: 4

2 x 700g (1lb 9oz) live lobster
2 tablespoon salt
Serve with mayonnaise and green salad

COOKING LOBSTER: Fill a large pot with water, add salt and bring to the boil. Immerse lobster and hold under the surface for two minutes. Simmer for 15 minutes. Allow an extra five minutes for each additional pound. Remove and leave to cool.

PREPARING: Snap off the eight legs close to the body. Break legs at joints and pick out meat with shellfish pick or skewer. Remove each claw and crack with a wooden mallet. Lay the lobster on its back and cut with a heavy sharp knife along its entire length. Pull away the bony covering on the underside. Starting at the tail, prise away the tail meat in one piece. Strip off the brown-grey feathery gills and remove the stomach sac and dark intestinal cord. Scoop out the soft grey-green liver and save. Lay the tail meat on a chopping board and slice into pieces about 2cm thick.

SERVING: Return the tail meat and the liver to the empty shell. Serve on a large blue and white ashet with the legs and claws with mayonnaise, green salad, crusty bread and unsalted butter.

Oysters in their Shells

Cook's Tip: It's worth investing in oyster shucking equipment.

Yield: 4

8-10 oysters per person depending on size, chilled
Seasoning to taste: lemon juice, cayenne pepper, Tabasco

OPENING: Hold the oyster in a cloth in your left hand with the flat side uppermost - so that the juice is not lost - and the hinge end towards you. Or use a special oyster holder. Push an oyster knife with a strong sharp point and a short rounded blade (most kitchen knives are unsuitable) into the muscle at the hinge end. While pushing hard, give a twist upwards which will cut the muscle and release the shell. Remove any shell fragments. Loosen the oyster by running the knife carefully underneath the muscle.

SERVING: Serve on a bed of crushed ice with condiments to taste along with crusty bread and unsalted butter and a chilled dry white wine or champagne.

Norway and Squat Lobsters

WITH MUSSELS AND SCALLOPS IN THEIR SHELLS

This seafood platter creates the most colourful and attractive display of prime seafood. It's how it would have been eaten in the past, with the minimum of fuss.

Yield: 4

8 medium-sized Norway lobsters (langoustines)
1kg (2lb 4oz) squat lobster, washed
1kg (2lb 4oz) princess scallops, washed
1kg (2lb 4oz) mussels, washed and de-bearded

PREPARING SHELLFISH: Put on a large pan of lightly salted water and bring to the boil. Drop in the Norway lobsters and cook for three to four minutes. Remove. Return water to the boil and drop in squat lobster. Cook for about 60 seconds and remove. Strain cooking liquor. Pour about an inch into the base of the pan and drop in the scallops. Cover with a lid. Shake the pan several times and steam until all the shells are opened (one to two minutes). Remove and repeat with the mussels.

SERVING: Using large deep white plates, fill with crushed ice. Arrange shellfish in a pile on top. Serve with lemon wedges and crusty bread and unsalted butter. Provide finger bowls and shellfish picks.

Scallops an' Bacon

This was a favourite fisherman's breakfast-at-sea with scrambled eggs and toast.

Yield: 4

250g (4oz) Ayrshire bacon or other unsmoked bacon
25g (1oz) butter
500g (1lb 2oz) queen scallops, shelled

Scrambled Eggs:
6 eggs
2-3 tablespoons single cream
Salt and pepper

COOKING THE SCALLOPS AND BACON: Heat a frying pan and chop the bacon roughly. Fry gently in the dry pan till lightly browned and crisp. Remove and keep warm. Add butter to bacon fat and heat through. Add the scallops and toss in the pan, turning frequently till cooked. They should only take about a minute and should not be overcooked. Remove and keep warm.

COOKING THE EGGS AND SERVING: Break the eggs in a bowl and beat with two tablespoons of cream. Drain off a few tablespoons of the cooking fat in the frying pan and put into a pan. Heat up and add the eggs. Stir till set but still soft. Stir in another tablespoon cream (optional). Season with salt and pepper. Place on heated serving plate, place scallops and bacon on top. Serve with crusty bread and unsalted butter.

GAME CLASSICS

Red Deer Venison

It is summer 1700, and the clan chieftain lives with his wife and extended family in a square, six-foot thick walled tower on the edge of a cliff. Through the great front door and up a narrow flight of stone steps is the communal hall where a fire burns in the cooking-hearth and a side of venison roasts on a spit. Slices are carved from the hot roast for the main meal of the day and on the thick oak table are the remains of a salmon, thin, soft barley bannocks, butter, sheep's milk, cheese and a bowl of wild berries which the children have gathered.

Roast venison and other wild game birds appear regularly on the table. They are among the rich bounty which is free for the taking, before Highland chieftains lose their lands and Queen Victoria popularises the Highlands as a sporting playground by creating the royal holiday home at Balmoral.

While the Highlands become a playground for sportsmen, the kitchens of the shooting lodges they frequent are usually supervised by a Highland cook. These are the women who have the knowledge – passed down through the generations – of cooking the challenging game meat. Women like Margaret Fraser, whose *Highland Cookery Book* (1930) contains 90 recipes, 66 on cooking venison from the deer's head to its feet.

To roast a haunch of venison, she says: 'Trim the haunch and flour it well, taking special care that the parts which were cut are well coated. Place in a roasting-tin with plenty of beef dripping, and let it have a very hot oven to start it – or hang before a very bright fire and roast in the usual way for four hours, basting frequently. Season and dish on a hot plate with plenty of good brown gravy and redcurrant jelly.'

Red Grouse

Tomorrow is the Glorious Twelfth. There is the usual flurry of excitement as some attempt to fly in the 'first grouse', shot in the early morning, to appear that night on the restaurant menu. But when a London restaurant offers Winston Churchill roast grouse on 12 August, he chooses a steak and kidney pie instead. Two, if not three, days later the grouse might be worth eating, he opines, but not on the day it was shot.

'Grouse, and its kindred, require longer keeping than any other of the game birds,' says HBC Pollard in *The Sportsman's Cookery Book* (1926), 'and should hang from a minimum of three days to over a fortnight, according to the weather and the larder.'

In their heyday, before the moors became depleted, grouse were roasted on a spit, or in a very hot oven, and served up in their entirety. Usually they were placed on a slice of bread to catch the juices. And when it came to removing the meat from the bones, eaters were not shy about chewing bones. It was the only way to enjoy the full flavour from every nook and cranny of the delectable bird. Etiquette allowed it. Finger bowls were provided.

The medieval meeting of bread sauce with all richly flavoured game birds - as well as turkeys – pre-dates the French flour-thickened roux. Bread was the most common thickening agent for soups and sauces in medieval European cookery and remains popular in many countries, though bread sauce is Britain's only modern descendent.

Scotland's first published cookbook – Mrs McLintock's *Receipts for Cookery* (1736) – recommends bread sauce flavoured with nutmeg and a little claret wine for grouse, while Ronald Eden of Cromlix estate in Perthshire, author of *The Sporting Epicure*[ita] (1991), suggests a simpler version:

'Put one pint of new milk to boil with one onion and a few white peppercorns. Let it simmer for a while; steam it, and return it to the fire. Add two handfuls of breadcrumbs, one gill of cream, pepper and salt and serve hot.'

Game Seasons, all dates inclusive:

Red Deer is the commonest breed in Scotland and inhabits rough, wild, hill country. A Stag weighs about 14-16 stone (cleaned); Hind: 7–11 stone.
Scottish Season for stags: 1 July–20 October; for hinds: 21 October–15 February.
Best time for eating stags: early autumn; for hinds: November to mid January.

Roe Deer: Inhabits forests, weighs about four stone.
Scottish Season for bucks: 1 May–20 October; for does: 21 October–28/29 February.
Best time for eating bucks: October; for does: December to February.

Fallow Deer: Inhabits forests and parklands, weighs about 12 stone.
Scottish Season for bucks: 1 August–30 April; for does: 21 October–15 February.
Best time for eating bucks: October to November; for does: December to February.
Sika Deer: Stag weighs 6-7 stone; Hind: 4½–5 stone.
Scottish Season for stags: 1 August–30 April; for hinds: 21 October–15 February.

Hare: Season: no close season but may not be sold March to July inclusive. The best time for eating is October to January.

Pheasant: Season: 1 October – 1 February.

Mallard Duck: 1-1.3kg (2½ -2¾ lb), two to three servings. Season – below high tide mark: 1 September–20 February. Elsewhere: 1 September–31 January.
Teal 300-370g (11-13oz), one serving. Season: as for Mallard.
Widgeon 700-900g (1½-2 lb), two servings. Season: as for Mallard.

Goose: Pink-Footed Goose 2.7-3.2kg (6-7 lb), six servings. Season – as for Mallard. Greylag Goose 3.7-5kg (8-11lb), six servings. Season: as for Mallard.

Woodpigeon: 500-600g (1-1½ lb), one serving. No close season.

Red Grouse: 700-900g (1½-2lb). Season: 12 August–10 December.

(Red grouse live on the high heather moors eating, besides heather, a number of other herbs and grasses that give them their special flavour. Native to Scottish moors, they are wild birds and cannot be hand-reared. However their survival can be enhanced by human 'management' of the areas in which they live. To create a mosaic of heather plants at various stages of growth for the grouse habitat, different areas of the hill are burnt each year to help them regenerate. This system provides plenty of young shoots important for their diet plus older well-grown heather as cover for nesting birds. Availability is variable depending on how well grouse moors have been managed and the weather. Cold wet conditions when the young chicks are vulnerable leads to fatalities. Grouse shoots are usually highly organised with groups of beaters driving the birds forward towards the guns.)

Blackgame: 1.4-1.8kg (3-4 lb), three servings. Season: 20 August–10 December.

Ptarmigan: 400-600g (1-1½ lb), one serving. Season (Scotland only): 12 August–10 December.

Partridge Cock: 350-450g (13-15oz); Hen: 400g (12½-14½ oz), one to two servings. Season: 1 September–1 February.

Common Snipe: 100-130g (3½–4½ oz), one to two per person. Season: 12 August–31 January.

Woodcock: 230-400g (8-14oz), one serving. Season: 1 September–31 January.

Braised Haunch of Red Deer with Redcurrant Jelly

Cook's Tips: Deer must be skinned soon after they are shot then hung in a cool place so that the surface of the carcass is properly sealed. If this is done correctly, the meat can be hung until tender for several weeks without going 'moochie' (mouldy from warmth and/or damp). Age and hanging time greatly affect the quality of venison. Older animals will be tough, sometimes very tough, and possibly also dry so must be braised or stewed rather than roasted. Game dealers and butchers should be knowledgeable about the likely tenderness of the meat and should advise accordingly. Properly hung meat should be well dried out and 'sit up like a good piece of beef'. Enzyme action will have tenderised it and developed a rich gamey flavour. The meat should be dark crimson with pure white fat. It is the fat that signals the condition of the meat.

Yield: 8-10

50g (2oz) butter
500g (1lb 2oz) streaky bacon, unsmoked
500g (1lb 2oz) carrots, peeled and chopped
500g (1lb 2oz) celery, cleaned and chopped
1kg (2lb 4oz) onions, peeled and sliced
250g (9oz) dried ceps, soaked in hot water to just cover for 2 hours

Several sprigs of parsley and thyme, plus 3 bay leaves tied in a bundle with celery stalk or leek leaves
2 heads of garlic, whole cloves peeled
12 juniper berries, crushed
1 haunch of wild venison, on the bone with lower shin removed to fit roasting tin (or shoulder and front leg, suitably jointed)
Sea salt and black pepper
1 bottle robust red wine
1 jar redcurrant jelly

Large Roasting Tin
Preheat the oven to 50°F/180°C/Gas 4.

PREPARING THE VEGETABLES: Put the butter into the roasting tin and put onto the heat. Melt gently and sweat the bacon till beginning to crisp. Add the carrots, celery and onions and continue to sweat for about 5-10 minutes, stirring frequently to prevent sticking. Drain the ceps (reserving the liquid) and add.

THE VENISON: Remove vegetables from the heat, add garlic, herbs, juniper berries and place venison on top. Add salt and pepper, wine and water from ceps. Cover tightly with foil and place in a medium oven for three to four hours or until the meat is tender.

SERVING: Remove foil and serve in the roasting tin with its accompanying vegetables and cooking juices. Serve with Creamed Potatoes (see p95) and redcurrant jelly.

Venison Collops with Sloe Jelly

Cook's Tips: The tender cuts – that is the meat farthest away from the head and feet: the loin, tenderloin, steaks and chops – are cooked hot and fast. Without fat layers to cook through, the heat penetrates through the muscle, cooking the meat to rare or medium-rare in just minutes thus minimising the loss of juices. When game meat is over-cooked, the connective tissue in the muscle contracts, squeezing out all the juices, making the meat dry, tasteless and tough.

Yield: 4

1 tablespoon oil
25g (1oz) melted butter
4 x 175g (6oz) thick haunch steaks, or sinew-free meat from the loin
Sea salt and pepper
4 tablespoons robust red wine
2 tablespoons port
1 tablespoon sloe jelly – or redcurrant, rowan, bramble, blackcurrant
Lemon juice or red wine vinegar to taste
Salt and pepper
25g (1oz) butter to finish sauce

Garnish: fresh berries in season
Serve with: Creamed Potatoes (see p95)

COOKING VENISON: Heat the oil and butter in a frying pan and quickly fry the meat at a high heat for about two minutes on both sides. Tender meat should be served pink in the middle to retain as much of the natural flavour as possible. Remove and keep warm.

MAKING THE SAUCE: Add the red wine to the pan and boil up to reduce, scraping the residues from the meat from the pan. Add the port and reduce a little more. Add the jelly and stir in. Reduce a little more. Finish with lemon juice to balance the sweetness and salt and pepper and a knob of butter to give the sauce shine and body.

FINISHING AND SERVING: Strain the sauce onto heated serving plates. Place the venison on top and garnish with fresh berries. Serve with creamed potatoes.

Venison Pasty

'A modern pasty,' says Meg Dods in *The Cook and Housewife's Manual* (1826), 'is made of what does not roast well, as the neck, the breast, the shoulder. The breast makes the best pasty.'

Yield: 6-8

1.5kg (3lb 5oz) neck, shoulder, breast of venison
250g (9oz) firm lamb fat
2 tablespoons oil
2 onions, finely chopped
Sea salt and ground pepper
$\frac{1}{2}$ teaspoon each ground mace and allspice
300ml (10 fl oz) robust red wine
2 tablespoons wine vinegar
250g (9oz) puff pastry
1 egg yolk with 1 teaspoon water for brushing

Preheat the oven to 400°F/200°C/Gas 6 for first 30 minutes then turn down to 350°F/180°C/Gas 4 for another 80 minutes.

PREPARING THE MEAT: Cut the meat and lamb fat into small even sized pieces. Heat the oil in a pan and brown the onions lightly. Add the meat and continue to brown. Mix in the seasonings and add the wine and vinegar. Pour into a pie dish. Leave to cool slightly.

MAKING THE PASTY: Place a pie funnel in the centre of the pie dish. Roll out the pastry about 2cm wider than the rim of the dish. Place the dish on top of the pastry and cut round. Wet edges of the dish and put extra strip round, pressing down well. Wet this edge and put the rest of the pastry on top. Press down well to seal the edge. Decorate the edge and also the top of the pastry with scraps made into leaves. Make a hole for the steam to escape and brush with egg. Bake for 30 minutes at high heat, reduce and bake for another 60-80 minutes. Serve.

Roast Young Grouse
with Bread Sauce and Berries

Though the grouse season begins on the Glorious Twelfth, they are at their peak in September, coinciding with tangy brambles and mountain blaeberries which make the perfect partnership.

Yield: 4

4 young, oven-ready grouse
125g (4oz) butter, softened
Herbs/berries for the cavity: thyme, tarragon, bay leaf, juniper berries
Sea salt and pepper
600ml (20fl oz) robust red wine
125g (4oz) brambles (blackberries) or blaeberries

Skirlie (see p93)
4 slices of hot toast

Preheat the oven to 450°F/230°C/Gas 8.

PREPARING THE GROUSE: Rub the birds with butter then divide the remainder into four pieces and insert in the cavity of each bird. Add selection of herbs. Place in a roasting tin, cover with foil and leave overnight for flavours to mingle.

ROASTING: Heat a large frying pan and when hot, sear the birds on all sides. This starts the roasting quickly, put birds back into the roasting tin and roast for 15 minutes. Remove from the oven, cover and leave in a warm place for 10 minutes for the flesh to relax.

FINISHING AND SERVING: Meanwhile, add red wine to the pan juices. Bring to the boil and reduce. Taste and season. Strain, mix with brambles/blaeberries and place on serving plates. Place grouse on top. Serve with skirlie (see p93) mixed with 50g (2oz) softened butter and spread on toast.

Roast Pheasant with Tarragon

To keep this dry bird moist and succulent it should be roasted quickly and turned frequently so that it self bastes. Most of the roasting time should be on its breast so that the juices are running into it, rather than out. Ideally it should be roasted on a spit. All the problems of basting and turning vanish if you have one, while the results are the best ever.

Yield: 2-3

4 sprigs of parsley
4 sprigs of tarragon
125g (4oz) butter
1.5kg (3lb 5oz) young pheasant, hung for at least 4-5 days
Strip of pork fat or 4 rashers of unsmoked streaky bacon

Preheat the oven to 375°F/190°C/Gas 5.

PREPARING THE BIRD: Put a few sprigs of parsley and tarragon into the cavity of the bird along with about half the butter. Spread the remaining butter over the breast. Put the remaining herbs on top and cover with pork fat or bacon. Truss with string or thread to secure fat or bacon. Leave overnight, if possible, in a cold place for flavours to mingle.

ROASTING: Place the pheasant on its side on a rack in a shallow roasting tin and roast for 10 minutes. Turn onto the other side, baste and roast for another 10 minutes. Turn onto its breast, baste and roast for about 20 minutes. Remove from the oven. Take off the fat or bacon and return to the oven for another five minutes to brown the skin. It should take about 45 minutes in total. To test for doneness, pierce the meat near the thigh and leg joint. If the juices that run out are still pale pink the bird will be juicy but slightly underdone. If the juices are clear, it will be well done. This may take up to an hour so be prepared to continue with the basting since the breast meat loses its juices very quickly if overcooked.

SERVING: Put the bird onto a heated ashet, cover with foil and keep warm. Put the roasting tin onto the heat and add the red wine. Boil up, scraping the pan to release all the flavour. Simmer to reduce a little. Taste for seasoning and serve in a sauce boat with the pheasant. Serve with roast potatoes and skirlie (see p93).

Braised Pheasant
with Whisky and Juniper

Cook's Tips: This slow braising method overcomes the dryness of pheasant. It's best to use a gentle whisky with no peaty overtones.

Yield: 2

2 tablespoons oil or butter
1kg (2lb 4oz) pheasant, hung for at least 4-5 days
1 onion, finely chopped
150ml (5fl oz) light, aromatic Lowland malt such as Auchentoshan
150ml (5fl oz) water or game stock
1 tablespoon juniper berries, crushed
Sea salt and pepper
150ml (4fl oz) whipping cream
Lemon juice, to taste

Preheat the oven to 375°F/190°C/Gas 5.

BRAISING THE PHEASANT: Heat the oil or butter in a casserole (cast-iron, enamelled) and brown the pheasant on all sides. Remove, then add the onions and cook till golden brown. Return the pheasant to the pan and pour over half the whisky. Flame, and when the flames subside, add the water, juniper berries and seasoning. Cover and bake in the oven for 45 minutes or until tender. It could take longer depending on the age of the bird. Remove and joint the bird with a sharp knife into two breasts and two legs.

FINISHING THE DISH: Put the joints on a heated plate, cover with foil and keep warm. Strain the cooking liquor and return to the pan. Add the remaining whisky, cream and lemon juice and bring to the boil. Reduce to a good consistency. Taste and season. Return pheasant to the casserole and serve with Creamed Potatoes (see p95).

Rabbit an' Onions

Well-flavoured rabbits have a better flavour than some modern chicken. They are best eaten fresh though they can be hung. They should be skinned first (see instructions for Preparing the Hare p55).

Cook's Tips: Look for soft ears and sharp teeth which indicate a young rabbit. They should be plump with a smooth fur. There is no close season. They can weigh from 500g-1.5kg (1-3lb) – 2 small or 1 large for 4 servings.

Yield: 4

2 tablespoons oil
1 rabbit, skinned and jointed
2 onions, peeled and chopped
1 potato, peeled and chopped
2 leeks, washed and chopped
4-5 cloves garlic, peeled and chopped
Several sprigs of parsley and thyme, plus 3 bay leaves tied in
    a bundle with celery stalk or leek leaves
600ml (20fl oz) water or stock
Sea salt and pepper
350g (12oz) fresh or frozen peas
350g (12oz) beetroot, cooked
1-2 tablespoons chopped mint
2-3 tablespoons vinaigrette

PREPARING AND COOKING RABBIT: Heat the oil in a large cast-iron casserole or pot and brown the rabbit. Remove. Add the onions and sweat till soft and lightly browned. Add the potato, leeks and garlic and sweat for another five minutes, stirring frequently. Return the rabbit to the casserole and add the seasoning, herbs and water. Bring gently to the boil and simmer for 40-45 minutes or until the rabbit is tender.

FINISHING: Remove the bundle of herbs and add the peas. Cook for another few minutes. Taste for seasoning. Garnish with chopped mint and serve with cooked beetroot, sliced and mixed with vinaigrette.

Bawd Bree

(HARE STEW)

Not so highly regarded as other game meat, yet Scottish hares which have exercised well on the mountains have a superb flavour. They need a 'slow and low' method of cooking which allows their rich flavour to develop to its full potential.

Cook's Tips: A young hare will have soft, thin ears which tear easily and white, sharp teeth whereas an older hare will have tougher ears and larger, yellowier teeth. The coat of an older hare will be rougher. The Blue or Mountain hare is regarded as a better flavour than the Brown hare.

Yield: 4

1 hare
Water to cover
Several sprigs of parsley and thyme, plus 3 bay leaves tied in a
    bundle with celery stalk or leek leaves
3 carrots, cleaned
4 stalks celery
$^1/_2$ medium turnip (swede)
1 large onion stuck with 6 cloves
2 tablespoons flour
2 tablespoons dripping or oil
3-4 tablespoons port
Sea salt and black pepper

Serve with: Boiled mealy potato and rowan jelly

PREPARING THE HARE: Hares should be hung head downwards, ungutted and unskinned for one to two weeks, depending on the weather, taste and toughness of the hare. Place a bowl with a teaspoon of vinegar in it (this stops the blood congealing) underneath the head to catch the blood. To skin: make a circular cut through the fur just above the back heel joints. Make a lengthwise cut along the inside of the leg on both sides and pull the skin off both legs. Tie the paws together and hang up somewhere. This is not essential but makes the skinning job easier and means that the blood is collecting at the top end and is therefore less likely to spill out all over the place when the belly is opened up. Make a slit at the base of the tail from the top of one hind leg to the top of the other. Peel the skin back gently, turning it inside out and leaving the tail attached to the body. Now peel the skin down over the body and forelegs to the shoulders. Make a circular cut through the fur on the front legs just above the paws and then slit the skin along the inside of the leg. Peel back the skin on both legs. Peel the skin from the neck and then over the head as far as the ears, cut off the ears at the base and pull away the rest of the skin. It may be necessary to loosen round the eyes and mouth. Lay the hare on its back and with a very sharp knife open up the belly. Draw out and discard all the intestines leaving the liver, heart, lungs and kidneys. Now take out the kidneys; remove the liver carefully, remove the gall bladder and discard. Put the liver into a bowl with one teaspoon of vinegar. Position the bowl underneath the body and make a slit in the diaphragm at the base of the chest and allow the blood to run out into the bowl with the liver and vinegar. When you have collected the blood, pull out the heart and lungs. Remove the meat from the back and legs and cut into neat pieces. Place the remainder of the carcass into cold water and leave overnight.

MAKING THE STOCK: Bring the carcass and water to the boil, skim and add the herbs. Simmer for one hour and then add the vegetables. Cook for another hour. Strain. Dice the vegetables and return to the stock or sieve into the stock.

FINISHING THE DISH: Flour the hare flesh. Slice the kidneys and heart and flour. Melt dripping or oil in a pan and fry till lightly browned. Add to the stock and simmer gently till the meat is tender. Add diced vegetables and any edible carcass meat. Press liver through a sieve and mix with the blood. Pour some of the hot stock into the liver and blood and stir. Pour back into the pan and heat through. It should not boil or it will curdle. Add port. Taste for seasoning and serve in deep wide Scots soup plates with rowan jelly and a boiled mealy potato in the centre of the plate.

Jugged Hare

Cook's Tip: Long slow cooking will produce the best results.

Yield: 4-6

1 hare, skinned and gutted with
blood reserved and mixed
with a teaspoon of red wine
vinegar to prevent it curdling
4 tablespoons oil
3 medium onions, finely chopped
3 carrots, finely chopped
Half a head of celery, finely chopped
Several sprigs of parsley and thyme,
plus 3 bay leaves tied in a bundle
with celery stalk or leek leaves
1 teaspoon mace

$\frac{1}{2}$ teaspoon cloves
1 teaspoon allspice
1 tablespoon plain flour
$\frac{1}{2}$ bottle of red wine
1 tablespoon redcurrant jelly
Sea salt and pepper
Water or chicken stock to cover
1-2 tablespoons port
Lemon juice or red wine vinegar to taste
Serve with: Creamed Potatoes (see p95)

Preheat oven to 325°F/170°C/Gas 3.

PREPARING HARE: Skinning and gutting (see p55). Joint hare.

BROWNING: Heat the oil in a cast-iron, enamelled casserole and add the hare. Toss in the oil till lightly browned on all sides. Remove, and add onion. Cook till lightly browned. Add the carrots and celery and continue to toss in the oil for about five minutes. Add bundle of herbs.

COOKING: Crush all the spices roughly in a mortar or grinder. Sprinkle over the vegetables, add flour and mix in. Return hare to the casserole with the wine, redcurrant jelly, salt and pepper. Just cover with water or chicken stock, cover with lid and cook in the oven for two to three hours.

FINISHING: When cooked, remove the hare and strain the cooking liquor. Discard vegetables. Return sauce to the casserole, add port and simmer for about five minutes to reduce a little. Taste and season adding more redcurrant jelly if too bitter and more lemon juice if too sweet. Reduce the heat so the sauce is not boiling and stir in the blood, allow to thicken for a few minutes, return the hare and serve with creamed potatoes.

Roast Chicken and Oatmeal Skirlie

Cook's Tip: The attraction of this recipe for the cook is that the chicken and vegetables are cooked together. The attraction for the eater is that the vegetables cook underneath the chicken and absorb some of its flavour.

Yield: 4

1 x 1.6kg (3½ lb) free range, preferably
   organic chicken
4-5 tablespoons melted dripping
   or olive oil
Sea salt to taste
4 medium potatoes, peeled, washed
   and dried
4 medium onions, peeled
4 medium parsnips, peeled
4 heads of garlic

Skirlie:
4 tablespoons bacon fat, or other fat or oil
1 large onion, finely chopped
125g (4oz) medium oatmeal
Sea salt and pepper

Preheat the oven to 425°F/220°C/Gas 7.

ROASTING: Rub chicken with oil and season with salt. Cut potatoes, onion and parsnips into roughly the same size. Put into the roasting tin with garlic, drizzle all over with melted dripping or oil and turn, to coat evenly. Make a bed for the chicken in the middle and place it on one side. Roast for 30 minutes. Remove from the oven and turn the chicken onto its other side. Turn the vegetables. Roast for another 30 minutes. Remove from the oven and turn the chicken onto its back so the breast is up. Turn vegetables. Roast for another 30-40 minutes.

TEST FOR READINESS: Pierce with a skewer through the thickest part of the thigh and the juices that run out should be clear. If slightly pink, return to the oven for another 10-15 minutes. Cover the breast with foil to prevent drying out if it is getting too brown.

RESTING AND SERVING: Leave to rest for 10 minutes in a warm place. Strain off the juices. Decant the excess oil/fat and use for other cooking. Add some cold water to the remaining gravy, put into a pan and bring to the boil. Taste for seasoning and serve with the chicken.

TO MAKE SKIRLIE: Heat the fat in a frying pan and cook the onion till soft and lightly browned. Add the oatmeal and cook for another five minutes stirring occasionally. Season to taste and serve with the chicken.

Chicken Stovies

Also known as Stoved Chicken, this Highland dish combines chicken with traditional slow cooked 'stovies' in a pot. The word comes from an early use of the verb ' to stove' as in: 'Add the boiling water and let the preparation stove slowly till wanted,' says Meg Dods in *The Cook and Housewife's Manual* (1826).

Yield 4

4 chicken joints
2 tablespoons seasoned flour
50g (2oz) butter
500g (1lb 2oz) onions, sliced
1kg (2lb 4oz) potatoes, peeled and sliced
Sea salt and pepper
250ml (8fl oz) water
Melted butter for brushing
1-2 tablespoons chopped parsley

Preheat the oven to 350F/180C/Gas 4.

BROWNING THE CHICKEN: Flour the chicken and heat the butter in a frying pan. Brown the chicken on all sides.

ASSEMBLING THE DISH: Place a layer of onions and potatoes (about a third) in the base of a casserole. Season and place two joints on top. Cover with another layer (second third) of potatoes and onions, season and add remaining joints. Finish with remaining third of potatoes and onions. Add water.

BAKING AND SERVING: Cover with a tight-fitting lid and bake for one and a half hours. Remove the lid about 20 minutes before the end of the cooking time and brush the top with butter. Return to the oven, leave the lid off and bake till lightly browned on top. Sprinkle over parsley and serve.

Roast Duck
with Fried Potatoes and Oranges

Cook's Tip: This recipe produces a crisp well-cooked duck plus a supply of good flavoured dripping which can be used to add flavour to soups and stews. Here, it's used to make fried potatoes.

Yield: 4

2.7kg (6lb) fresh, free range duck
Sea salt, ground
1kg (2lb 4oz) floury potatoes
6-8 tangerine oranges

Serve with watercress or other piquant leaf salad

Preheat the oven to 425°F/220°C/Gas 7.

ROASTING: Dry bird thoroughly, leave in a cool draught to dry off skin. The dryer the skin, the crisper the duck. Prick the duck skin all over, through to the subcutaneous fat, with a thick needle or skewer, to allow the excess fat to run out of the bird while cooking. Place duck on a rack in the roasting tin to allow the heat to circulate better. Season surface with salt and put into the oven. After 20 minutes, turn the heat down to 350°F/180°C/Gas 4 and roast slowly for two and a half to three hours for a crisp well-done bird, removing from the oven after the first hour and a half to drain off excess fat and reserve. To check for doneness, prick the leg with a skewer to check that the juices run clear. If still pink return to the oven.

MAKING POTATOES: Boil potatoes gently till just soft. Drain and peel. Cut into thin slices. When duck is almost ready, heat some of the duck dripping in a frying pan and fry the potatoes on either side till browned and crisp. Season with salt.

PREPARING TANGERINES: Remove skin with a sharp knife. Cut in slices, remove any stones.

FINISHING: Remove duck from the oven and leave to rest. Strain off the rest of the surplus fat and reserve. Add a little water to the pan juices and bring to the boil. Reduce for about 5-10 minutes, scraping the debris from the base of the roasting tin. Season and pour into a heated sauceboat. Serve duck with gravy, fried potatoes, watercress and oranges.

Roast Goose with Apple Stuffing

Cook's Tips: Like duck, one of the perks of this recipe is the fat that it produces. An essential ingredient in bean stews, it also adds great flavour to soups and roast potatoes.

Yield: 8	Gravy:
4.5-5kg (10-12lb) young goose	Goose giblets or carcass of other
with giblets	poultry
Sea salt, ground	1.2L (2pt) water
900g (2lb) small cooking apples	1 carrot, chopped
2kg (4lb 8oz) potatoes, peeled	1 onion, quartered
	1 celery stalk
	1 leek, sliced
	1 tablespoon black peppercorns
	1 bay leaf
Preheat the oven to 425°F/220°C/Gas 7.	A few parsley stalks

MAKING GRAVY: Put all the ingredients into a pan, bring to the boil, skim surface to remove scum. Simmer gently for about two hours. Strain.

ROASTING: Dry off goose thoroughly, prick the skin all over, through to the subcutaneous fat, with a thick needle to allow the excess fat to run out of the bird while cooking. Wash apples and remove the centre cores. Fill body cavity with the apples. Place goose, breast downwards, on a rack in the roasting tin to allow the heat to circulate better. Season surface with salt. Put into the oven. After one hour, remove the bird and turn onto its back. Sprinkle with salt. Drain off excess fat and reserve. Turn the heat down to 350°F/180°C/Gas 4 and roast slowly for another two hours for a crisp well-done bird. To check for doneness, prick the leg with a skewer and check that the juices run clear. If still pink return to the oven. About an hour before its is ready, put the potatoes into another roasting tin and pour over some goose fat. Turn them in the fat until thoroughly coated and roast for about an hour till browned.

FINISHING: Remove goose from the oven and leave to rest for 10-15 minutes. Strain off the rest of the surplus fat and reserve. Add the strained gravy to the pan juices and bring to the boil. Reduce for about five to ten minutes, scraping the debris from the base of the roasting tin. Season and pour into a heated sauceboat. Serve goose with gravy, apples which will have softened, and roast potatoes.

MEAT CLASSICS

Haggis, Tatties and Neeps

A candlelit glow lightens the dim interior of the recess known as the 'coffin' – on account of its shape – in Dowie's tavern in Liberton's Wynd, just off the Royal Mile. Snug, cosy and free from outside cares, its other attraction is the landlord's kindliness and discretion.

Dowie's has become a favourite haunt of the poet Robert Burns, since he arrived from his native Ayrshire on 29 November, 1786 for his first visit to the capital. Burns rates John Dowie one of the finest landlords he has come across in the city.

Tonight he is holed-up with some of his cronies, including Willie Nicol and Allan Masterton, drinking the excellent Edinburgh Ale brewed by Archibald Younger. Later there will be the 'rascally' Highland gill. But as the night wears on, they call on Dowie to find out what's for supper.

In the flexible tavern system, there is a range of dishes which vary in price from tatties on their own – the cheapest supper – to slices of roast or boiled meat with greens. Neeps are never eaten as a supper on their own but are used to flavour the otherwise monotonous tattie supper in the days when meat-eating in Scotland – for most people – is largely confined to high days and holidays.

Dowie also has a haggis pudding, which he recommends to Burns and his friends. This economical dish, which his wife has made using a pluck (innards) of a sheep, has taken her the best part of the morning to prepare.

She boils it first, then chops up all the bits, mixing this with oatmeal and seasonings then stuffs it all into the sheep's stomach bag. It is a dish of peasant virtue and strength, strongly influenced by images of slaughter, which Burns recognises for its sense and worth. It is far superior, he thinks, to all the elaborate Frenchified food he has eaten during his socialising in the smart New Town houses of Edinburgh's intelligentsia.

When Dowie's haggis arrives, 'filling the groaning trencher', all gather round for the ritual stabbing to release the glorious sight: 'Warm-reeking rich!'. Then the communal eaters take up their horn spoons and delve in for their share of the 'Great Chieftain o' the Puddin-race!'.

Five years after his death in 1801, the first Burns Club is formed in Greenock. But it is in 1815 that the Edinburgh literati, including Sir Walter Scott, hold the first national Burns celebration with a formal supper including a rendering of 'The Address' accompanied by platefuls of haggis. At the end of the century there are 51 Burns clubs. And by then mashed tatties and neeps have been added to the menu as The Burns Supper sets off to travel the globe.

Mince an' Tatties/Doughballs

A pound of mince for a family of four does two days in the tenement kitchen, with the black-leaded coal range and the 'wally dugs' guarding either end of the mantelpiece. It's so simple to make. Item: one pot. Into it put a lump of dripping for browning the chopped onion. Then add the mince. Break it up with a fork, while it sizzles and browns, so you don't get lumps. Next, add chunks of carrots, peeled and chopped. Fill up with water, preferably already boiled. Add salt and pepper, put on the lid and remember to turn the handle in to avoid accidents in the cramped kitchen where the family lives, eats, sleeps and washes.

Never a week passes without the legendary pot of thin, but good flavoured, mince to-do-two-days. Cheap and sustaining, it has the added merit of being the perfect partner for inexpensive carbohydrates. The first day is with doughballs (or 'baas'); the second is with boiled potatoes ('tatties'). Always on the dinner table is a spicy condiment: thick brown HP (Houses of Parliament) sauce and/or thinner darker brown Yorkshire Relish. Everyone takes their pick and seasons to taste.

For the doughballs, spoonfuls of a suet dumpling mixture are dropped into the pot about half an hour before the mince is ready. The lid is replaced and the damp heat and steam make the doughballs swell and rise. Fluffy on top, soft and sappy from the mince underneath, they are sometimes speckled green with a handful of chopped parsley. This is the one-pot dinner.

A two-pot is when potatoes are the filler. Boiling in their skins is vital for 'floury' Golden Wonders that 'turn to soup' in an instant if they're boiled peeled. Peel while they are still hot: holding each potato with a fork, take off the skin with a knife. Once it is peeled, it's put back into the pot with a lump of butter, a splash of milk, some salt and pepper.

Then an old newspaper is put on the floor for the pot to sit on. And standing over it, the potato masher pulverises the hot potatoes till they blend with butter and milk into a steaming creamy mass. Lumps are not allowed.

And neither are whole potatoes according to the poet J K Annand (1903-1993) in 'Mince and Tatties' from his book *A Whale O' Rhymes*:

I dinna like hail tatties	*Sae mash and mix the tatties*
Pit on my plate o mince	*Wi mince intil the mashin,*
For when I tak my denner	*And sic a tasty denner*
I eat them baith at yince.	*Will aye be voted 'Smashin!'*

Scotch Pie and Bovril

In one hand is the pie – thin crisp pastry, moist meaty filling – in the other the mug of steaming hot Bovril. Both are sustenance at half-time, before returning to the wet and windy terraces for the remainder of the match.

It's been a partnership at football grounds for decades. At least since the convenient mass-produced Scotch pie became a staple item for urban industrial workers and their families. It was first made by itinerant 'pie-wives' who baked them at home and hawked them about the streets for a living.

According to one St Andrews professor, writing of the 1920s, his pie-wife's mutton pies were something of a gourmet treat: 'Delightful as were her pigeon and apple pies, her chef-d'oeuvre was a certain kind of mutton pie. The mutton was minced to the smallest consistency, and was made up in a standing crust, which was strong enough to contain the most delicious gravy. There were no lumps of fat or grease in them at all. They always arrived piping hot. It makes my mouth water still when I think of those pies.'

Scotch pies of this quality continued to be made with tasty mutton until sheep that were over a year old, went out of fashion around the 1950s. Beef was then substituted for mutton in the Scotch pie. A really cheap pie was full of starchy filler and a great deal of pepper to compensate for the lack of meaty flavour.

The pie's history has not always been a happy one, though today some dedicated pie-makers have revived its quality and brought back its gourmet status with an annual Scotch pie award when bakers and butchers compete for the title of the best Scotch Pie.

The pie's partner, Bovril, was invented in 1874 by a Scottish butcher, John Lawson Johnston, when he emigrated to Canada. At first he called his thick, meaty-flavoured paste 'Johnston's Fluid Beef' which he promoted as a hot drink at Ice Carnivals in Montreal.

On the back of this success, he moved to London and set up a much larger operation making a thicker and stronger meat extract that he renamed Bovril. ('Bo' from Latin = ox; and 'vril' from vrilya = life force.) We know better now, but at that time most people believed the extravagant claims that 1lb of Bovril was equal to 36lb of meat, though of course it is made from beef, steeped in water, boiled, strained and then the liquid reduced by boiling to a pasty consistency.

A Scotch pie is a round, raised pie, made by bakers using special moulds, of about 9cm diameter and about 4cm high. The top edge extends by about 1cm beyond the round of pastry covering the pie, which makes a central space for holding fillings, sauces or gravy. They are pale golden with the top edge darker brown.

Their popularity developed in the late nineteenth century as industrialisation brought large numbers of people into cities where wages were low and living (and cooking) conditions poor. Never made at home, they were among the first convenience food, sold hot from the bakers ('het peys' in Dundee). Tinned beans, mashed potatoes and gravy were popular fillings.

Tripe and Onions

For the gentlemen of Edinburgh (circa 1800), the late afternoon and early evening is spent in John's Coffee House, reading and debating the news in the London papers which have just arrived by stage coach two days after publication. The women are at home, drinking tea and playing cards. Sometimes the men join them, but here, in the warm den of the coffee house, there is the tempting allure of wafting aromas, and other enticements.

At Douglas's tavern, the cook makes the best minced collops in town. Everyone says so. Just as everyone agrees that the best puddings are at Lizzie's, the best sheep's heid at Duddingston and the best tripe suppers at the Guildford.

Their one-pot supper arrives in a deep plate, a mix of different kinds of tender, light grey tripe. There are some 'thick seam', meaty chunks from the first stomach, as well as interesting pieces of 'honeycomb' from the second and some finer textured 'reed' and 'bible' tripe from the third and fourth stomach.

The cook collected these 'pluck meats' ('offal' is an English word not yet used in Scotland) from the fleshmarket three days ago. To make a supply of cooked tripe for tripe suppers, she cuts up the cleaned and blanched (but not bleached) tripe into cutlet-sized pieces and puts them into a large earthenware pot with a knuckle bone.

She covers the pot with a thick piece of linen cloth then ties it on firmly with string. It sits in a cauldron of hot water and is left at the side of the fire to simmer gently for a day and a night. By this time the tough tripe has softened and absorbed the good flavour of the bone.

The bone is removed, and the pot goes into the larder to be kept for another day to cool and set firmly into a jelly. It will keep like this for a month in winter. To make a tripe supper for her gentlemen customers, she simply cuts out a chunk of jellied tripe, heats it through and serves it with salt and pepper, mustard and a roasted onion.

Other tripe-lovers of the day elaborate on the tavern cook's basic recipe. They thicken the cooking liquor with flour and butter. Milk, mustard, mushroom ketchup, herbs, chives and a glass of wine are among a variety of other additions. Button onions are fried in butter to accompany...

Forfar Bridies

Don't horseshoes bring luck? And what do you need more than anything else when setting out on married life? With these thoughts in mind, Mr Jolly, an enterprising Forfar baker of the 1850s, sets about creating a pastry in the shape of a horseshoe for a wedding breakfast.

This is prime beef breeding Angus country, so he can make it with the best quality beef. He needs some suet for lubrication and onions for more flavour. All are chopped finely and used for a tasty filling. The horseshoe-shaped pastries are a great success, and soon they are essential fare at every wedding, far and wide. Jolly names his good-luck symbols – the 'bridie' – after the bride's meal.

In Jolly's bakery a young apprentice baker, James McLaren learns, among other skills, the craft of the bridie according to the Jolly recipe:

'Take a pound of the best steak. Beat it with the paste roller, then cut it in narrow strips, and again cut these into inch lengths and season with salt and pepper. Divide into three portions. Mince, finely, three ounces of suet. Make a stiff dough with flour, water and a seasoning of salt and roll out thin into three ovals. Cover half of each oval with the meat: sprinkle with the suet and a little minced onion if desired; wet the edges, fold over, and crimp with finger and thumb; nip a small hole on top of each. Bake for about half an hour in a quick oven, then at a moderate temperature until the steak is tender. They should be eaten hot.'

Besides being made for weddings, they are sold in the shop and prove very popular among the women of Forfar as a weekend, take-away treat. They are a hit, too, with local farm hands who visit Forfar on market day and queue up in the back court of Jollys, ordering three 'het bradies' at a go. One enthusiast munches his way through eight bridies without stopping.

'In the normal bridie, you used to get one-sixth of a pound of stewing steak and kidney, diced by hand,' says an old Forfarian. 'A hole was made in the paste to let off steam. If you got a bridie with two holes in it, it had onions.'

By 1893, James McLaren has prospered sufficiently at Jolly's bakery to have enough resources to set up a bakery of his own in the town. Such is the demand for bridies that he carries on the tradition: passing the recipe on to his son who follows him in the bakery. He in turn is followed by his grandson, William McLaren, who continues the family tradition.

The luck of the bridie, I am happy to report, still survives.

Meat and meat processing traditions

Aberdeen Angus; Beef Shorthorn; Galloway: Highland Beef breeds: The oldest native breeds are the Galloway and Highland. With their thick coats and sturdy feet, they can be kept on exposed hill and marginal land, which Scotland has in abundance. It's their natural habitat, where they eat a natural diet, thriving on low-cost winter and summer rations, that they convert into high-quality beef with marbled fat. It makes environmental and agricultural sense to breed beef in Scotland. The other native breeds – Aberdeen Angus and Beef Shorthorn – are less hardy and are wintered inside but are still fed a high-quality natural diet based on silage (preserved grass), converting this into early-maturing, high-quality beef with marbled fat. Around three-quarters of the beef produced in Scotland comes from beef-suckler herds where the calves are allowed to feed from their mothers until they can feed for themselves. Cattle from these beef-breeding herds command the highest prices for the prime quality. Cheaper beef comes from dairy cattle, past their age of useful milk production or from herds, known as 'bull beef', which have been intensively reared indoors and fed on a less natural diet.

Ayrshire Bacon: This is Scotland's only distinctive bacon cure and was first developed in the South-West where pigs were reared as an adjunct to a flourishing dairy industry. Unlike most bacon cures, the back (cutlet) and the streaky (flank) are not separated. Once boned out it is skinned and salted in wet brine for two days, then dried out before it is rolled up tightly with the fat side outermost and the streaky wrapped round the back. Because it is skinned, the carcass is not scalded after slaughter to remove the bristles. This produces an end product with a finer colour and firmer texture than bacon which has been scalded. When sliced thinly and fried the round shape makes a convenient filling for bacon rolls.

Blackface; Cheviot; Shetland; North Ronaldsay Sheep breeds: All native sheep breeds are hardy and can be kept on exposed hill and marginal land throughout summer and winter, eating a natural diet which they convert into high quality lamb. There are rare breeds, like the sheep on North Ronaldsay, which live entirely on the shoreline, eating mostly seaweed which they convert into a distinctive flavoured lamb. None of the native breeds are large but what they lack in size, they make up for in flavour. Until the mid-twentieth century, most sheep was eaten as mutton rather than lamb. Then a meat industry policy concentrated on producing under-a-year-old lamb instead of mutton which disappeared from the menu. Used for pies, it was also exported to countries where it was appreciated for its flavour and suitability for long-cooked stews. A few butchers have revived mutton, or young mutton as it is sometimes called, since it is usually not more than two years old. Salting was the original method of preservation and continues in some areas (see Reestit Mutton on following page).

Black and White (or Mealie) Puddings: These were originally made at the killing of a pig to make use of the surplus blood and intestines. Recipes vary around the country, some with more, or less fat. Some are more highly spiced than others. Black have blood added, while White or Mealie are made with just oatmeal fat and onions.

Pig-killing was a communal time when everyone gathered to help. As a contributor to the *North East Review* remembers: 'Come time the skins were a' filled up, and tied, and jabbit wi' a darner (needle), and they were ready for the pot. They were biled an oor. It wis easy the langest oor I mind on. My teeth wid be watering till I slivert, and when they lifted the lid o' the pot to see the water wisna biling in – oh! the guff (smell) that filled the kitchie. The tastings, or the preens, as my mother ca'ed them, were first oot and nae wirds could tell ye fit they tastit like – as the poet his't – "warm reeking rich", ye dinna see the like the day.'

Haggis, tatties and neeps: see Meat Classics p61

Lorne, Square or Sliced, Sausage: An uncased, fresh beef sausage made in a large rectangular block and cut in slices approximately 10cm square. Known as a Square or Sliced sausage everywhere besides Glasgow where it is known as a Lorne sausage after the popular Glasgow music hall comedian, Tommy Lorne, whose derogatory remarks about the square sausage 'doormats' became legendary. Its shape was a convenient fit for a morning roll, making a favourite breakfast with a fried egg on top.

Reestit Mutton: This originated in the days before refrigeration and survives in Shetland and other islands. The meat is cut up and put into brine, the recipes for which are secret, but are approximately 80% salt to 20% sugar. The meat is left for about 10-21 days then hung up on hooks to dry. One Lerwick butcher had a notice in his window for visitors unfamiliar with the tradition: 'Reestit Mutton, What is it? Traditionally it was salted lamb or mutton dried above a peat fire. It will keep for years if you keep it dry. Reestit mutton soup is an acquired taste that you acquire at the first taste. A small piece is enough to flavour a pot of soup which should include cabbage, carrots, neeps and tatties.'

Sassermeat: This is a sausage-like mixture of minced beef – now made mostly by butchers in Shetland – salted and spiced, and sometimes moulded into 'square' sausages in a tin of the type used for Lorne Sausages. It is thought to be of Scandinavian origin (Shetland was once part of Norway) and was originally a heavily salted and spiced mixture which was packed into an earthenware crock for use throughout the winter when fresh meat was not available.

Roast Rib of Scotch Beef

Cook's Tips: The best flavour, texture and quality comes from native breeds that have been well fed and show a good marbling and covering of fat. Quality also depends on butchering; ie the meat should be hung long enough to develop a mature flavour. Well-hung meat is dark red and 'sits up' well with no wetness on the surface. A pinkish-wet piece of meat can shrink to almost half its size in cooking.

Yield: 6-8

2 to 2.5kg (4½ – 5½ lb) rib eye on the bone
50g (2oz) butter
½ teaspoon sea salt
1 teaspoon ground black pepper
1 teaspoon powdered English mustard
1 tablespoon flour

Roast Root Vegetables:
1 small turnip, peeled and chopped roughly
4 medium parsnips, peeled and sliced
4 medium carrots, peeled and sliced
4 medium potatoes, peeled
4 medium onions, peeled
2–3 tablespoons oil (preferably olive)

Yorkshire Puddings:
125g (4oz) plain flour
Pinch of salt
1 large egg
300ml (10fl oz) milk
50g (2oz) lard

Pre-heat the oven to 475°F/240°C/Gas 9.

PREPARING: Rub the joint all over with butter. Mix the salt, pepper, mustard and flour and coat meat all over. Cover and leave overnight to absorb flavours.

ROASTING: Place the vegetables in the roasting tin, drizzle with oil, season and put into the preheated oven. Cook for 30 minutes, turning occasionally. Add the beef, skin side up. Return to oven. After five minutes reduce the heat to 400°F/200°C/Gas 6 and from this point, time the meat roasting, allowing 15 minutes per 500g (1lb 2oz) for medium rare. This produces a joint with enough medium well-cooked meat at either end for two or three portions while the rest will be medium rare. Allow 20-25 minutes for well-cooked meat. Remove any of the vegetables that are ready before the meat, and keep warm.

TO MAKE THE PUDDINGS: Sift the flour into a bowl and add salt. Make a well in the centre and add the egg and milk. Whisk together to make a thick pouring consistency (you can also mix in a blender). Put a knob of lard into each pudding mould and place in a very hot oven 475°F/240°C/Gas 9 till almost smoking hot (about five minutes). Remove and pour in the batter. Bake for 10 minutes. Remove and serve with gravy as a first course.

FINISHING AND SERVING: Remove the meat and vegetables onto a serving ashet, cover and keep warm. Meanwhile decant the fat from the roasting tin. Add red wine and reduce over a high heat for a few minutes, scraping up the bits of debris from the base of the tin. Season, strain and serve in a sauceboat with the meat and vegetables. Also serve with Horseradish Sauce (see p201) and mustard (see p200).

Mince an' Tatties

*Cook's Tip:*The secret of the best mince is to brown both onions and the mince separately, and thoroughly. This gives a natural flavour to the gravy and there's no need for stock cubes et al.

Yield: 4

2 tablespoons oil
2 medium onions, finely chopped
500g (1lb 2oz) stewing steak, minced
Salt and pepper

Optional vegetables:
2-3 carrots, diced
$\frac{1}{2}$ medium turnip (swede), diced
2-3 stalks celery, diced

Serve with: Creamed Potatoes (see p95)

BROWNING AND COOKING: Heat the oil in a pan and add the onions. Cook gently, stirring occasionally, until they begin to brown. When they are an even, rich brown, remove from the pan. Add the mince and break up with a fork, stirring well. Continue to brown until all the excess moisture is evaporated and the mince is dry and well-browned. Return the onions. Stir well and add salt and pepper. Just cover with water and bring to a simmer. Add the other vegetables (optional). When the vegetables are cooked stir in parsley. Serve with creamed potatoes.

MINCE AN' DOUGHBALLS: follow the above recipe, use recipe for Dumplings (see p72), and add dumplings 20 minutes before the mince is ready. Put on lid and cook till they are risen and light.

Beef Olives and Skirlie

Cook's Tip: To save time, buy butcher's ready-made beef olives.

Yield: 4

500g (1lb 2oz) rump steak, cut thinly
250g (9oz) sausage meat
Cocktail sticks for securing
2 tablespoon oil
1 medium onion, finely chopped
Water to three-quarters cover
Sea salt and pepper

For the skirlie (see p93)

PREPARING THE OLIVES: Cut the steak into strips about 5cm (2 inch) wide. Remove the sausage meat from its casing and divide up evenly between the strips of beef. Roll up and secure with a cocktail stick.

COOKING: Heat the oil and add the onion. Cook till lightly brown, then add the olives and brown on all sides. Add the water to come about three-quarters of the way up. Add salt and pepper and simmer gently till tender.

SERVING: Remove meat and keep warm. Reduce cooking liquor to a rich glaze and pour over the olives. Serve with Skirlie (see p93) and Creamed Potatoes (see p95).

Boiled Beef
with Carrots and Dumplings

Cook's Tip: A favourite variety of zesty sauces, such as horseradish or mustard, or pickled walnuts or chutney, will liven up boiled meat and vegetables.

Yield: 6

2.5kg (5lb 8oz) brisket or silverside
Water to cover
Several sprigs of parsley and thyme, plus 3 bay leaves tied in
    a bundle with celery stalk or leek leaves
4 stalks celery, chopped
6 medium onions, peeled
6 medium carrots, peeled
6 leeks, cleaned and cut into thick chunks

Dumplings:
225g (8oz) self-raising flour
100g (3½ oz) prepared suet
Sea salt and pepper
Water to mix

Serve with: horseradish, mustard sauce, pickled walnuts or chutney

BOILING MEAT: Put the beef into a large pot and cover with cold water. Bring to the boil and skim. Add herbs, salt and pepper and continue to simmer for about one and a half to two hours or until the meat is just tender. After the meat has been cooking for about one and a half hours, add the celery, onions and carrots. About 10 minutes before it is ready add the leeks. If the beef takes a bit longer, remove the vegetables once they are cooked. Remove the meat and vegetables and place on a large heated ashet. Moisten with a little stock and place in a warm place.

DUMPLINGS: Bring the cooking liquid up to boiling point. It should be boiling gently when you add the dumplings. Sift the flour into a bowl and add the suet, salt, pepper and mix with water to a soft consistency. Shape into walnut-sized balls and drop into the simmering broth. Put on lid and leave to cook for about 10 minutes (reserve the remaining stock and use for making soup).

SERVING: Serve dumplings with the meat and vegetables and with pickled walnuts and Horseradish Sauce (see p201).

Steak and Kidney Pie

This is a traditional New Year's Day dinner. Often it's made by a favourite butcher who will happily make a 'Desperate Dan' (giant pie) to feed a large family gathering – sausages are the filler for the less well-off.

Yield: 4-6

2 tablespoons beef dripping or oil
1 large onion, finely chopped
250g (9oz) lamb's kidney or beef sausages
500g (1lb 2oz) rump or pope's eye steak
1 tablespoon plain flour, seasoned with salt and pepper
Water
2 bay leaves
250g (9oz) mushrooms or use a pie funnel or small cup
200g (7oz) puff pastry
1 beaten egg for brushing

Preheat the oven to 450°F/230°C/Gas 8.
Grease a 1.2L (2pt) pie dish.

MAKING THE FILLING: Heat the oil and brown the onions until dark, but not burnt. Brown the sausages (if using). Skin, split, core and cut up the kidney. Using a rolling pin or meat bat, beat out the rump steak till thin. Cut into long strips and coat the meat with seasoned flour. Cut the sausages in half. Roll the meat round either the sausages or the kidney. Put into the base of the pie dish and cover with onions. Add the bay leaves, and pile mushrooms on till they come high above the rim to hold up the pastry. Or place pie funnel or cup in the centre of the meat. Pour in enough water to come half-way up the filling.

BAKING THE PIE: Roll out the pastry an inch or so larger than the pie. Place the pie dish on top of this and cut round the pie. Wet the rim of the pie dish and cut a thin strip from the leftover pastry and place round rim. Wet edge and place pastry lid on top – seal down well. Use any leftover pastry to make pastry leaves and place these on top. Brush pastry top and leaves with beaten egg, and make two holes for the steam to escape. Bake for about 30 minutes in the hot oven until the pastry is risen and browned. Reduce the heat to 350F/180C/Gas 4 and bake for another hour until the meat is tender. Cover the pastry with foil if it is browning too much. Fill up with hot water or stock through one of the holes until it's about three-quarters full before serving.

Grilled Steak and Chips

Cook's Tip: Though the fillet is the most tender steak, it is also the one with the least fat and therefore the least flavour.

Yield: 4

4 x 200-225g (7-8oz) grilling steak
    (sirloin, rib eye or fillet)
Oil for brushing
Ground black pepper
Sea salt
Mustard
500g (2lb 4oz) potatoes for chips (see p33)

PREPARING AND GRILLING: Preheat the grill to a high heat. Brush steaks with oil and season with pepper. Grill on both sides, turning every few minutes for 5-10 minutes depending on thickness.

TEST FOR DONENESS: Still bouncy when pressed with turning tongs = rare; slightly firm = medium rare; very firm = well-done.

SERVING: Serve on heated plates with mustard, a green salad and chips.

Scotch Beef in French Claret

'We have one great advantage, that makes amends for many inconveniences, that is, wholesome and agreeable drink, I mean French Claret.'

Edward Burt (Chief Surveyor to General Wade during the making of roads through the Highlands) *Letters from a Gentleman in the North of Scotland* (1724-28).

Cook's Tips: With so much borrowing back and forth between Scotland and France, the use of French claret to cook Scottish beef seems an obvious combination. The cheapest cut of bee can be used with no loss of flavour, in fact the harder working muscles like the leg will have more flavour than other less active ones.

6-8 servings

For the meat:
4 tablespoons beef dripping or oil
1.5kg (3 lb 5oz) stewing steak, cut into 4cm (1½ inch) cubes
5 cloves garlic, crushed
2 tablespoons flour
1 bottle fruity young claret (Burgundy, Cotes-du-Rhone or Beaujolais)
Salt and freshly milled black pepper
1 teaspoon sugar
Several sprigs of parsley and thyme, plus 3 bay leaves tied in a bundle
    with celery stalk or leek leaves

For the trimmings:
150g (5oz) lean bacon
6-8 very small onions
400g (14oz) button mushrooms, chopped

Serve with: chopped parsley and boiled potatoes.
Pre-heat the oven to 300°F/150°C/Gas 2.

COOKING MEAT: Heat the oil in a frying pan and brown the pieces of meat. Put the rest into the casserole, add the garlic and sprinkle over the flour. Leave uncovered in the oven to continue browning for 15 minutes, stirring from time to time. Add the wine, season lightly, and add herbs. Cover and simmer until the meat is tender (about one to two hours).

PREPARING TRIMMINGS AND SERVING: Meanwhile, cook the trimmings. Heat a frying pan and fry the bacon till light browned. Add the onions and cook uncovered for about 10 minutes. Then add the mushrooms, stir, cover and cook gently for another 10 minutes. Keep aside till serving. Remove meat from the oven and stir in the trimmings. Heat through for five minutes and serve with chopped parsley and boiled potatoes.

Spiced Beef

This treatment adds a rich mellow flavour to beef and is a useful joint for impromptu eating through the mid-winter festive season or for other celebrations. Early methods involved burying the meat in dry salt in a stone trough during the winter months; spices were added but the proportion of salt was high and therefore it dominated the flavour of the meat. Today there is less need to use so much salt and more modified versions depend on subtle blends of spices making a rich and distinctive flavour in the meat.

Cook's Tips: It is not really worth spicing anything under 2kg (4 lb 8oz) since the point is to have enough to last several meals. The best size is 3.5kg (7lb 8oz) and the best cuts are silverside, rump and 'Salmon' cut, as well as the cheaper brisket. There should be a good mixture of fat and lean. The fat is necessary to keep the meat moist during cooking, but fat is also a good absorber of flavour during the spicing process. The meat should have all bones removed and should also be left unrolled. Penetration of the spices is quicker and more thorough in unrolled meat. Also, because the meat is flatter, more of it is sitting in the spicing liquor. It is important, from this point of view, to have a bowl or dish that fits the meat neatly. Pieces which are a fairly uniform shape like the salmon cut or silverside will not need rolling or tying before cooking but rib roast and brisket may need some tying.

2-3.5kg (4lb 8oz -7lb 8oz) middle rib, silverside, rump or brisket
125g (4oz) soft brown sugar
25g (1oz) allspice
25g (1oz) juniper berries
25g (1oz) black peppercorns
15g (½ oz) coriander seeds
½ nutmeg grated
1 head garlic
125g (4oz) salt

SPICING: Put the meat into a fairly closely fitting dish and cover with sugar. Cover well and leave for two days in a cool place, turning each day. Pound spices and garlic together in a mortar. The spices may be ground coarsely in a grinder but they should not be finely powdered or it will be difficult to remove them from the outside surface of the meat at the end of the spicing – especially important if it is to be baked. Mix the spices with salt and rub into the meat. Cover with lid or foil. Rub and turn meat every day. The length of time the meat should be left depends on how heavily or lightly spiced you like the meat. A 2.25kg (5lb) piece of silverside, left in the above mixture for a fortnight, will be very strongly spiced and not to everyone's palate. All old recipes recommend a month minimum – palates were more robust in those days. The pickling time also depends on the thickness of the meat – flat brisket will be quite well spiced in five to six days while a thick piece of rump will need about nine.

COOKING:

For boiling — (best for tougher cuts like brisket) wipe off excess spice and put in a pot of boiling water, bring to the boil and skim well. Add one stick of celery; an onion stuck with a few cloves; one carrot; one small piece of turnip; bunch of parsley and thyme; a tablespoon peppercorns. Bring back to the boil, skim and simmer very gently, allowing 30 minutes per pound plus 30 minutes till tender.

For braising — wipe off the excess spice. Melt two tablespoons oil in a pan and add two to three chopped carrots; one small turnip and one medium onion, chopped, and sauté till lightly browned. Place the meat on top – cover with a skin of fat if necessary. Add enough water to cover the vegetables completely and come about halfway up the meat. Cover with a double layer of foil and then a tightly fitting lid and bake slowly at 300°F/150°C/Gas 2 until tender.

PRESSING: Remove when cooked, wrap tightly in foil while still hot and put between two boards with a weight on top. Leave overnight.

SERVING: It can be eaten hot, but the spice flavour is best appreciated when cold. Serve with grated boiled beetroot, seasoned with salt and pepper and mixed with a well-flavoured vinegar and olive oil. In a sandwich, flavour with mustard or chutney. Store in the fridge. It will keep for at least a month.

Roast Rack of Lamb

Using this method means there is bone on one side and fat on the other, so that the meat in the middle is protected and is therefore juicier and better flavoured than other methods.

Yield: 2

2 tablespoon dripping or oil for basting
1 rack (4 chops)
Ground black pepper
Sea salt

Serve with: green salad and redcurrant jelly.
Preheat the oven to 450°F/230°C/Gas 8.

ROASTING: Heat the dripping or oil in a roasting tin in the oven. Season meat. When the fat is very hot, add the meat and turn to brown and begin the roasting. Allow 15 minutes per 500g (1lb 2oz) for medium-rare. Rest in a warm place for another 10 minutes.

SERVING: Serve two chops per person with a green salad and redcurrant jelly.

Braised Lamb Shoulder
with Carrots

A convenient meal in a pot, it's best to treat this as a soup-stew and serve in deep soup plates.

Yield: 6-8

3 tablespoons dripping or oil
2kg (4lb 8oz) lamb shoulder on the bone
2 large onions, finely chopped
3-4 carrots, roughly chopped
$\frac{1}{2}$ medium turnip, roughly diced
3 leeks, cleaned and sliced into 2cm (1 inch) pieces
Water
Several sprigs of parsley and thyme, plus 3 bay leaves tied in a
    bundle with celery stalk or leek leaves
Sea salt and ground pepper

Serve with: Creamed Potatoes (see p95).
Preheat the oven to 325°F/170°C/Gas 3.

PREPARING MEAT AND VEGETABLES: Heat the dripping or oil in a large cast-iron, enamelled casserole. Add the meat and brown on all sides. Remove. Add the onions and cook, stirring over a medium heat, till well browned. Put the meat back in the dish.

BRAISING: Add the herbs and water to come half-way up the meat. Season and cover with a tight-fitting lid. Cook slowly for one and a half hours or until the meat is tender. Add the carrots, turnip and leeks about 30 minutes before the meat is ready. To crisp the surface: remove the lid and turn up the oven to 450°F/230°C/Gas 8 and brown the surface for about 15-20 minutes.

FINISHING AND SERVING: Remove the herbs and meat, and take the meat off the bones. Cut roughly into wedges and place in the centre of a heated ashet. It should slip easily off the bone. Pile the vegetables round the meat. Taste the cooking liquor for seasoning and adjust. Pour over enough to moisten the meat and vegetables. Sprinkle over parsley. Serve with creamed potatoes and some of the remaining cooking liquor in a sauce boat. Use remaining stock for broth.

Pickled Lamb or Mutton

A preservation method that adds flavour to the meat and great character to soups and stews.

Pickle:
2L (3pt 10fl oz) water
550g (1½ lb) coarse sea salt
250g (9oz) brown muscovado sugar
1 sprig bay leaves
1 sprig thyme
1 tablespoon crushed juniper berries
1 tablespoon crushed peppercorns

1.8kg (4lb) leg of lamb or mutton
on the bone
2 onions
3-4 cloves
2 medium carrots
1 bay leaf
1 tablespoon peppercorns

MAKING THE PICKLE: Put the pickle ingredients into a pan and bring to the boil. Stir to dissolve the salt and sugar and boil vigorously for about five minutes. Leave to cool.

PICKLING THE MEAT: Put the pickle into a well-washed earthenware crock or plastic bucket with a lid. Immerse the meat, keeping it below the surface by laying a heavy plate, or other weight, on top. Cover and keep in a cool, dry place. Pickling time will depend on the thickness of the meat. Thicker joints can be left a bit longer than thin. 24-48 hours for a mild cure; 48-72 hours for a stronger cure; and 72 upwards for a very salty cure such as Shetlanders use for Reestit mutton (see p67).

COOKING THE MEAT: Remove the meat from the pickle and wash well. Put it into a pan with the onions which have been stuck with cloves, carrots, bay leaf and peppercorns. Cover with water and bring slowly to the boil. Skim. Simmer until the meat is just tender, then leave to cool overnight in the liquid. The next day, skim off the fat and reserve for future use as dripping. Remove the meat and slice.

SERVING: Serve cold with a salad, or reheat with some of the stock (check first for saltiness and add water if too salty). Serve with glazed carrots and boiled potatoes, butter and chopped parsley. Use the remaining cooking liquor to make broth (see Chapter 1).

Pickled Chicken: Pickle a 2-3kg (4-6lb) chicken in the pickle liquid for about 24-48 hours. Roast with vegetables (see p57).

Baked Ham on the Bone

Cook's Tip: Check with your butcher if the ham is very salty and needs an overnight soak to remove excess salt (most hams for cooking on the bone are not usually as heavily salted as bacon). Either on or off the bone, the system is the same. The aim is to cook the meat in an envelope of steam, so there must be some space above the meat when wrapping it in foil.

Yield: 8-12

7kg (15lb) ham (on the bone for larger sizes)
1½–3 heaped tablespoons soft brown sugar
1–2 tablespoons whole cloves
Extra-width foil
Roasting tin

Serve with: Creamed Potatoes (see p95) and green vegetables.
Preheat the oven to 325°F/160°C/Gas 3.

PREPARING HAM: Put two pieces of double-thickness foil large enough to cover the ham comfortably, crosswise in the roasting tin. Place the ham on top and bring up each piece of foil to meet in the middle making an enclosed 'tent' over the ham. Do not wrap tightly since the ham should cook in the steam. Twist all edges together to make a perfect seal.

BAKING: Put the ham into the oven and bake for 30 minutes per 500g (1lb 2oz). Slice off a piece with a sharp knife near the end of the cooking time to test that the meat is tender. When ready, remove from the oven.

GLAZING: Turn up oven to 435°F/220°C/Gas 7 and fold down the foil. Remove the skin with a very sharp knife taking care not to remove too much fat. Score the fat lightly with the sharp knife into a diamond pattern. Push a clove into the joins of all the diamonds. Rub the whole surface with sugar and return the ham to the oven for about 30-40 minutes till crisp and browned.

SERVING: Serve hot with creamed potatoes and green vegetables.

Meat Loaf

This is a soft and moist rather than a dense and firm version.

Yield: 6

500g (1lb) white bread, roughly cubed
1 egg
150ml (5fl oz) milk
1kg (2lb 4oz) minced beef
250g (9oz) smoked bacon, finely diced
1 medium onion, finely chopped
2-3 tender inner stalks of celery with leaves, finely diced
2-3 tablespoons parsley, chopped
1 tablespoon Dijon mustard
$\frac{1}{2}$ grated nutmeg
2 teaspoons salt
Ground black pepper

Serve with: chutney, pickles or cooked beetroot sliced with vinaigrette.
Grease or line a 20 x 12cm (8 x 5 inch) loaf tin.
Preheat oven to 350°F/180°C/Gas 4.

MIXING LOAF: Put the bread cubes into a large bowl and add the egg and milk.
Mix and mash and leave to stand for five minutes while the bread absorbs all the
liquid. Add all the other ingredients, season and mix well. To check seasoning:
fry off a spoonful in a pan and taste. Pour into lined tin and leave overnight to
allow flavours to develop.

BAKING: Level the top and bake for about an hour.

SERVING: Turn out and serve either hot with Creamed Potatoes (see p95),
chutney and pickles, or cold with sliced cooked beetroot tossed in a vinaigrette.

Grilled Black and White Puddings

WITH AYRSHIRE BACON AND POACHED EGGS

Cook's Tip: Some tart apples sliced and fried in butter, served with the black and white puddings, are an alternative to bacon and eggs.

Yield: 4

4 slices black pudding
4 slices white pudding
4 rashers Ayrshire bacon
4 large free range eggs

GRILLING: Heat the grill to a medium heat. Remove casing from puddings. Grill the black and white puddings on either side for two to three minutes depending on thickness. Remove and keep warm. Grill the bacon till crisp.

POACHING EGGS: Break the eggs into a pan of boiling salted water with a teaspoonful of vinegar added. Poach gently till set but still runny in the centre.

SERVING: Pile the puddings and bacon in the centre of the plate. Place poached egg on top. Finish with a grinding of black pepper and serve.

Jellied Tripe

This is a butcher's speciality that can be found at the made-up meats counter. Theirs is a simpler affair than this version which is based on the jellied tripe made by the inspirational Fergus Henderson at his restaurant, St John in Smithfield, London. See also in his book *Head to Tail Eating* (1999).

Yield: 4-6

2 pig's trotters
1 head of garlic
Several sprigs of parsley and thyme, plus 3 bay leaves tied in a
    bundle with celery stalk or leek leaves
1L (1pt 15fl oz) dry cider
1kg (2lb 4oz) tripe
3 shallots, peeled and finely sliced
2 carrots, finely sliced
3 cloves of garlic, crushed
2 tinned, plum tomatoes
Sea salt and pepper

Serve with: chicory salad and capers.

COOKING TROTTERS and TRIPE: Put the trotters, garlic and herbs into a pot, cover with cider and bring to the boil. Reduce and simmer, covered for about two hours. Add the tripe and cook for another one to two hours or until the trotters and tripe are cooked and tender. Strain.

MAKING JELLY: Put the cooking liquid on to cook again and bring to the boil. Reduce to a simmer and cook without a lid till reduced by half. In another pan melt the lard or duck fat and add the shallots and carrots. Sweat for five minutes and add the garlic and tomatoes. Mix through and continue to cook. Meanwhile, remove the meat from the trotters. Add the meat to the vegetables along with the tripe and add half of the cooking liquid. Season and simmer for about 20-30 minutes to cook the vegetables.

FINISHING: Line a terrine or a pie dish with clingfilm and fill with the tripe mixture. Add more cooking liquid to cover, making a moist mixture. Cover and put in the fridge to set overnight. Slice when cold and serve with a chicory salad and capers.

Tripe and Onions

Cook's Tip: The nineteenth-century tavern cook livened up this dish with mustard, mushroom ketchup, herbs, chives and a glass of wine. They also served it with button onions fried in butter. (see Meat Classics p64)

Yield: 4

1L (1pt 15fl oz) milk
1 teaspoon mace blades
3 medium onions, finely chopped
1.5kg (3lb 5oz) white honeycomb tripe, cut into bite-sized strips
Sea salt and pepper
25g (1oz) butter
25g (1oz) flour

Serve with: Creamed Potatoes (see p95) or hot buttered toast.

COOKING TRIPE: Put the milk into a large pot and add mace and onions. Bring to the boil and simmer gently for about 20 minutes. Add the tripe, salt and pepper, and continue to simmer for about an hour. Test tripe for tenderness. It should not be overcooked.

THICKENING: Melt the butter in a pan and add the flour. Stir constantly over a low heat. Add a cupful of the hot cooking liquid and stir in. Continue with another two cupfuls, stirring all the time. Bring to the boil and allow to thicken. Return to the tripe and stir in. Taste for seasoning.

SERVING: Serve with creamed potatoes or hot buttered toast.

Haggis Neeps an' Tatties

Cook's Tip: Mix the neeps and tatties together and make Clapshot and Burnt Onions (see p96) As with tripe and onions, mustard also makes a good accompaniment to haggis.

Yield: 6-8

1 sheep's stomach bag
1 sheep's pluck (including heart, lungs attached to windpipe and liver)
Water to cover
250g (9oz) coarse or pinhead oatmeal, lightly toasted
25g (1oz) butter
4 medium onions, finely chopped
200g (7oz) prepared suet
Sea salt and ground pepper
Ground allspice
Large needle and strong thread for sewing up

Serve with: Creamed Potatoes (see p95) and mashed turnip or Clapshot (see p96).

PREPARING BAG AND PLUCK: Wash the bag in cold water, clean well and leave overnight in the water. Wash the pluck and put in a large pot. Cover with water. Add 2-3 teaspoons salt. Hang the windpipe over the side of the pot and place a jar or bowl beneath it to catch the drips.

BOILING PLUCK: Bring to the boil and simmer gently till all the meat is tender, skimming occasionally. It should take about two hours.

MAKING HAGGIS (the next day): Toast the oatmeal and put it in a large bowl. Melt the butter in a frying pan and cook the onions till soft and translucent but not browned. Add the suet. Remove the pluck meats from the liquid. Cut off the windpipe and any other fibrous tubes and discard. Mince all the meat coarsely, or chop very finely, and add to the oatmeal and onions. Add the salt, pepper and allspice and mix thoroughly. Taste for seasoning and adjust. Add enough cooking liquid to make a moist consistency and fill the stomach bag about three-quarters full, leaving room for expansion. Press out any air and sew it up with a needle and strong thread. Wrap it in foil (this protects it from bursting) and place in a pot of boiling water and simmer for three hours.

SERVING: Remove from the pot and take off the foil. Slice open the stomach bag and serve with creamed potatoes, mashed turnips and Dijon mustard.

GRAIN AND
VEGETABLE CLASSICS

Porridge and Cream

The long wooden porridge stick, known as the 'spurtle', is stirred through the heaving grey mass that fills a large black iron pot hanging over the fire in the farmhouse kitchen. Soon, it comes to a boil. Volcanic eruptions make the familiar noise. The 'parritch' is ready.

The pot is taken to the table, the stick is removed and the family gathers round, each holding their wooden bowl of freshly skimmed cream in one hand and in the other, a long-handled, carved horn spoon.

In communal eating like this you take your turn to delve into the pot for a steaming spoonful before dipping it into the cream. Hot porridge: cold cream. And once everyone has had their fill, the leftovers are poured into the 'porridge drawer' of the Scotch dresser. When cold and set like jelly, the 'parritch' is called 'caulders' and is cut up into slices – like Italians cut up leftover polenta – to fry up later, or take to the fields as a midday snack. From about the beginning of the eighteenth century, it's a common ritual for most Scots, as oats begin to replace barley as the country's staple grain.

The twentieth-century's multimillion pound breakfast cereal market may have threatened the survival of porridge and cream, but oats were given a popularity boost in the 1980s when an American professor discovered that they contain a gummy, fibrous material that reduces 'bad' cholesterol and blood sugar. Added to this, oats have a higher food value than any other grain, with more protein, more iron, more B vitamins and more calcium.

The first recipe for classic porridge appears in F M McNeil's *The Scots Kitchen*, 1929: 'Allow for each person one breakfast cupful of water, a handful of oatmeal (about an ounce and a quarter) and a small salt-spoonful of salt. Use fresh spring water and be particular about the quality of the oatmeal. Bring the water to the boil and as soon as it reaches boiling point add the oatmeal, letting it fall in a steady rain from the left hand and stirring briskly with the right. A porridge stick, called a spurtle, is used for this purpose. Be careful to avoid lumps. When the porridge is boiling steadily, draw the mixture to the side and put on the lid. Let it cook for twenty to thirty minutes and do not add the salt until it has cooked for at least ten minutes. Ladle straight into porringers or soup plates and serve with small individual bowls of cream, or milk or buttermilk. Each spoonful of porridge, which should be very hot, is dipped into the cream or milk, which should be quite cold, before it is conveyed to the mouth.'

Mealy Tatties

The farm cart leaves for the weekly trip to the town filled with a load of boiled-in-their-skins potatoes. 'Mealy tatties', cries the farm hand as he leads his horse through the streets. People come out of their houses with basins to collect a supply. The mealy tattie cart trundles through the Scottish streets for the best part of the nineteenth century. The potatoes, cooked on the farm, are a specially dry, mealy or floury, variety. They are the preferred Scottish choice, rather than wet, waxy varieties.

Potatoes have been accepted slowly in Scotland, compared to their wholesale acceptance in Ireland, but now they are well established. They fulfil a vital role as a filling, cheap carbohydrate and become a staple item of the diet throughout the country. 'Fish, with oat bread or potatoes, without any accompaniment at all, forms three daily meals of the Shetland cottager,' says E Edmondston in *Sketches and Tales of the Shetland Isles*.

Several floury varieties are grown. But it is the late nineteenth century before popular varieties are named and established. W Sim of Aberdeenshire raises a low-yielding potato with a very high dry matter content in 1891 that he names Duke of York. John Brown of Arbroath is another pioneer who, in 1906, registers the Golden Wonder. A year later, another very good floury potato is grown by James Henry in England, but he does not recognise its merits as a dry potato with flavour, possibly because the English like wetter, more waxy potatoes, and he sells it to a seedsman (Mr Kerr) who names it Kerr's Pink in 1917.

All mealy tatties have low yields making them less profitable to grow than bigger, wetter potatoes and are, therefore, more expensive to buy. Their advantage, however, is their good flavour. This is important if they are to be served by themselves and not just as a cheap adjunct to meat. Of the old varieties, the most popular mealy tattie remains the Golden Wonder which has a russet skin and white, creamy flesh with a distinctive flavour and an elongated, pear shape. A very popular old variety is Kerr's Pink which has a pinkish skin, cream flesh, round shape its own distinctive flavour.

During the 1950s, 60s and 70s the Scottish Plant Breeding Institute at Pentlandfield produced the mealy Pentland varieties: Pentland Crown, Pentland Dell and Pentland Squire. Other mealy varieties include: Arran Consul, Arran Victory, Catriona, Di Vernon, Dunbar Rover, Dunbar Standard, Edzell Blue, Epicure, King Edward, Maris Piper, Record and Red Craigs Royal.

Grain and vegetable traditions

Oatmeal: The sweet, creamy flavour of oatmeal depends on Scotland's favourable growing conditions: long, cool, moist summers allowing the oat grains to ripen slowly and grow fatter than they do in drier, hotter climates. Their suitability to the climate established oats as a staple grain and in the seventeenth century they began to take over from barley, which in most places became the brewing grain. Oatmeal contained valuable oil and was a richer source of nutrients. It was also more versatile, and could be milled into many different 'cuts', providing more interesting textures with 'pinhead', 'coarse' and 'medium' used in dishes such as haggis, porridge, brose and oatcakes.

By the end of the eighteenth century, oatmeal had become the people's grain: 'Oatmeal with milk, which they cook in different ways, is their constant food, three times a day, throughout the year, Sundays and holidays included,' says Donaldson, in *A General View of Agriculture in the Carse of Gowrie* (1794). With industrialisation and the move northwards of a diet based on tea and cheap white bread, the people's diet of milky porridge suffered and it was only in the latter half of the twentieth century that the nutritional value of oats in the diet was recognised and consumption increased.

There are still a few water-powered stone-grinding mills, as well as several factory mills that kiln-dry oatmeal in the traditional way. The careful drying on a kiln floor, of perforated metal sheets with a smokeless fuel furnace some 20-30 feet below, allows the oats to develop their mild, nutty flavour. Other factors that determine the good flavour of oats are the district where it is grown, its oil content, and whether it has been stone ground without heating, thus protecting its flavour, or roller ground with heat which will alter the flavour and destroy some of the nutrients.

Beremeal and Common Barley: Like oats, the quality of common barley and its Neolithic ancestor, bere (a four-rowed barley Hordeum Vulgare), depends on the favourable growing conditions in Scotland: long, cool, moist summers allowing the grains to ripen slowly and fill out better than they do in drier, hotter climates. Until the late seventeenth century, bere was the people's grain. It was overtaken by oats, except in areas beyond the Central Belt that were cut off by lack of communications. In these areas, bere continued to be the favoured grain, and so it's in the North of Scotland and on Orkney and Shetland that the old bere still survives. Ground finely into beremeal, and made into the traditional beremeal bannock, it has a greyish-brown colour and an astringent earthy tang: perfectly complemented with mellow Orkney butter and creamy farmhouse cheese – a traditional high tea when dinner was the midday meal.

In comparison, common barley flour is a pale imitation, though pot or pearl barley remains the traditional grain for adding character to Scottish broths. Pearl barley is the whole grain which has had its bran layer polished. Pot or Scotch barley has less of the bran removed than pearl barley. Pearl barley cooks quicker, releases its starch to the broth, and will almost disintegrate if cooked for too long. The preferred pot or Scotch barley, on the other hand, takes longer to cook and retains its character in a broth.

Peasemeal: This is ground from roasted yellow field peas. The roasting process caramelises some of the sugar as well as making the starch and protein more digestible. It is traditionally used in pease brose: boiling water, stirred into the meal and seasoned with salt and pepper, some butter and sometimes raisins. It is also used in bannocks and scones, in a mix with other flours since it has no gluten.

Kail (English spelling: kale): The kail-yard (kitchen garden) was to the Scots what the potato-plot was to the Irish peasant. Kail was so much part of the eating tradition that dinner became known as 'kail'. The bells of St Giles Cathedral in Edinburgh that chimed at two pm were known as the 'kail bells'. Though used in Scotland in broths or as a vegetable, in England kail is largely used as a feed for cattle. The advantage of kail in the Scottish climate is its hardiness throughout the winter. Unlike most vegetables it benefits from a frost, which improves its flavour.

Leek: Thought to have been introduced to Britain by the Romans, the Scots have made good use of leeks in soups and stews and particularly in the classic combination with chicken: Cock-a-Leekie. A variety of the Common Long Winter Leek, raised on the fertile soils of East Lothian, with a longer thicker stem and broader leaves was known as the Musselburgh Leek. In *The Vegetable Garden* (1885) William Robinson says that the 'fine qualities of this vegetable are much better known to the Welsh, Scotch and French than to the English or Irish'.

The regions of Fife and Lothian, with their fertile soils, continue to be important for leek growing. Small to medium-sized leeks have the sweetest flavour. The hardy, winter growing Musselburgh Leek is no longer grown commercially although it continues to be grown in domestic gardens.

The use of leeks as a vegetable in its own right, rather than a flavouring for soups, has been encouraged by the fact that they are no longer only a winter vegetable but are grown year-round. Scots have always liked a longer green leaf, 'green flag', and shorter 'blanch', since this gives a better colour and flavour to soups. A supply of young, tender leeks can be used instead as a salad vegetable with vinaigrette.

Swede Turnip: 'Our club [The Cleikum] put a little powdered gineger [sic] to their mashed turnips, which were studiously chosen of the yellow, sweet, juicy sort, for which Scotland is celebrated...' says Meg Dods in *The Cook and Housewives Manual* (1826).

This yellow variety that she refers to is the same variety that accompanies haggis and mixes so well with Orkney Clapshot. It is a variety of Brassica Campestris, which is known as a Swedish turnip, swede or Rutabaga – Brassica Napus. It came from Sweden to Scotland in the late eighteenth century and is known in England as a swede. Brassica Rapa, the white-fleshed cultivated turnip, is the plant from which many other turnips, oil seed rape and many varieties of Chinese cabbage, have been developed. Brassica Rapa is related to the ordinary cabbage and was originally crossed with it to form the swede. It is likely that swedes first appeared in medieval gardens where turnips and varieties of cabbage were growing together.

GRAINS:

Oatmeal Porridge

Cook's Tip: From thick and grainy to thin and custardy, the texture of porridge is entirely a matter of taste. Its flavour is also up for individual choice; from a homely, classic mix of hot, mealy oats and cold, rich cream to a more modern purée with raspberries finished with crème fraiche or a zany black and white number swirled through with Greek yoghurt and drizzled with black treacle.

Yield: serves 1

2 tablespoons medium oatmeal and/or a mix with coarse and pinhead
300ml (10fl oz) water

SOAKING OVERNIGHT: This allows the grains to swell and makes for a creamier porridge. Essential if coarse or pinhead oatmeal is being used.

COOKING: Put the water on to boil and sprinkle in the oatmeal, stirring all the time with a wooden spurtle (porridge stick) or wooden spoon. Bring to the boil and continue to stir. Simmer for about five minutes, longer if coarse or pinhead oatmeal is used. It will reduce as it thickens, so it is very much a question of how you like your porridge: creamy and runny or thick and stodgy. Remember also that it will thicken as it cools. Accidental lumps are known as 'knots' and some porridge lovers rather like them, while others regard 'knotty' porridge as totally inedible.

SERVING and EATING TRADITIONAL: Add salt to taste. Pour into a bowl and serve with a small bowl of cream. Eat by dipping spoonfuls of hot porridge into the cold cream.

EATING MODERN: Sweeten with golden syrup, black treacle, brown sugar (mixed with a teaspoon of cinnamon if you like) or honey. Stir in some butter. Add chopped fruit such as bananas, soft fruit such as raspberries, or nuts and raisins. For a coarse, textured porridge, add a spoonful of muesli. Honey and whisky are favourite winter warmers. The permutations are endless.

Pease Brose

Cook's Tip: More easily digested than either uncooked oatmeal or beremeal, this is the favoured brose meal. It is, like porridge, entirely a matter of personal taste what you mix it with, but it is a stronger taste than oatmeal or beremeal and it works less well with sharp fruits and better with more mellow raisins, apricots, dates and nuts.

Yield: 1

2 tablespoons peasemeal
250ml (8fl oz) boiling water or hot milk
Knob of butter
Salt
1 tablespoon currants
Honey or sugar to taste

MIXING AND EATING: Put the peasemeal into a bowl. Pour over the boiling water or hot milk and stir in. Then add the knob of butter and stir. Season with salt and mix in the currants. Finally, sweeten to taste and serve with more butter.

Oatmeal Skirlie

This was originally a peasant family dinner, with potatoes and/or vegetables, but it's eaten now mostly with roasts or as a stuffing for poultry and game. In some parts it is a popular accompaniment to mince, stews and beef olives (see p71).

Yield: 4

4 tablespoons bacon fat or other fat or oil
1 large onion, finely chopped
125g (4oz) medium oatmeal
Sea salt and pepper

FRYING AND SERVING: Put the fat into a frying pan and heat. Add the onion when hot and cook till soft and lightly browned. Add the oatmeal and cook for another few minutes over a moderate heat, stirring occasionally. The oatmeal should be only lightly browned. Season and serve as an accompaniment to meats and vegetables.

TO MAKE SKIRLIE TOAST: Butter some hot toast and mix the skirlie with some beef dripping or a knob of butter to make it easier to spread onto the toast. Serve hot with cold meat for high tea or with roast grouse or other game birds as well as chicken and turkey.

Sweet Haggis

A homely version of a mealy pudding with dried fruit. It's made in a dumpling cloth and cooked like a 'clootie' and was a favourite early-twentieth-century Saturday night tea speciality. Leftovers, fried up with bacon etc, make a sustaining Sunday morning breakfast.

350g (12oz) medium oatmeal
125g (4oz) plain flour
300g (10oz) beef suet, finely chopped
125g (4oz) currants
125g (4oz) raisins
125g (4oz) soft brown sugar
Salt and pepper
Water to mix
Dusting: 2 tablespoons plain flour

Prepare cloth (cloot): 55cm (22 inch) square white cotton or linen. Fill a pan with boiling water and add the cloth. Boil the cloth for a few minutes, then lift out with tongs and spread out on the work surface. While still hot, sprinkle evenly with a thick dusting of flour. Shake to disperse evenly over all the cloth, then shake off excess.

TO MAKE HAGGIS: Place a grid or upturned saucer in the base of a very large pot to prevent sticking, add water and put the pot on to boil. Put all of the ingredients into a bowl and mix to a fairly stiff dough. The mixture should be neither too soft (when it will crack on turning out) nor too stiff (when it will be too heavy a texture). Pour into the centre of the cloth. Bring up the sides, making sure all the edges of the cloth are caught up. Tie with a string, leaving space for expansion. Hold up the tied ends and pat the haggis into a good, round shape and lower into the pot of boiling water. It should come about halfway up. Tie the ends of the string to the pot handle (if there are two handles on either side of the pot tie the two ends of string to either side so the pudding hangs in the middle) – this will prevent it rolling over and water getting in at the top. This also helps to keep it a good round shape. Cover tightly with a lid and simmer gently for four hours, checking the water level regularly.

TO TURN OUT AND SERVE: Fill the sink, or a large basin, with cold water and lift the haggis from the pot, holding it by the string. Submerge in the water and leave for one minute. This releases the cloth from the skin. Move into a bowl about the same size as the haggis. Cut the string and open out the cloth hanging the sides over the bowl's edge. Invert a serving plate on top and turn over. Remove the cloth carefully – it should come away cleanly – and put into a warm oven to dry off. When dry, cut into thick slices and serve with grilled bacon for breakfast or high tea. Leftovers can be sliced and fried with bacon.

VEGETABLES:

Boiled Floury 'Mealy' Potatoes

Cook's Tip: These must be boiled in their skins. Taking off a circle of skin at either end of the potato or taking a circle off round the potato allows the potato to expand without bursting its skin.

Yield: 4

1kg (2lb 4oz) floury potatoes, washed
   (Golden Wonder, Maris Piper, King Edward, Kerr's Pinks)
Sea salt

For Chappit Tatties:
50g (2oz) butter
3-4 tablespoons milk or cream
1-2 tablespoons chopped chives
Sea salt

For Fried Potatoes:
2-3 tablespoons of beef or poultry dripping
Sea salt

COOKING POTATOES: Peel off a thin strip of skin round the potato from top to bottom or take a circle off at either end. This prevents the potato bursting and makes it easier to peel. Cut the larger potatoes as they should all be roughly the same size. Put the potatoes into a pot of boiling water and add salt. Bring to the boil and simmer until they are just cooked, checking frequently as floury potatoes burst and 'go to soup' very quickly. Drain.

FOR CHAPPIT (CREAMED) TATTIES: Remove potatoes and peel. Return to the pan. Add butter and milk, then mash. Taste for seasoning. Sprinkle over chopped chives and serve.

FOR FRIED POTATOES: Heat dripping in the pan till very hot. Slice potatoes thinly and fry on both sides till golden. Season with sea salt and serve immediately.

Clapshot and Burnt Onions

Cook's Tip: Yellow, swede turnips are much hardier than the cultivated white turnip, and are at their best from August through to April. Late winter turnips will have much less water and more flavour. The outer layer of the smaller ones is less woody. They also have a milder flavour.

Yield: 4

500g (1lb 2oz) swede turnip, peeled and sliced roughly
Sea salt
500g (1lb 2oz) floury potatoes, washed and prepared as for
    Boiled Floury Potatoes (see p95) (Golden Wonder, King Edward, Kerr's Pinks)
25g (1oz) butter
Ground black pepper

Burnt onions:
2 tablespoons olive oil
1 large Spanish onion, sliced thinly
1 tablespoon granulated sugar

Serve with: meat, poultry or game or on its own with bannocks and cheese.

MAKING THE CLAPSHOT: Put the turnip into a pot of boiling water, add salt and simmer for about 10 minutes. Add the washed potatoes and bring back to the boil. Simmer until the potatoes are just cooked, checking frequently as floury potatoes burst and 'go to soup' very quickly. Drain, remove the potatoes and peel. Return to the pan, add butter and black pepper and mash. Taste for seasoning and place in a heated serving dish.

BURNT ONIONS: While potatoes and turnip are cooking, heat the oil in a frying pan and add the onions. Stir and fry onions till they are brown and crisp – for about 10 minutes – driving off as much moisture as possible. Sprinkle over sugar and stir for another few minutes until the sugar caramelises and the onions darken.

SERVING: Serve the burnt onions on top of the clapshot. It may be served with meat, poultry or game as a vegetable or on its own, as it is in Orkney, with beremeal bannocks and cheese.

Rumbledethumps

The story behind this unusual name is that in Scots 'rumbled' means 'mixed' and thumped means 'bashed' – just how you make this dish. It was originally a meatless peasant dinner.

Yield: 4

500g (1lb 2oz) floury potatoes, washed and prepared as for Boiled Floury Potatoes (see p95) (Golden Wonder, King Edward, Maris Piper, Kerr's Pink)
Sea salt
1 medium onion, finely chopped
500g (1lb 2oz) savoy cabbage, chopped
1-2 tablespoons chopped chives
Ground black pepper
50g (2oz) mature Scottish cheddar, finely grated

Serve with: meat, poultry or game or on its own as a main course.

COOKING POTATOES: Put the potatoes into a pot of boiling water, add salt and simmer until the potatoes are just cooked, checking frequently as floury potatoes burst and 'go to soup' very quickly. Drain, remove the potatoes and peel. Return to the pan, add butter and black pepper and mash.

COOKING CABBAGE: While potatoes are cooking, melt the butter in another pan and add the onion. Cook gently for about five minutes without browning. Add the cabbage, steaming gently until it wilts and season.

FINISHING AND SERVING: Add the onion, cabbage and butter to the potatoes. Mix well and season to taste. Add more butter if necessary. Place in a serving dish, sprinkle the top with cheese and brown under the grill. Serve with meats, birds or game or on its own as a main course.

Potato Stovies

Cook's Tip: The best stovies are made with leftover meat dripping and gravy. Butchers sell small pots of this, known as 'dripping for stovies' or 'stovie stock'. The trick is to cook the potatoes in as little liquid as possible. They should be moist but not too mushy. Chopping the potatoes in both large and small slices allows the smaller slices to soften and form a little mushiness while the larger pieces remain almost whole to provide a contrasting texture. The final flavour will always depend not just on the potatoes, but also on the meat dripping and gravy juices.

Yield: 4

3 tablespoons meat dripping
3 medium onions, finely chopped
1kg (2lb 4oz) floury potatoes, washed and peeled
  (Golden Wonder, King Edward, Kerr's Pinks)
125ml (4fl oz) meat gravy
125-225g (4-8oz) left-over roast meat
2-3 tablespoons finely chopped parsley, chives or spring onions
Sea salt and ground black pepper.

MAKING AND SERVING: Heat the dripping in a large heavy-based pan with a tight-fitting lid. Add the onions and cook lightly till brown. Slice potatoes – some thin, others thicker, for a more interesting texture. Some will soften to a mush while others will remain whole. Add to the pan and coat in fat. Season. Put the lid on the pan and leave on a low heat, stirring occasionally for about 10 minutes. Add the gravy and finish cooking over a very low heat. The potatoes should steam gently. When cooked they can be browned by turning up the heat. Stir in the meat, add the parsley, chives or spring onions, season and serve as a main course.

Roasted Leeks

Cook's Tips: Large leeks have a strong flavour and coarse texture and are best used in richly-flavoured soups and stews. If serving on their own as a vegetable or for salads always use young, tender leeks. Avoid leeks that have 'shot', ie started forming the flower head that makes a hard woody stalk in the centre.

Yield: 4

8 young leeks
2-3 tablespoons olive oil
Sea salt

Preheat the oven to 500°F/250°C/Gas 9.

PREPARING AND ROASTING LEEKS: Remove any wilted outer leaves and the root end. Slit open to just below the green stalk and wash well, then cut into two-inch pieces. Oil a large gratin dish and make a single layer of leeks. Cover with the remaining oil and sprinkle with salt. Roast for about 10 minutes, remove and turn. Roast for another 10 minutes – they should be soft and lightly browned. Serve hot with cheese and bread.

SERVED COLD WITH VINAIGRETTE and HARD-BOILED EGGS: Put one tablespoon of balsamic vinegar in a bowl and add about 4-5 tablespoons of extra virgin olive oil. Season with Dijon mustard, salt and freshly ground black pepper. Add 2 tablespoons chopped parsley. Pour over the roasted leeks while they're still warm and leave to marinate overnight.

TO SERVE: Chop two hard-boiled eggs finely and sprinkle on top of the marinated roasted leeks. Finish with a tablespoon of finely chopped parsley.

Young Leek Salad

Cook's Tips: A dish for small, slender young leeks that have a delicate flavour. They may also be added to other raw salads. Allow about two leeks per person depending on size.

Yield: 4

8 young leeks, prepared (see p99)

Dressing:
4-5 tablespoons oil
1 teaspoon mild mustard
1 tablespoon vinegar/lemon juice
Freshly ground sea salt and black pepper
Pinch of sugar
Handful of chopped parsley

MAKING: Put the dressing ingredients into a screw-top jar and shake well. Taste for seasoning. Clean the leeks and then chop them into one-inch slices. Put in a salad bowl and toss in the dressing. Good with cooked ham, spiced beef, mutton ham or pickled tongue.

Turnip Stovies

A winter dish that is a slow-cooked, buttery oven version of potato stovies. It can be served with cheese and bread or used as a vegetable with a gamey haunch of venison or well-hung pheasant.

Yield: 6

200g (7oz) butter
2 large onions, peeled and diced
1.2kg (2lb 12oz) turnip, peeled and sliced thinly
Sea salt and ground pepper

Preheat oven to 350°F/180°C/Gas 4.

PREPARING: With about 50g (2oz) of butter, grease the base and sides of a deep, cast-iron, enamelled casserole. Put the remaining butter into a pan and heat. When hot, add the onions and cook gently for about 20 minutes till they are soft and translucent.

BAKING AND SERVING: Put a layer of turnip into the casserole, cover with a layer of the onion and butter mixture and season. Continue layering, seasoning each layer and finish with a layer of butter and onions. Cover with a lid and bake for about an hour. Test with a knife or skewer to check that the turnip is cooked. Remove the lid for another 10 minutes to brown on top or place under the grill. Serve with roast meats.

Glazed Carrots

Cook's Tip: Do not use very young carrots, as they are best eaten raw, or very large, old carrots which will have lost their natural sweetness.

Yield: 4

500g (1lb 2oz) carrots, peeled
50g (2oz) butter
1 tablespoon soft brown sugar
Sea salt
Water
1 tablespoon chopped parsley
1-2 teaspoons lemon juice

COOKING: Cut the carrots into bite-sized pieces. Place them in a pan with the butter, sugar, salt and enough water to come halfway up the carrots. Simmer till the carrots are almost cooked. Most of the liquid should have evaporated. Shake the carrots in the pan over a high heat till almost all of the liquid has evaporated – take care not to brown the carrots.

SERVING: Add the remainder of the butter. Toss well and finish with parsley and lemon juice to taste.

Buttered Kail

Cook's Tip: The young leaves from the top of the plant are the best. Young kail is good raw, finely chopped in a salad, or stir-fried in butter with garlic, ginger and raisins. This peppery vegetable is best kept out of boiling water.

Yield: 4

50g (2oz) butter
3 cloves garlic, crushed (optional)
25g (1oz) fresh ginger, grated (optional)
375g (13oz) kail (English spelling: kale), washed, central stalk removed and finely chopped
50g (2oz) large Californian raisins (optional)

COOKING AND SERVING: Heat the butter in a wok. Add the garlic and ginger and cook for a few minutes to release the flavour. Add kail and stir-fry for a few minutes till it wilts. Add raisins and serve.

Roast Root Vegetables

An autumn or winter dish that can make a meal when served with cheese or cold meat and pickles. Or it can be cooked in the same oven as any roast.

Yield: 4-6

100ml (3½ fl oz) olive oil
1 small swede turnip
4 medium parsnips
4 medium carrots
4 medium potatoes
4 small onions
1 fennel bulb
Sea salt
2 sprigs rosemary
4 bulbs garlic
1 tablespoon chopped parsley
Ground black pepper

Pre-heat the oven to 450°F/230°C/Gas 8.

ROASTING: Put the olive oil into a large roasting tin and place in the oven. Leave for 5-10 minutes until it is very hot. Meanwhile, peel all the vegetables and cut into even-sized pieces. Remove the oil from the oven and add the vegetables to the roasting tin. Turn well in the oil so they are well coated. Season with salt and add rosemary sprigs. Cut the tops off the garlic bulbs and add. Roast until the vegetables are all tender, turning occasionally.

SERVING: Remove from the oven and keep in a warm place for five minutes. Push the insides out of the softened garlic and mix through the vegetables. Sprinkle over parsley and serve with a grinding of black pepper.

FRUIT AND PUDDING CLASSICS

McCallum (Ice Cream and Raspberry Syrup)

Cool, clean-tasting, refreshingly milky, Italian ice cream is scooped onto a cone. 'Raspberry?' 'Oh, yes please.'

Other topping options include a '99' milk chocolate flake, 'amaretto nibs' and 'hundreds and thousands'. But it's the partnership of dripping red raspberry syrup, as ice melts, which is childhood nostalgia in a cone.

One legend has it that red raspberry syrup met cool-tasting Italian ice cream in Glasgow when a Clyde football club supporter, named McCallum, persuaded his local Italian ice-cream maker to make an ice cream in the club colours – red and white. The 'club' ice cream was so popular that the inspired supporter was rewarded when the new creation was named after him. Another story is linked with an ice cream parlour in Rutherglen owned by a family of McCallums.

Whatever the truth of its origins, it's certain that the first McCallums were not take-away cones dripping in raspberry syrup, but sit-in-and-eat saucerfuls of several scoops of ice cream, with the red sauce poured over them in stripes. Special 'McCallum saucers' were stocked for the purpose as the popularity of the Italian ice cream parlours developed throughout the early decades of the twentieth century.

By this time, the first itinerant Italian ice-cream salesmen – who had begun by pushing their barrows around the city streets – had moved into small shops, mostly in slum areas. Then, armed with driving ambition, and much hard work, they began to move up into better areas. This is when they hit some local prejudice.

The Glasgow Herald (2 October, 1907 – *Ice Cream Hells*) reports a United Free Church conference held to discuss the growth of Italian ice cream shops. They were, so the churchmen opined: 'perfect iniquities of hell itself and ten times worse than any of the evils of the public house'. But Glasgow of the early twentieth century was a city of prospering classes looking for fun and entertainment in the many cinemas, dance and music halls. So despite the kill-joy church, there was a growing market for delectable Italian ice creams and everything that went with the classic Italian ice cream parlour. Then, a popular Glaswegian novelist of the day, A J Cronin, dared to take his upper-class heroine in *Hatter's Castle* (1931) into Bertorelli's café who knows, perhaps for a McCallum – and Italian ice cream parlours never looked back.

'He took her arm firmly and led her a few doors down the street, then, before she realised it and could think even to resist he had drawn her inside. Mary paled with apprehension, feeling that she had finally passed the limits of respectability and looking reproachfully into Denis' smiling face in a shocked tone she gasped:

'"Oh Denis, how could you?"

Yet as she looked round the clean empty shop, with its rows of marble topped tables, its small scintillating mirrors and brightly papered walls, she felt curiously surprised, as if she had expected to find a sordid den, suited appropriately to the debauched revels that must, if tradition were to be believed, inevitably be connected with a place like this.'

Cranachan

For days children have been scouring the countryside for ripe berries. It is late September and they find plenty of black, juicy brambles as well as smaller, sharper-tasting blaeberries. There are still a few late white raspberries for those who know where to find them. A large bowl is filled and placed in the middle of the table.

This is a special family gathering for Highland clanspeople (circa 1700) to celebrate the year's harvest. On the table too is a bowl of their own-grown meal ground finely. There is a large bowl of thick cream from their milking cow and another is filled with the soft, white 'crowdie' cheese that they make by cooking curdled milk and hanging it to drip in a cloth. There is a bowl of wild honey and the ever-available stoneware bottle of their own distilled water-of-life (*usquabae*), later to become known as whisky.

Everyone gathers round for the feast, and with carved horn spoons make up their own mix of the characterful ingredients.

Clootie Dumpling

My granny made a dumpling
She made it in a cloot
She put it in the kettle
And she couldn't get it oot

My granny made a dumpling
She made it in a cloot,
She took a stick of dynamite
And blew it oot the spoot!

My granny made her dumpling in a 'cloot' too, but she put hers in a large pot so there was no need for any dynamite. As I remember, she made it for

Cranachan

(SOFT FRUIT, CREAM AND TOASTED OATMEAL)

Cook's Tip: Making this up in advance misses the point of it as a communal celebration. Only by letting everyone make up their own – as they go – can they discover their own personal favourite mix of flavours and textures.

Yield: 6-8

425ml (15fl oz) double cream, whipped
125g (4oz) coarse or pinhead oatmeal, lightly toasted
225g (8oz) crowdie or other sharp soft cheese or crème fraiche
450g (1lb) soft fruit (rasps, strawberries, blackcurrants, brambles etc)
Bottle of light Lowland Malt Whisky to taste
Jar of runny flower honey to taste

2 medium sized bowls
1 small bowl

SETTING THE TABLE: Place the cream and crowdie in one bowl and mix well. Put the fruit into the other medium bowl and the oatmeal into the smaller one. Place three bowls in the centre of the table with the bottle of whisky and jar of honey. Provide each guest with a mixing bowl and spoon.

MIXING THE CRANACHAN: Begin with cream/crowdie, sprinkle with oatmeal and add fruit and honey. Finally pour over some whisky to lubricate and mix. Adjust whisky and honey to taste.

Hogmanay, as well as for all birthdays and we sat, expectantly, waiting for our share, hoping that it would contain a lucky piece of silver which would ensure our future prosperity.

The suet dumpling in a cloth has its origins in the primitive custom of boiling a pudding in an animal's stomach bag. It's where the haggis comes from, as well as the sweet clootie dumplings (bag-puddings in England) that became popular in the nineteenth century when spices and sugar became cheaper. They were the Scottish answer to the English fruit cake in households where all cooking was done on the top of the stove and baking in an oven was only done by the local baker.

'A huge pot hung over the fire which leapt in a shining black-and-steel range,' says Jennifer Gowan in 'Friendship is a Clootie Dumpling', *Scottish Field*, July, 1966. 'A black kettle stood on one hob, a brown teapot on the other. Steam rose gently from the kettle and thickly from the great black pot, whence also came a continuous "purring" noise and the wonderful smell.'

Fruit traditions

Apple and Pear: The familiar street cry for apples and pears in eighteenth-century Edinburgh was – 'Fine rosey-cheekit Carse o' Gowries, the tap o' the tree.' Today, neither apples nor pears are grown commercially in the Carse of Gowrie, or anywhere else in Scotland for that matter. Yet they grow particularly well in many parts of the country, and there are many domestic orchards where old varieties are still preserved.

Bilberry: A small, blue-black, wild berry which was once widely used in Scotland.

Blackcurrant and Redcurrant: These were at one time an important part of the Scottish kitchen garden. When made into preserves they were regarded as flavourings, not just to spread on bread, but to use in sauces with sweet puddings, or even to make flavourful drinks, often to cure colds. Now 90 per cent of blackcurrants are grown for the juice market, but there are also new hardier varieties that have been developed for growing in Scotland for the fresh market.

Blaeberry: Blaeberries are very small, deep purple-black berries growing wild on low bushes on large areas of Scottish hills. At one time they were picked annually by travelling people who sold them to the rural population. When fresh they were usually eaten with cream, then made into jam. The system of picking was with a large, wide-toothed comb and enthusiasts still head off for the blaeberry hills in August and September to make their picking.

Blueberry: Known as the High Bush American Blueberry, it is the same genus as the low-grown, wild blaeberry, both of which thrive on acidic peaty soil. The blue-black blueberry is larger than the blaeberry and has a powdery blue bloom, greenish to purple flesh and a winey flavour, less tart than a blaeberry. It adds character to fruit pies and is the most popular flavouring for American (blueberry) muffins. It has been made available to growers in Scotland by the Scottish Crop Research Institute, and some growers have taken up the crop. Though they take some time to establish, they can remain cropping for fifty years.

Bramble (blackberry): These grow wild in hedgerows and are picked by enthusiasts each September when they ripen. Some commercial varieties of brambles have been developed. These are a more fleshy fruit with less seeds, ripening earlier in August.

Gooseberry: Originally a wild fruit, growing naturally in the cool, moist, high regions of Northern Europe, thorny little gooseberry bushes were introduced to Britain in the thirteenth century. And while in England their popularity led to breeding larger and sweeter dessert varieties, in Scotland the hardier wild variety prevailed. They were named after the French 'groseille' rather than the English gooseberry and became known as 'grosets' or 'grosarts'. They thrived well in the cool, moist Scottish climate. So much so that on the isles of Orkney and Shetland, where no trees survived, gooseberry bushes were to be found in every back yard and it was said that when the people read in their Bibles of Adam hiding among the trees, the only vision they could imagine was of a naked man cowering under a thorny groset bush.

Raspberry: In the early 1900s it was a group of Scottish market gardeners in Angus who decided to move out of traditional strawberry production and into raspberries. They formed a co-operative and in subsequent decades established the Scottish crop as the dominant British supply. On the fertile Tayside soils – once favoured by the farming monks of the middle ages – the raspberry matures slowly, producing a flavourful berry around the beginning of July. The quest for perfection in raspberry quality is everlasting. Among the experimental raspberry canes at the Scottish Crop Research Institute (SCRI) at Invergowrie, there is endless variety of size, colour, brightness, firmness and flavour; all to be considered in the search for a perfect raspberry. Currently in production are Glen Clova, one of the oldest varieties (1969), and Glen Moy and Glen Prosen (both released in 1981). Other varieties include: Glencoe, a purple raspberry (1989), Glen Garry (1990), and Glen Lyon (1991). There is also the autumn fruiting variety, Autumn Bliss, which serves a niche market while Magna, Glen Ample and Glen Rosa are the newest varieties of the later 90s. Visual and taste differences between the main varieties are minimal. Clova is medium-sized, li[ght] to medium coloured fruit with a sweetish-sharp flavour. Prosen is medium-r[ed] coloured with a slightly sourer flavour but is a firmer, more easily transportabl[e] fruit, while Moy is a large berry, also medium-red coloured and generally regarded as the best flavoured of the three. Neither too sharp nor too sweet, its flavour is more rounded but it is also the one with the shortest shelf life.

Sloe: On his *Tour in Scotland* 1771, Thomas Pennant, one of the most eminent naturalists of the eighteenth century remarks on the fruits eaten on Jura – 'Sloes are the only fruits of the island. An acid for punch is made of the berries of the mountain ash (rowan): and a kind of spirit is also distilled from them.'
To make sloe gin, prick ripe sloes with a darning needle and pack them into jars. Pour in caster sugar to come one third of the way up the fruit and fill up with gin. Shake till the sugar is dissolved. Store in a cool place for at least a month, shaking occasionally. It will keep for a year and the liqueur can be drained off and bottled.

Strawberry: While turn-of-the-century Tayside growers moved out of strawberries and into raspberries, strawberry growing continued to flourish in the smallholdings of the Clyde valley. Now the Clyde valley has largely turned to other crops, such as tomatoes, and strawberry growing has been revived on the arable farms of Tayside, Fife and the North-East. The 1990s success story was the variety Elsanta, which was first developed for Dutch glasshouse growing, and not for an outdoor Scottish summer. It is a large, orange-red berry, with a deep, pinkish-red flesh, and when fully ripe is neither too soft nor too firm. It's a berry to be squashed when eating, when it releases its finely balanced flavours. Neither too sweet, nor too sharp, it's the gradual slow-ripening of the fruit in the long hours of summer daylight that develops the sugar content gradually to give the berries their superior taste. 'We sent our first consignment of Elsanta to France last week,' says William Halley of Scotfruit, Dundee distributors of Tayside soft fruits, 'and they have just multiplied the order by 10!' Other large eating varieties are Pegasus, Symphony and Hapil (EM227), a large, soft, juicy berry with a short shelf life which is only grown on pick-your-own farms. Cambridge Favourite and Tamella are smaller-sized, jam-making berries.

Tayberry: This is a hybrid cross between the American blackberry (bramble) and the European raspberry and is of similar type to the American Loganberry. The Tayberry has a strong personality, a sweet aromatic flavour and an exotic, deep, purple-red colour. It is a long firm, fleshy fruit (about 4cm) that cooks well. Though not widely available commercially, it is a very popular pick-your-own berry.

Caledonian Cream

An easy mix of lively flavours that were first combined by Mrs Dalgairns (circa 1829), the nineteenth-century cookery writer, when she mixed minced marmalade, brandy and the juice of a lemon through a couple of pints of cream.

Yield: 4

2 large sweet Spanish navel oranges
300ml (10fl oz) whipping cream
2 heaped tablespoons Seville marmalade
2-3 tablespoons brandy
Lemon juice to taste
Sugar to taste

MAKING: Strip the zest from the oranges with a zester into the bowl of a food processor. Cut off all the white pith and remove each segment of the orange with a sharp knife, avoiding the white pith. Squeeze out any remaining juice from the leftover pith and put it in the base of a glass serving dish. Add the marmalade and brandy to the orange zest in the processor and blend until smooth (this can also be used as a sauce). Add all but two teaspoonfuls to the cream. Mix and add sugar and lemon juice, and pour on top of oranges. Sprinkle the remaining teaspoonfuls on top and swirl with a knife. Serve chilled.

Ice Cream and Raspberry Sauce

This rich 'parfait' type of ice cream with a high proportion of egg yolks and cream is quite unlike Italian ice cream, with its milky and much more 'icy' texture.

Cook's Tip: This does not require any special ice cream-making equipment. The mixture can be set in a special mould and turned out for serving. It is best not to make it up in very large quantities since some of the delicate flavouring will be lost if kept in the freezer for longer than one month. Some flavours are more robust than others. Bear in mind, also that the frozen flavour will be less strong than unfrozen, so flavour strongly rather than mildly.

Yield: 4

3 egg yolks
3 tablespoons icing sugar
250g (9oz) strawberries and/or raspberries or any other fresh
   fruit in season
150ml (5fl oz) whipping cream, whipped
Lemon juice to taste
2 tablespoons flavouring liqueur, or to taste

Raspberry Sauce:
250g (9oz) raspberries
Lemon juice to taste
Sugar to taste

MAKING THE ICE CREAM: Put the eggs and sugar into a bowl over hot water and beat till thick and creamy. Press the fruit through a sieve to make the purée, or purée in the liquidiser or food processor and sieve. Add the lemon juice and liqueur. Mix the egg and sugar with the purée, folding in lightly and then fold in the cream. Taste for flavour and pour into a plastic container or special mould and freeze. To turn out, run the mould under the hot tap to loosen.

TO SERVE: Allow ice cream to soften slightly for about 30 minutes at room temperature, which will greatly improve the texture and also the flavour.

MAKING THE SAUCE: Either press the raspberries through a sieve to remove the pips, or blend in a food processor and sieve. Add lemon juice and sugar to taste. This will depend on the sharpness/sweetness of the fruit. Serve poured over the ice cream.

Blackcurrant Sorbet

(OR OTHER SOFT FRUIT)

Uncomplicated mixtures of fruit purée and sugar syrup give clean penetrating flavours that were often used in Victorian meals of many courses, somewhere about the middle, to 'refresh the palate'. Queen Victoria herself was particularly fond of a rum-flavoured sorbet. For eating styles today, they are usually served at the end of a meal with some fresh fruit.

Syrup:
250g (9oz) granulated sugar
300ml (10fl oz) water
Juice of 1 lemon
Juice of 1 orange

Fruit:
500g (1 lb 2oz) blackcurrants or any other soft fruit

1 large egg white, stiffly beaten

MAKING THE SYRUP: Dissolve the sugar in the water, bring to the boil and simmer for about five minutes. Cool and add the orange and lemon juice.

PREPARING FRUIT: Blend fruit in a processor. Mix into the syrup.

MAKING WATER ICE: Pass the purée and syrup through a sieve. Pour into a plastic container with a lid. The shallower it is, the quicker it will freeze. Put into the freezer and remove every half-hour or so to stir in the crystals that have formed, giving it a beat to prevent large crystals forming. When it is uniformly solid, but not too hard, it can be beaten with an electric beater into one stiffly beaten egg white to give it more volume and a lighter texture. Beat the egg white in the bowl first, and then gradually add spoonfuls of the water ice. It must not be too hard or it will be difficult to mix in. Re-freeze. Like all ices it should not be kept for too long in the freezer since the flavour will begin to fade after a month or so.

Hazelnut Meringue

WITH CREAM AND RASPBERRIES

This was first created in the 1970s at the Laich Bakery in Edinburgh's Hanover Street. The crunchy meringue – slightly chewy in the centre and heavy with hazelnuts – is sandwiched with a thick layer of whipped cream and an equally thick layer of raspberries.

Cook's Tips: It is best made up a few hours before eating so that the flavours mingle and the raspberry juice seeps a little into the top layer of meringue. The nuts can be either finely or coarsely ground, the latter giving a crunchier texture. This is a good cook-ahead-and-stop-worrying cake, since the meringues will keep for several weeks if they are tightly, but carefully, wrapped in foil and kept in an airtight tin.

For the meringue:
250g (9oz) hazelnuts
4 egg whites
250g (9oz) caster sugar

For the filling:
300ml (10fl oz) whipping cream, stiffly whipped
250g (9oz) raspberries

Icing Sugar for dusting

Line 2 x 20cm (8 inch) sandwich tins.
Pre-heat the oven to 350°F/180°C/Gas 4.

MAKING MERINGUE: Toast the hazelnuts in a cool oven for about 10 minutes, then cool. Grind them fairly fine (this is a matter of taste, coarser will give a rougher textured meringue). Whisk the egg whites till well bulked up but not too stiff and then add the sugar a tablespoon at a time, beating well. Finally fold in the nuts and pour into the prepared tins. Bake for 20 minutes till the meringue is set but not dried out. Remove from the tins and leave to cool.

ASSEMBLING CAKE: Spread the cream thickly on one half of the meringue, cover with raspberries and place the other half on top. Dust thickly with icing sugar and leave for at least an hour before serving.

Raspberries and Meringues

A simple mix of outstanding flavours and textures that can be assembled in minutes.

Yield: 4

500g (1lb 2oz) raspberries
4 tablespoons Frangelica liqueur
425ml (15fl oz) whipping cream
8 meringues (shop-bought will do)

Four bowls

MAKING: Divide raspberries equally into four bowls. Add one tablespoon of liqueur to each bowl. Whip cream till fairly stiff. Crumble meringues roughly and mix through the cream. Pile on top of raspberries and stir through, or leave in two layers. Serve immediately.

Strawberries and Cream
with Shortbread

Though Scots might claim the partnership of strawberries and shortbread, it's our English neighbours who have perfected the union of strawberries and cream.This is an amalgam of the two, largely inspired by Dorothy Hartley in *Food in England* (1954): 'Take a deep cold bowl half full of cream (an old punch bowl is excellent for this purpose). Whip the cream slightly, but do not make it too stiff. Then drop into it as many strawberries as it will hold, the smaller ones being put in whole, the larger, cut up. Stir as you go, mashing slightly, and when the cream really won't cover another strawberry, leave it to stand for an hour. It will then be a cold level, pale-pink cream. Crust it over with dredged white sugar and serve forth in June, on a green lawn, under shady trees by the river.'

Yield: 4-6

600ml (1pt) whipping cream
500g (1lb 2oz) strawberries
2 tablespoons caster sugar
8 Balmoral Shortbread biscuits (see p159)

MAKING: Put the cream into a bowl and whip lightly. Wash and shaw the strawberries, cut up larger ones, and drop into the cream, stirring and mashing. Leave to stand for an hour. Dredge the top with caster sugar and serve with the shortbread biscuits.

Fruit Crumble

Cook's Tip: When mixing different fruits, it's worth adding a handful of berries – brambles, rasps, strawberries, blackcurrants, blueberries – which will add flavour and colour as well as excellent juices.

Yield: 4-6

700g (1½lb) apples OR plums, gooseberries, rhubarb, blackcurrants, brambles
125-175g (4-6oz) granulated sugar
125g (4½oz) butter
250g (9oz) plain flour
50g (2oz) soft brown sugar
Grated rind of an orange or lemon

Serve with: custard or cream.
Preheat the oven to 400°F/200°C/Gas 6.
1.3L (2½pt) pie dish.

MAKING AND BAKING: Prepare the fruit. Peel, core and slice apples, stone plums and chop rhubarb. Grease the pie dish and put in the fruit in layers with the sugar. Rub butter into the flour until it resembles fine breadcrumbs (this can be done in a food processor). Mix in the sugar and grated orange or lemon rind. Pile on top of the fruit. Spread evenly and press down. Bake for 35-40 minutes. Serve with custard or cream.

Morayshire Apple Crumble with Oatmeal

Hazelnuts and oatmeal make this a variation on the crumble topping, while the apple filling is spiced with cloves.

Yield: 4-6

5 tablespoons water
4 cloves
75g (3oz) granulated sugar
50g (2oz) beef or vegetarian suet
125g (4oz) soft brown sugar
125g (4oz) medium oatmeal
25g (1oz) hazelnuts, finely chopped
700g (1½ lb) apples

Serve with: whipped cream.
Preheat the oven to 350°F/180°C/Gas 4.
Grease a 1.3L (2½ pt) pie dish.

INFUSING CLOVES, MAKING FILLING: Bring the water to the boil and add the cloves. Take off the heat and leave for 10 minutes. Add the granulated sugar and boil up to dissolve. Remove from the heat. In a bowl mix the suet, half – 50g (2oz) – of the soft brown sugar, the oatmeal and nuts. Peel, core and slice the apples.

ASSEMBLING AND BAKING: Place the apples in the base of the dish and pour over the clove syrup. Cover with the topping mixture spread evenly and, lastly, spread over the remaining brown sugar. Press down and bake for about an hour till the apples are cooked and the top browned. Serve hot with whipped cream.

Eve's Pudding

Cook's Tip: It's worth adding a handful of berries – brambles, rasps, strawberries, blackcurrants, blueberries – which will add flavour and colour as well as extra juices.

Filling:
900g (2lb) cooking apples
1 lemon, grated rind and juice
1 tablespoon water
75g (3oz) soft brown sugar

Sponge Topping:
125g (4½ oz) self-raising flour
125g (4½ oz) caster sugar
125g (4½ oz) butter, softened
2 eggs
2 tablespoons milk

Serve with: cream, custard or milk.
Preheat the oven to 350°F/180°C/Gas 4.
Grease a 1.3L (2½ pt) pie dish.

PREPARING FILLING: Peel, core and slice the apples thinly. Place in layers in the pie dish, sprinkling each layer with grated lemon rind, juice and water, then sugar.

MAKING SPONGE AND BAKING: Put the flour and sugar into a bowl and beat for about one minute. Add the butter, eggs and one tablespoon of the milk and beat for another minute, or until it changes colour and becomes creamy. Add the remaining milk and beat for another 30 seconds. It should be a soft dropping consistency. Add more milk if necessary. Spread evenly on top of the apples and bake for about 40 minutes until the sponge is risen and browned and the apples tender. Serve with cream, custard or milk.

Apple Dumplings

Cook's Tip: It's best to choose apples of an equal size so they will all be cooked at the same time.

Yield: 4

Shortcrust pastry:
100g (3½ oz) unsalted butter
200g (7oz) plain flour
1-2 tablespoons cold water
Pinch of salt

4 large cooking apples
50g (2oz) soft brown sugar
1 teaspoon cinnamon
Pinch of ground cloves
Beaten egg to glaze
1 tablespoon caster sugar

Serve with: custard, whipped cream or créme fraiche.
Preheat the oven to 425°F/220°C/Gas 7 and bake at this temperature for 10 minutes. Reduce heat to 325°F/170°C/Gas 3 for about 30 minutes.

MAKING PASTRY: Put the butter into the mixer bowl (or food processor) and add half the flour. Beat on a slow speed until they have combined into a soft paste. Add the remaining flour, salt and one tablespoon of water and mix at a slow speed till it becomes a smooth, firm paste. Add more water if necessary. Do not over mix. Wrap in clingfilm and leave to rest in a cool place for at least an hour before use.

MAKING DUMPLINGS: Divide the pastry into four and roll out each piece into a round wide enough to cover the apples completely. Cut off any surplus pastry and reserve for decoration. Peel the apples and remove central core with the vegetable peeler. Place each apple in the centre of the pastry round. Mix the sugar with the cinnamon and cloves and use to fill the core space. Wet the edges of the pastry and gather them up round the apple, moulding them into a neat join at the top. Turn over and press to neaten. Make some pastry leaves and decorate the tops. Brush with egg and dust with caster sugar. Bake for 10 minutes in a hot oven to set the pastry, then turn down to cook the apple. Test with a skewer after about 30 minutes when the apple should be soft.

Apple Frushie (Pie)

'Frushie' is the Scots for crisp and was often used to describe anything with a short pastry.

Yield: **4**

Sweet shortcrust pastry:
100g (3½ oz) unsalted butter
50g (2oz) icing sugar
1 egg yolk
175g (6oz) plain flour

Filling:
1kg (2lb 4oz) tart cooking apples
100g (4oz) soft brown sugar
1 teaspoon cinnamon or mixed spice
1 lemon, juice and zest

Dredging: caster sugar

Serve with: cream or custard.
Preheat the oven to 350°F/180°C/Gas 4.
Use a 1.3L (2½ pt) deep pie dish.

MAKING THE PASTRY: Beat the butter and sugar in a mixer (or blend in a food processor) till light and fluffy. Add the egg and beat for a minute to mix in, then add the flour and mix on a slow speed till it forms a smooth paste. Do not overmix. Wrap in clingfilm and leave to rest in a cool place for at least an hour till ready to use.

MAKING THE PIE AND BAKING: Roll out the pastry about 2.5cm (1 inch) larger than the rim of the pie dish. Invert the pie dish and place on top of the pastry. Cut round to fit and wet the pie dish rim. Cut the excess pastry into a long strip and place on the rim. Press down well and wet the edges. Peel, core and slice the apples. Mix the sugar and cinnamon. Put apples into the pie dish in layers, sprinkling with lemon juice and zest and the spiced sugar. They should be heaped well above the rim of the pie dish. Place on the lid and press down well to seal. Make a small hole in the centre for the steam to escape. Pinch the edge to make a decorative finish, or mark with a fork. Bake for 40–50 minutes till the apples are cooked. Cover the pastry with foil if it darkens too much. Dredge with caster sugar and serve hot or cold with cream or custard.

Lemon Meringue Pie

Soft, lemony filling is topped with a marshmallowy meringue, set in a crisp pastry crust to make the perfect contrast of flavours and textures.

Yield: 12 from 25 x 3.25cm deep (9$\frac{1}{2}$ x 1$\frac{1}{2}$ inch deep) flan tin with removable base.

Pastry:
100g (3$\frac{1}{2}$ oz) unsalted butter
50g (2oz) icing sugar
1 egg yolk
175g (6oz) plain flour
Beaten egg for brushing

Filling:
125g (4oz) sugar
25g (1oz) cornflour
4 lemons, zest and juice
6 egg yolks
200ml (7fl oz) milk
50g (2oz) butter
2-3 tablespoons single cream

Meringue:
6 egg whites
Pinch of salt
175g (6oz) caster sugar

Preheat the oven to 350°F/180°C/Gas 4 then turn down to 300°F/140°C/Gas 2. Grease a flan tin.

MAKING PASTRY: Beat the butter and sugar in a mixer (or blend in a food processor) till light and fluffy. Add the egg yolk and beat for a minute to mix in. Add the flour and mix on a slow speed until it forms a smooth paste. Do not overmix. Wrap in clingfilm and leave to rest in a cool place for at least an hour before use.

LINING FLAN, BAKING BLIND: Roll the pastry out on a lightly-floured work surface to a circle large enough to fill the base and sides of the flan tin plus about 1cm (½ inch) extra. Lift the pastry over a rolling pin into the flan tin and press into the base and sides. Do not cut off the overhang. Place a sheet of foil in the base, pressing the foil into the corners and up the sides. Fill with dry beans or rice. Bake blind for 18–20 minutes or until pastry is set. Remove from the oven and take out the foil and beans. Brush the base and sides with a little beaten egg and return to the oven to dry out for another 10 minutes or until crisp. Trim off the surplus pastry with a sharp knife.

MAKING THE FILLING: Put the sugar, cornflour, lemon juice and yolks into a bowl and beat together till the sugar is dissolved. Heat the milk, butter and lemon zest in a pan and slowly bring almost to the boil. Leave to infuse for five minutes. Strain over the egg mixture, whisking constantly. Return to the pan and cook slowly over a low heat, stirring all the time, until the custard has thickened. Add cream to thin down a little and pour into prepared flan tin.

MAKING THE MERINGUE: Whisk the egg whites and salt till they form peaks and then add about half the sugar gradually in tablespoons, beating between each addition. Stir in the remaining sugar gradually and when mixed in, pipe on or pile on top of the filling. Dust with caster sugar on top to give a crisp finish.

BAKING: Bake at the cooler temperature for about 30-40 minutes till lightly browned.

Ecclefechan Butter Tart

A rich, fruity tart that is a popular Borders teatime speciality, but can also be served with cream as a dessert.

Yield: 12 from 25 x 3.25cm deep (9$\frac{1}{2}$ x 1$\frac{1}{2}$ inch) deep) flan tin with removable base.

Pastry:
100g (3$\frac{1}{2}$ oz) unsalted butter
50g (2oz) icing sugar
1 egg yolk
175g (6oz) plain flour
Beaten egg for brushing

100g (4oz) melted butter
175g (6oz) soft brown sugar
2 eggs
2 dessertspoons apple cider vinegar
100g (4oz) chopped walnuts
250g (9oz) mixed dried fruit

Serve with: whipped cream.
Preheat the oven to 375°F/190°C/Gas 5.
Grease a flan tin.

MAKING PASTRY: Beat the butter and sugar in a mixer (or blend in a food processor) till light and fluffy. Add the egg yolk and beat for a minute to mix in. Add the flour and mix on a slow speed until it forms a smooth paste. Do not overmix. Wrap in clingfilm and leave to rest for at least an hour in a cool place till ready to use.

LINING FLAN: Roll the pastry out on a lightly-floured work surface to a circle large enough to fill the base and sides of the flan tin plus about 1cm ($\frac{1}{2}$ inch) extra. Lift the pastry over a rolling pin into the flan tin and press into the base and sides. Trim off the overhang.

MAKING TART: Mix all the ingredients together and pour into the pastry. Bake for 30 minutes. Serve hot or cold with whipped cream.

Burnt Cream

A rich custard topped with sugar, which is burnt to a crunchy layer of burnished caramel.

Yield: 4 x 150ml (5fl oz) bowls or pots

75ml (3fl oz) milk
50g (2oz) caster sugar
6 egg yolks
275ml (9fl oz) double cream
1 vanilla pod
2 tablespoons caster sugar for caramelising

MAKING MIXTURE: Put the milk, sugar and egg yolks into a bowl and beat well with a whisk. Put the cream into a pan. Split the vanilla pod in half and scrape the seeds into the cream in the pan. Add the pod and bring the cream gently to simmering point so the full flavour of the vanilla is infused into the cream. Remove from the heat and leave to infuse for another 10 minutes. Remove the vanilla pod, then pour half the cream over the egg and sugar mixture, beating well. Pour this back into the pan with the remaining cream. Cook gently, stirring all the time, till the mixture thickens. Strain and pour into the pots.

FINISHING: Cover the surface with sugar and caramelise under a hot grill or use a pastry blowtorch. Serve immediately.

Whipkull

This is an old Shetland New Year's Day breakfast that was eaten with rich shortbread as a memorable start to the year. It's thought to be of Scandinavian origin.

Yield: 8-12

4 egg yolks
175g (6oz) caster sugar
125ml (4fl oz) rum
500ml (18fl oz) whipping cream

MAKING: Beat the egg yolks and sugar till thick and foamy. This can be done in a bowl over a pan of hot water or in a double boiler. Add the rum. Beat the cream in another bowl until stiff and add to the mixture. Serve with thin Petticoat Tails (see p158) or Balmoral Shortbread (see p159).

BAKING CLASSICS

Dundee Cake

Janet Keiller has a shop on the south side of the Seagate in Dundee where she has spent the best part of her life – besides raising seven children – making preserves, jellies, biscuits, sweeties and cakes. She has always believed in diversifying into unique lines and it has certainly paid off. Now she is almost 60 and is ready to retire. She has a tidy sum put by and is keen to use it to help her son, James, develop the business. He is the only son who has shown an interest in her enterprise and has also developed her innovative flair. He is just 22 when she hands over the running of the Keiller shop in 1797.

Marmalade, of course, becomes the Keiller's biggest success story (see p180). But as the small city shop grows into a factory, marmalade can only be made for a few months in the year when the Spanish fruit ripens. There are factory hands to be kept busy for the rest of the year and so James Keiller continues with his mother's good sweeties, soft fruit preserves made from the fruit grown in the Dundee hinterland – and cakes.

Soon, Keiller's Dundee Cake becomes as popular as their marmalade. Quality ingredients, which the family pride themselves on using throughout their range, are used for the cake. Of course they use the best butter and the finest sultanas. But it is the flavouring of preserved orange peel – saved from the marmalade making – and the cake studded on top with roasted whole almonds that give it the Janet Keiller unique selling point.

According to David Goodfellow, of Dundee bakers Goodfellow and Steven, the Keiller's Dundee Cake recipe was passed on by an old master baker who had worked for Keiller's, and wrote it down before going off to fight in the First World War. There are no cherries and no spices, just a buttery rich sultana cake flavoured with orange peel and almonds.

Oatcakes and Crowdie

On the coal-less Isle of Lewis in the Outer Hebrides, ovens are a rarity. 'Bread' is baked on a girdle over the gentle heat of a peat fire by all nineteenth-century crofters. Not a soft yeasty loaf, but a hard oatmeal 'cake' that these Gaelic speakers call a 'bonnach' (bannock) and non-Gaelic Scotland calls an 'oatcake'.

This 'cake' refers back to the old meaning – a 'cake of bread' which is thin, flat, round and usually baked hard – as in something 'caked' hard, such as a cake of soap.

Their Hebridean 'bonnach' is much thicker and heavier than the Lowland version and they often use it as travelling food. It is easy to carry and is eaten with butter and cheese. Not a hard-pressed, mature cheese as found in the Lowlands, but the soft, fresh, crofter's crowdie.

It is a fine feast of textures and flavours in hard, mealy oatcake and soft, citric cheese. Even better if there is a layer of creamy butter in-between. With a glass of milk, it is a meal that sustains them for many an hour's hard labour:

'They make a kind of bread, not unpleasant to the taste, of oats, and barley, the only grain cultivated in these regions, and, from long practice, they have attained considerable skill in moulding the cakes,' says G Buchanan in his *Description of Scotland* (1629).

'Of this they eat a little in the morning, and then contentedly go out a-hunting, or engage in some other occupation, frequently remaining without any other food till evening.'

Their crowdie-making was part of a pastoral system where every crofter had at least one milking cow. Spring and summer were the peak times of production, the cheese was made without rennet or souring agents, but followed the natural division of the milk into curds and whey. It's an old lifestyle which may have gone, but the crofter's crowdie is still made by Scottish cheese makers. Its method was recorded in an anonymous collection of Lewis recipes, said to have been collected by a teacher at the Nicholson Institute in Stornoway, possibly during the 1960s:

'Set a pan with freshly sour or thick milk on a slow heat and watch till it curdles, not letting it simmer or boil or it will harden. When set, let it cool before drawing off the whey. Use a muslin cloth. When whey is completely squeezed out, mix crowdie with a little salt until you find it very soft in your hands, mix with cream or top of milk and set out in dishes. The mixture can also be pressed in a colander to remove whey and a weight placed on top. The crowdie can then be sliced like cheese.'

Selkirk Bannock

Sir Walter Scott is dead some 30 years when Queen Victoria calls for tea with his granddaughter, still living at Abbotsford in 1867. The tea table is spread with a fine array of Scottish baking from light, floury scones to rich gingerbread. What interests the Queen, however, is the round, golden sultana bun with the wonderful buttery flavour. She has one slice and is hooked, eating nothing else from the tea table.

The bun that has just received such enthusiastic royal approval is, of course, a Selkirk Bannock. Bannocks from Selkirk were already something of a speciality and Scott himself mentions them in *The Bride of Lammermoor*: 'Never was such making of car-cakes (Scots crumpets) and sweet scones and Selkirk bannocks,' he says. But the one made for the Queen's tea comes from a particularly skilled local baker, Robbie Douglas, whose fame is spread far and wide.

Royal seals of approval notwithstanding, it is Robbie Douglas's search for perfection that is the more important factor in ensuring the bannock's long term success.

'Robbie's first bannock,' says F M McNeill in *The Scots Kitchen* (1929), 'was much more than a mere mixture of flour, butter and fruit. He found that the flavour was influenced by different butters, and finally he chose a butter made from milk produced on certain neighbouring pastures. If for any reason this butter could not be procured, well, no bannocks were made. That was one reason why there were no bannocks during war-time. Similarly with the sultanas. They had to be of a certain kind, specially imported from Turkey.'

McNeill includes a traditional recipe: 'Make or procure from the baker two pounds of dough. Into this rub eight ounces of butter and flour of lard until melted but not oiled; then work in eight ounces of castor sugar and two pounds of sultanas. Mould in the form of a large round bun, place in a buttered tin, let it stand in a warm place for thirty minutes to rise, and bake in a moderate oven until lightly browned (about an hour and a quarter).'

Tea and Scones

Described as 'a soft, flat cake of barley meal, oatmeal or flour', the first mention of a 'scone' is in 1549. Its origins appear to be Germanic, from 'schoonbrot', meaning 'fine bread'. It was a Glasgow tea merchant, however, who provided the meeting place for tea and scones.

Stuart Cranston had already been selling 'sampling' cups of tea to his customers at 44 St Enoch Square when he decided to open a proper tearoom in 1875. It was the beginning of a flourishing tearoom era in the city. Though he created the first, it was his sister, Kate Cranston, aided by the architect Charles Rennie Mackintosh, who is credited with inventing the tearoom. Mackintosh's avant garde interiors, and Cranston's stylish teas – both 'afternoon' and 'high' – achieved sight-of-the-city status with art-lovers from all over Europe making a pilgrimage to the city for a Cranston tea in a Mackintosh setting. The Scottish scone, including its many variants, taking its place on elegant, tiered cake stands.

Baking traditions:

Aberdeen Rowie (roll) or Butterie Golden: Rustic, misshapen, crispy, salty and flaky, this is Scotland's peasant version of the aristocratic French croissant. Rowies, like croissants, depend for their character on layers of fat – originally butcher's dripping, though today's are made with vegetable fat – between thin layers of yeast dough. They were made originally for fishermen at sea who needed a roll with a longer keeping quality. While it's known in the North-East as a rowie, its national tag is butterie, though it has never contained butter. Its texture should be very crisp and flaky, though some bakers make a less crisp more 'bready' version which is not regarded by aficionados as a 'real' rowie. A 'wee' rowie is half-sized. Two stuck together with butter is a 'double' rowie. A bag of bities is a bag of broken rowies. A 'cremated' rowie is a well-fired rowie. The first literary mention of a 'butterie' is recorded in the Scottish National Dictionary in an account of an Arbroath Street seller (circa 1899). 'Between butteries, Rob Roys (a kind of Bath Bun), an' turnovers, her basket was weel filled.'

Abernethy Biscuit: A pale golden, shortbread-type biscuit, pricked on top and made with reduced butter and sugar. Its name comes, not from the town of Abernethy, but from a Scots surgeon John Abernethy (1764–1831) who suggested the recipe to his local baker.

Bannock: A round, unleavened bread of barley and/or oats made in the days before raising agents. For most of Scotland, oats and barley were the staple crops, but in the more fertile areas with a drier, warmer climate wheat was also used. The bannock was usually rolled out to fit the size of the family girdle, and baked over an open peat fire. It was the early Scots equivalent of an oven-baked loaf. While this was the everyday bannock, special bannocks were made for festive occasions – its round shape was symbolic of the cycle of life, death and resurrection. The Beltane bannock, baked on May Day, was also coated in a symbolic custard made of eggs – so the hens would lay – milk – so the cows would produce milk – and grain – so the crops would grow. Variations of this custom were practiced around the country.

Border Tart: A shortcrust pastry flan filled with a mixture of dried fruit, sugar, melted butter and egg. When baked it is usually coated with white water icing. Ecclefechan Butter Tart is a variation.

Cumnock Tart: A sweet variation of the Scotch pie, made with apples or rhubarb. It was originally made by an Ayrshire baker, Mr Stoddart, around 1920 and is presently made by Hugh Bradford of Glasgow, whose father was apprenticed to Mr Stoddart. It's a hand-crafted, oval-shaped, double-crust individual tart with a sugary-browned surface and lightly burnt edges.

Glasgow Roll: A morning roll with a hard outer surface and a light, very open, well-aerated texture inside. Sometimes described as a 'chewy' roll. It was specially designed as a roll for hot fillings, with its hard crust and airy centre. The traditional filling was bacon and egg or square sausage and egg. It's made with a very high gluten flour and is entirely hand-crafted. The largest bakery in Glasgow makes 300,000 a night.

Kirriemuir Gingerbread: This was first made by Walter Burnett in Kirriemuir who sold his recipe to a large plant baker in East Kilbride near Glasgow in the 1940s. It was made in this bakery until 1977 when the recipe was sold again to Bell's of Shotts who continue to make it. It is a light-textured, dumpling-type gingerbread which is sweetly-malted and lightly-spiced.

Parkin: Also known as 'perkin'. The recipes vary according to the baker but they range from thick, biscuity cakes to thin, hard biscuits. They are a light, ginger-brown, with a sweet, ginger flavour and most have some oatmeal added.

Softie: This is an East Coast description for a round bun. The name was used to distinguish it from a hard, crisp 'rowie'. It contains double the amount of sugar that is in a plain bap.

Square Loaf: A loaf specially designed for making 'pieces' (sandwiches) that fit into a square lunch box. It is also known as a 'plain' loaf (distinguished from a 'pan' loaf which used to be considered a posher version, since it was made in a tin, and became a slang term for those who had aspirations above their station), or 'batch bread' in a system of baking bread where the loaves are tightly packed on a tray and rise upwards rather than outwards giving them their tall shape. It is the half slice which is square.

Water Biscuit: A thick, circular biscuit that is made in Orkney. They are an irregular cream to pale golden colour, blistered in places with gold-brown bubbles and docked with small holes. They are a rich, nutty flavour and are extremely crisp with a flaky texture. A development of the old ship's biscuit, they were originally used as a bread substitute.

BAKING CLASSICS:

Oatcakes

Cook's Tip: These are best made with Scots oatmeal which has the finest flavour because the kernels ripen slowly, intensifying their flavour.

Yield: 12

200g (7oz) medium oatmeal
50g (2oz) plain flour, sifted
75ml (2½ fl oz) boiling water
40g (1½ oz) softened vegetable cooking fat or butter
1 level teaspoon honey or sugar

Preheat the oven to 350°F/180°C/Gas 4.
Lightly oil two baking sheets or a round (8 inch) or rectangular (7 x 11 inch) baking tin.

MIXING: Put the oatmeal and flour into a bowl and make a well in the centre. Measure the boiling water into a pan and cut up the fat into small pieces. Add the fat to the boiling water and heat (this can also be heated in the microwave). Add honey or sugar and pour all the liquid into the dry ingredients. Mix until it forms a soft pliable dough, adding more boiling water if it is too stiff. It should not crack when rolled out.

SHAPING – METHOD 1: Divide the dough into three pieces. While still hot, roll thinly into two rounds about 18cm (7 inch) diameter. Cut each round into 4 triangles (farls). Place on baking tin and bake for 30-40 minutes until they turn a light, sandy colour. Cool on a rack and store in an airtight tin.

METHOD 2: Place the dough in a round or rectangular tin and press out thinly, then spread evenly with a palate knife. Cut into six or eight (squares in the rectangular tin or triangles in the round tin). Bake as for method 1.

Beremeal (Barley) Bannocks

Once the everyday bread of the whole country – originally without raising agents – these are now mostly made in Orkney, Shetland and some of the islands. The flour is milled on Orkney and at Golspie in Sutherland.

Yield: 1 large round

175g (6oz) beremeal (barley flour)
50g (2oz) plain flour
Pinch of salt
1 teaspoon cream of tartar
1 teaspoon bicarbonate of soda
250ml (9fl oz) buttermilk or fresh milk soured with a tablespoon of lemon juice

Pre-heated girdle: The girdle is ready when you hold your hand above the surface and it is pleasantly hot. Another test is to dust with flour which should colour slightly. If it burns too quickly, it is too hot.

MIXING AND BAKING: Sift all of the dry ingredients into a bowl and make a well in the centre. Add the buttermilk and mix with a knife to a soft elastic dough. Flour the work surface and roll the dough out into one round about 1cm (½ inch) thick. Sprinkle the girdle with a thin layer of beremeal and bake the bannock on both sides (three to four minutes on each side) until cooked through. Remove and wrap in a towel to keep warm and soft. Serve warm with butter and farmhouse cheese.

Shortbread

Shortbread was raised to 'flour confectionery' status by the Scottish Master Bakers Association who considered it a class above the common 'biscuit', which is largely the reason it became – in its tartan box – such an export success.

Cook's Tips: Butter is the determining flavour in shortbread, so tasting it before using will give some idea of its quality and suitability. Texture depends on the flour used. Cornflour will make it less crunchy. Rice flour on the other hand will make it more crunchy.

(6 inch) round shortbread moulds

280g (10oz) plain flour, sifted
55g (2oz) cornflour or rice flour, sifted
110g (4oz) caster sugar, sifted
225g (8oz) butter, softened and
cut into small pieces
Dredging: caster sugar

Preheat the oven to 325°F/150°C/Gas 3.
Depth of shortbread for thick fingers 2cm (³/₄ inch).
For thin fingers 5mm (¹/₄ inch).
Dust baking tin or shortbread mould lightly with flour.

MIXING BY HAND: Sift the flours on the work surface. Put the sugar onto the work surface and place the butter on top. Knead all the sugar into the butter, then add a little flour and gradually work into the butter and sugar. Continue adding the flour until the mixture becomes firm and pliable but not too stiff. It should not be difficult to roll out and should not crack.

MIXING BY MACHINE: Put all the ingredients into the mixing bowl and mix at a slow speed until the dough begins to come together. Then raise the speed a little until it forms a smooth dough. Test the consistency and add more flour if it is too soft.

SHAPING THIN FINGERS: Roll the dough out to 5mm (¼ inch) and cut in fingers approx 6.5cm (2½ inch) long and 2.5cm (1 inch) wide. Put onto a baking tin. Mark all over with a fork to prevent rising and rest in a cool place for one hour before baking.

SHAPING THICK FINGERS: Roll the dough out into a large square or press into a tin. It should be approximately 2cm (¾ inch) thick. Mark in lengths 7.5cm (3 inch) long and 2.5cm (1 inch) wide. Mark with a fork to prevent rising and rest in a cool place for one hour before baking.

SHAPING INTO LARGE ROUND: Roll the dough out into a large round about 2cm (¾ inch) thick and place on a baking tray. Pinch the edge with first finger and thumb to decorate or use the flat edge of a fork to mark the edge. Mark into triangles and mark all over with a fork to prevent rising. Rest in a cool place for one hour before baking.

USING A SHORTBREAD MOULD: Divide dough equally into three and press one piece into the floured mould. Run a rolling pin over the top to level it. With fingertips, pull out the edges all round so they are not ragged and come away cleanly. Reverse and – holding your hand underneath to catch the shortbread as it comes out – knock out the dough by hitting the edge of the mould on the edge of a table. It may be necessary to hit it in several places before it comes out. Place the dough on a baking tin and mark with a fork. Repeat with the other two pieces of dough. Rest for one hour in a cool place before baking.

BAKING: Bake till evenly golden brown. Thin fingers will take 20–30 minutes, thicker fingers, round and mould, 45–50 minutes. Dredge with sugar while still warm. Remove from the tin and put to cool on a rack. Store in an airtight container.

Mixed Grain Mashlum Bannock

This moist, aromatic bread is made from a mixture of meals grown in the same field. It was once known as 'mashlum' meal.

Cook's Tip: This is best eaten with cheese or a thick soup-stew. It can either be baked in a round bannock shape and cut in wedges or put into a 25cm (10 inch) cast-iron pot with a lid in the style of an Irish bastible pot. A chicken brick also works well though the finished loaf is a slightly odd shape.

> 125g (4½ oz) medium oatmeal
> 125g (4½ oz) beremeal or barley flour
> 350g (12oz) wholemeal flour
> 50g (2oz) wheatgerm
> 1 heaped teaspoon bicarbonate of soda
> 1 tablespoon heather honey
> 1 egg
> 4 tablespoons extra virgin olive oil
> 1 teaspoon salt
> 425ml (15fl oz) buttermilk or fresh milk soured with the juice of a lemon
> Oil for greasing

Pre-heat the oven to 450°F/230°C/Gas 8.
Grease a baking tray if making round bannock or grease a 1kg (2lb) loaf tin or round pot with lid that can be put in the oven or a chicken brick.

MIXING: Put all the meals, the wheatgerm and the bicarbonate of soda into a large bowl and mix well. Make a well in the centre and add the honey, egg, oil, salt and buttermilk/soured milk. Mix this together with the outstretched fingers of one hand. Once it is well mixed, begin bringing in the flour from the sides. The mixing should be done as quickly as possible and it is important to have a large enough bowl. When the mixture comes together as a soft, but not sloppy, elastic dough it is ready. If it is too stiff the bread will be heavy.

SHAPING and BAKING: Either shape the dough into a round bannock, divide into four, dust on top with oatmeal or barley flour and bake on a greased baking tray, or put the mixture into a loaf tin or into a pot with a lid, dusting on top with oatmeal or barley flour. Bake the round bannock for 40-50 minutes. The covered loaf will take longer, about an hour. To test, remove from the tin and knock on the base: it will make a hollow sound if ready. Remove and cool thoroughly.

Oven Scones

There are three ways of rising this scone, the most traditional is with buttermilk and soda. This gives the most moist, airy texture. The other methods make a drier scone.

Yield: 8 quarters or 12–24 depending on thickness and cutter size

Either:
225g (8oz) plain flour
1 teaspoon bicarbonate of soda
1 teaspoon cream of tartar
125ml (4fl oz) buttermilk, or fresh milk
soured with the juice of half a lemon
or
225 (8oz) plain flour
2 teaspoons baking powder
125ml (4fl oz) fresh milk
or
225g (8oz) self-raising cake flour
125ml (4fl oz) milk
50g (2oz) butter or 2 tablespoons oil
1 egg, beaten

Preheat the oven to 450°F/230°C/Gas 8.
Grease and flour baking tins or use silicone paper.

MIXING AND SHAPING: Sift the flour and raising agent into a bowl and rub in the butter or blend in a blender. Make a well in the centre and add the milk and egg. Mix to a soft, elastic consistency. Dust with flour and knead lightly on a floured working surface. Roll out to 2.5cm (1 inch) thick, either into two rounds, cut into four quarters or cut with a cutter. Dust with flour and bake till risen and golden brown, 15–20 minutes. Wrap in a towel, place on a rack and serve slightly warm with butter and jam.

CAKES AND TEA BREADS:

Vanilla Butter Sponge

Cook's Tip: This is a quick, no-creaming method with excellent results. The basic method is to put special 'cake' flour (this is finer than other flours and achieves the best texture) and caster sugar into a bowl and mix with an electric beater for 30 seconds. This brings the flour and sugar particles closer together when the sugar crystals puncture the flour particles, allowing more liquid to be absorbed faster. Three-quarters of the eggs/liquid is then added along with the soft butter, and beaten for about 90 seconds until it becomes creamy and light. This is when the strength of the cake is developed. The remaining liquid is beaten in for another 30 seconds. Total time to mix: two-and-a-half minutes.

250g (9oz) self-raising cake flour
250g (9oz) caster sugar
250g (9oz) unsalted butter, softened
4 eggs, beaten
2–3 tablespoons milk
2 teaspoons vanilla extract

Preheat the oven to 350°F/180°C/Gas 4.
Line 23–25cm (9–10 inch) round cake tin; or 2 x 20cm (8 inch) sandwich tins with silicone baking paper, or foil, or grease and flour.

HEATING THE EGGS: Put the eggs, still in their shells, into a bowl of very hot, but not boiling water. Leave for two minutes to heat the eggs without cooking.

MIXING: Sift the flour into a bowl and add the sugar. Beat with an electric beater for about 30 seconds. Add the butter. Mix the eggs and two tablespoons of milk together and add about three-quarters of this mixture to the flour, sugar and butter. Beat for about 90 seconds till the mixture becomes light and creamy. Scrape down the sides. Add the remaining eggs, milk and vanilla and beat for another 30 seconds. Add the remaining tablespoon of milk if necessary. Pour into prepared tin(s).

BAKING: Bake a large cake for 50–60 minutes or until a skewer inserted into the centre comes out clean. Bake sandwich cakes for 25–30 minutes. Cool in the tin(s) for 10 minutes, then turn out onto a rack.

Variations:

Chocolate Coated

Coat with Chocolate Cream Icing: Break up 200g (7oz) best quality plain chocolate and put it into a bowl. Put 200ml (7fl oz) double cream into a pan and bring to the boil. Pour over the chocolate and blend in. Stir till smooth. Leave to cool slightly, or until it begins to thicken a little, but not too much. Put the cake on a rack. Pour chocolate on top of the cake and spread evenly with a large spatula over the top and sides. Shake before it sets to make a smooth surface. For a rough surface beat the mixture with an electric beater till thick and creamy then spread over cake.

Madeira cake

Make the basic cake mix, flavouring with the grated zest of a lemon. Bake in one large cake tin. Decorate on top with a slice of crystallised lemon.

Lemon Cake

Make the basic cake mix; flavouring with 1 tablespoon of grated lemon zest. Shortly before the cake is ready, boil 75g (3oz) granulated sugar with the juice of 2 lemons. When the cake comes out of the oven, prick all over the top with a skewer and using a pastry brush, coat the top of the cake with about half the syrup. Leave to cool in the tin. Remove and invert the cake. Prick all over the base and brush with syrup, then brush sides with syrup. Allow to cool before wrapping in clingfilm. Store for 24 hours to allow the syrup to distribute evenly.

Victoria Sandwich

Make the basic cake mix. Bake in two sandwich tins.
Fill centre with:
(1)
250ml (8fl oz) whipped cream,
3–4 tablespoons jam or flavoured butter cream.
Dust top with caster sugar.

(2)
100g (3½oz) unsalted butter, softened
125g (4½oz) icing sugar

Flavouring options:
1 teaspoon vanilla extract
2 tablespoons milk
or
2 tablespoons liqueur, rum or brandy
or
2 tablespoons orange or lemon juice
or
25g (1oz) cocoa powder
2 tablespoons boiling water

TO MAKE FILLING (2): Put the butter in the mixing bowl and beat till soft and fluffy. Add the flavourings and beat till mixed in. Add the icing sugar gradually until light and smooth. Spread on one half of the cake. Place the other half on top.

Date and Walnut Chocolate Loaf

This is a moist, full-flavoured cake made in a loaf tin so that the slices resemble dark chocolate bread.

Cook's Tip: It's made using the quick sponge method (see Vanilla Butter Sponge p138). Mixing the cocoa powder with boiling water releases the cocoa flavour.

    25g (1oz) best quality cocoa powder
    3 tablespoons boiling water
    3 large eggs, beaten
    125g (4½ oz) self-raising cake flour
    150g (5½ oz) caster sugar
    150g (5½ oz) butter, softened
    125g (4oz) dates, stoned and chopped
    125g (4oz) walnuts
    2 teaspoons vanilla extract
    Icing sugar for dusting

Preheat the oven to 350°F/180°C/Gas 4.
Line 20 x 10cm (8 x 4 inch) loaf tin with silicone baking paper, or foil, or grease and flour.

HEATING THE EGGS: Put eggs, still in their shells, into a bowl of very hot, but not boiling water, leave for two minutes to heat the eggs without cooking.

MIXING: Whisk the cocoa powder and hot water together until smooth, then beat in the eggs. Sift flour into a separate large bowl and add caster sugar. Whisk for about 30 seconds using an electric beater. Add all the butter and two thirds of the egg and cocoa mixture to the flour and sugar and beat for about 90 seconds to develop the cake's structure. It should become light and creamy. Scrape down the sides. Add the remaining egg and cocoa mixture, plus the vanilla, and beat for another 30 seconds. Scrape down the sides again and beat for another 30 seconds. Reserve a few walnuts to decorate the top and chop the rest roughly. Add with the dates and mix through.

BAKING: Pour the mixture into the prepared tin. Place the walnuts on top and bake for 40–50 minutes or until a skewer inserted into the centre of the cake comes out clean and the cake springs back when pressed lightly in the centre. Cool in the tin for 10 minutes and then turn out onto a rack. Dust lightly with icing sugar and allow to cool before wrapping in clingfilm to store.

Cream Sponge

An everyday family cake and a Scottish favourite which is finished with a layer of double cream and raspberry or strawberry jam in the centre.

Cook's Tips: This cake method creates the lightest sponges. The technique involves trapping air – created by beating a large amount of eggs with the sugar – so the mixture is extremely delicate and airy and must be treated with care. It is particularly suitable for sponges that are to be served as desserts, especially with cream. The texture is too delicate for heavy icings such as fondant and marzipan.

Always use caster sugar. The best results are achieved if eggs are warmed slightly, and always fold the eggs in very gently with a large metal spoon. Work quickly once the eggs are mixed in so that they do not deflate. Bake immediately after mixing, taking care not to knock the tin or shake the mixture. Allow to cool in the tin before removing. Keep cooling cake out of draughts.

    6 large eggs
    175g (6oz) caster sugar
    175g (6oz) plain fine cake flour, sifted

    Filling:
    300ml (10fl oz) whipped cream
    250g (8oz) fresh fruit in season

Preheat the oven to 425°F/220°C/Gas 7.
Use 2 x 25cm (10 inch) round cake tins or 3 x 20cm (8 inch) sandwich tins and line with silicone baking paper, or foil, or grease and flour.

HEATING THE EGGS: Put the eggs, still in their shells, into a bowl of very hot, but not boiling water, leave for two minutes to heat the eggs without cooking.

MIXING: Put the sugar into the mixing bowl and break in the eggs. Mix at top speed until the mixture turns white and creamy and you can see the trail of the whisk marks in the mix. The mixture should triple in volume. With a large metal spoon, fold in the flour gently with a cutting and folding movement until all the flour is mixed in, then pour into cake tin(s).

BAKING: Bake for 20–25 minutes. To test for readiness, the top should be golden brown, firm and springy to the touch. Leave to cool in the tin. When cool, remove from the tin and cool on a rack.

FINISHING: Beat the cream till stiff and spread half on top of one cake. Cut the fruit up finely and place evenly on top. Spread the remaining cream on top of the fruit. Cover with the other cake half and dust on top with icing sugar.

Dundee Cake

(SEE BAKING CLASSICS P127)

Cook's Tips: Use only special, fine, sifted cake flour for the finest texture. Always use caster sugar. All dry ingredients should be at room temperature, eggs and butter slightly warmed. Always beat at the highest mixer speed. Cool in the tin for 10 minutes before removing to allow the cake to 'set'.

5 large eggs
250g (9oz) unsalted butter
250g (9oz) caster sugar
300g (10½ oz) plain fine cake flour
75g (3oz) ground almonds
1 lemon, zest
1 orange, zest
350g (12oz) sultanas, washed
50g (2oz) crystallised orange peel, finely
    chopped (or 2 tablespoons thick cut marmalade)
3 tablespoons milk

Topping:
50g (2oz) whole almonds, blanched and halved

Preheat oven to 350°F/180°C/Gas 4.
Line round cake tin 20cm (8 inch) with silicone baking paper or foil.

HEATING THE EGGS: Put eggs, still in their shells, into a bowl of very hot, but not boiling water. Leave for two minutes to heat the eggs without cooking.

MIXING AND BAKING: Beat the butter and sugar till light and fluffy. Add the eggs in four separate additions, beating well in between. Add a little flour if the mixture curdles and beat well. Gently fold in the remaining flour and ground almonds. Add orange and lemon zest, sultanas and orange peel or marmalade. Mix in with milk to dropping consistency, then pour into a prepared tin. Cover the top with halved blanched almonds and bake for about one and a half hours. Test for readiness – a skewer should come out clean. Cool, wrap and store in an airtight tin.

Fochabers Gingerbread Loaf

A subtly spiced loaf flavoured with beer.

250g (9oz) plain flour
1 heaped teaspoon each of ground ginger, mixed spice and cinnamon
½ teaspoon ground cloves
1 teaspoon bicarbonate of soda
50g (2oz) soft brown sugar
125g (4oz) butter, softened
1 egg
125g (4oz) treacle
125ml (4fl oz) dark beer
50g (2oz) currants
50g (2oz) sultanas
50g (2oz) candied peel

Preheat the oven to 350°F/180°C/Gas 4.
Line a 20 x 10cm (8 x 4 inch) loaf tin with silicone baking paper, or foil, or grease and flour.

MIXING: Sift the flour, spices, soda and sugar into a bowl. Beat with an electric beater for about one minute to mix. Make a well in the centre and add the butter. Mix the egg and treacle together with the beer. Add about three quarters to the flour mixture and beat for about one minute or until the mixture lightens a little and becomes creamy. Add the remaining liquid and beat for another minute. It should be a soft dropping consistency. Add more beer if necessary. Add currants, sultanas and candied peel and mix through. Pour into a loaf tin.

BAKING: Bake for about an hour. Test for readiness by inserting a skewer which should come out clean. Cool on a rack. To store, wrap in clingfilm and/or foil.

Sticky Gingerbread

To be properly 'sticky' this rich gingerbread should sink a little in the middle.

250g (9oz) unsalted butter, chopped small
275g (10oz) soft dark brown sugar
175g (6oz) black treacle
1 tablespoon ground ginger
1 tablespoon ground cinnamon
4 eggs, beaten
275g (10oz) regular plain flour (not for cakes), sifted
1 teaspoon bicarbonate of soda, sifted
75g (3oz) crystallised ginger, finely chopped
200ml (7fl oz) buttermilk OR fresh milk soured with the juice of a lemon
OR natural yoghurt

Preheat the oven to 350°F/180°C/Gas 4.
Grease and line a round 23-25cm (9-10 inch) cake tin.

MIXING: Put the butter, sugar, treacle and spices into a pan and heat gently to melt the butter and soften the treacle. Take off the heat and when cool, beat in the eggs. Then stir in the flour sifted with soda. Mix together. Finally add the ginger and soured milk/yoghurt and mix in. It should make a fairly runny consistency.

BAKING: Pour the mixture into the tin and bake for 45–60 minutes. Test by pressing on the top. It should spring back easily when ready. Allow to cool in the tin and wrap in clingfilm and/or foil to store.

Granny Loaf

A 'boiled' fruit cake which is very quick and easy to make.

300ml (10fl oz) hot water
150g (5oz) soft or dark brown sugar
75g (3oz) unsalted butter
350g (12oz) mixed dried fruit
2 teaspoons mixed spice
150g (5½ oz) plain flour, sifted
150g (5½ oz) self-raising flour, sifted
1 level teaspoon bicarbonate of soda, sifted
2 eggs

Preheat the oven to 350°F/180°C/Gas 4.
Grease or line a 21 x 11cm (8 x 5 inch) loaf tin.

MIXING: Put the water, sugar, butter, dried fruit and mixed spice into a pan. Simmer for three minutes then leave to cool. Add the flours and bicarbonate of soda along with eggs and mix to a soft dropping consistency. Pour into a baking tin.

BAKING: Bake for about one and a half hours. Test for readiness with a skewer, which should come out clean. Cool in the tin. To store, wrap in clingfilm or foil.

Rock Buns

Cook's Tip: Substitute chocolate chips for the currants.

Yield: 8–10

225g (8oz) self-raising plain flour
75g (3oz) butter
50g (2oz) caster sugar
1 egg
75g (3oz) currants
50ml (2fl oz) milk
1 egg beaten with 1 teaspoon water for glazing
1 tablespoon granulated sugar

Preheat the oven to 470°F/230°C/Gas 8.
Grease trays lightly with oil or use silicone paper.

MIXING AND BAKING: Sieve the flour into a bowl. Rub in the butter (or mix in a blender) till the mixture resembles fine breadcrumbs. Add the sugar, egg, currants and most of the milk and mix to a fairly stiff dough. Add more milk if necessary. Drop buns onto the tray in spoonfuls, spacing well. Glaze with the beaten egg and sprinkle with granulated sugar. Rough up the sides with two forks. Bake till risen and browned, 15–20 minutes.

Girdle Oatcakes

(TRADITIONAL METHOD)

Cook's Tip: The less water used the crisper the oatcake and the more likely it is to curl – the sign of a good oatcake. Work quickly since it is easier to shape and roll out thinly when the dough is still warm.

Yield: 1 round, 4 triangles

125g (4½ oz) medium oatmeal
Pinch of salt
1 tablespoon melted dripping or butter
125ml (4fl oz) boiling water

Heat the girdle and grease. Test heat by sprinkling on some flour which should turn a light brown in a few minutes. Also judge heat by holding your hand over the girdle. It should feel hot, but not fiercely so.

MIXING AND SHAPING: Put the oatmeal into a bowl and add the salt. Make a well in the centre, add the dripping or butter and mix through. When well mixed, add the boiling water and mix to make the mixture come together into a firm, but not crumbly, ball. Dust the work surface with oatmeal and press the mixture out roughly into a round. Roll out to about 5mm (¼ inch) thick. Keep pinching the edges together to keep them even. Cut into four triangles (farls) and leave to dry for an hour. This helps them to 'curl'.

BAKING: Place the four triangles on the girdle and leave to bake till they have dried out and are curled at the edges. This will only happen if they are thin enough. Thick oatcakes will not curl and may need to be baked on both sides. If very thin and well curled, remove and stand on end – in a toast rack if possible – in a warm place to dry out completely. Store in an airtight tin or in oatmeal – the traditional method – which gives them a special mealy taste. They may be dried out in a warm oven before use.

Potato Scones

Usually eaten hot, rolled up with butter, but also an essential item in a Scottish breakfast/high tea fry-up.

Cook's Tips: The thinner the dough is rolled the better the scone. To test for the best potato scone hold one corner and shake – it should give a good 'wiggle'. If too thick and stodgy there will be no wiggle.

Yield: 8

225g (8oz) floury potatoes, mashed
75g (3oz) plain flour
25g (1oz) butter
Pinch of salt

Heat the girdle and grease. Test heat by sprinkling on some flour which should turn a light brown in a few minutes. Also judge heat by holding your hand over the girdle. It should feel hot, but not fiercely so.

MIXING AND SHAPING: Put the mashed potato into a bowl and sift in the flour. Add the butter and salt and mix to a smooth dough. It should be soft and pliable. Add some water if required. Divide into two, knead into round balls and roll into 2 circles 3-5mm ($^1/_8$ –$^1/_4$ inch) thick. Cut each circle into four.

BAKING: Bake on the girdle until brown on one side (about three minutes), then turn and brown the other side. Wrap in a tea towel and serve warm with butter. Fry with bacon and eggs etc. for a 'full' Scottish breakfast.

Soda Scones

Cook's Tip: These can be made into a more rustic wheaten scone, like Irish soda bread, by substituting half the plain flour with a coarse granary flour.

Yield: 2 rounds, 8 scones

225g (8oz) plain flour
1 level teaspoon bicarbonate of soda
1 level teaspoon cream of tartar
1 tablespoon vegetable oil
150ml (5fl oz) buttermilk or sweet milk soured with the juice of a lemon
Pinch of salt

Pre-heat the girdle and grease lightly. Test heat by sprinkling the girdle with some flour which should turn a light brown in a few minutes. Also judge heat by holding your hand over the girdle. It should feel hot, but not fiercely so.

MIXING AND SHAPING: Sift the flour, bicarbonate of soda and cream of tartar into a bowl. Make a well in the centre and add the oil, sour milk and salt. Mix to a soft pliable dough. Do not overmix or the scones will shrink when baked. Turn out onto a floured board. Flour on top and divide into two. Roll each piece into a circle about 1cm (½ inch) thick and cut each round into 4 quarters.

BAKING: Bake on the girdle for about four to five minutes on one side. Turn and bake on the other side till cooked through. Fold in a tea towel when cooked and serve warm with butter and strawberry jam.

Currant or Sultana Scones

Cook's Tip: Substitute black treacle or golden syrup for the sugar to add more flavour.

Yield: 24 with 5cm (2½ inch) cutter
225g (8oz) self-raising flour
25g (1oz) caster sugar
2 tablespoon vegetable oil
1 egg
150ml (5fl oz) milk
50g (2oz) currants

Preheat the girdle and grease lightly. Test heat by sprinkling on some flour which should turn a light brown in a few minutes. Also judge heat by holding your hand over the girdle. It should feel hot, but not fiercely so.

MIXING AND SHAPING: Sift the flour into a bowl and add the sugar. Make a well in the centre. Mix the oil and egg together. Add this, along with most of the milk and the currants. Mix to a soft dropping consistency, adding more milk if necessary. Leave to rest for three minutes. Roll out on a floured board to a large round of 1.5cm (¾ inch) thick. Cut into triangles or cut with a scone cutter into rounds.

BAKING: Put the triangles or rounds onto the girdle and bake on one side for about five minutes until lightly browned. Turn and bake on the other side. Wrap in a tea towel and place on a wrack. Serve warm.

Scots Girdle Pancakes (Dropped Scones) and Girdle Crumpets

Cook's Tip: The secret of making good pancakes is practise.

Yield: 24-28 Pancakes – 16-18 crumpets

225g (8oz) self-raising flour
2 eggs, beaten
1 level tablespoon golden syrup/ honey/ treacle or sugar
1 tablespoon vegetable oil
175ml (6fl oz) milk for pancakes

Additional For Crumpets:
1 egg
250ml (9fl oz) milk
$\frac{1}{2}$ teaspoon bicarbonate of soda

Heat girdle and grease. Test heat by sprinkling on some flour which should turn a light brown in a few minutes. Also judge heat by holding your hand over the girdle. It should feel hot, but not fiercely so.

TO MAKE PANCAKE MIX: Sift the flour into a bowl and make a well in the centre. Add the eggs, syrup, oil and most of the milk. Mix to a thick 'pouring cream' consistency adding more milk if necessary.

TO MAKE CRUMPET MIX: As for pancakes BUT add 1 extra egg and $\frac{1}{2}$ teaspoon bicarbonate of soda which makes more bubbles while cooking. Use more milk to make a runnier mixture. Sift flour, bicarbonate of soda into a bowl and make a well in the centre. Add the eggs, sugar and most of the milk. Mix to a thin cream consistency adding more milk if necessary.

TO BAKE PANCAKES AND CRUMPETS: Drop in spoonfuls onto a hot girdle. Use a ladle for the crumpets which should spread to about 15mm (6 inch). When bubbles appear on the surface, turn. Crumpets should be thinner than pancakes with a lacy effect on one side. Pancakes are usually smaller. When bubbles appear on the top surface, turn. They should be an amber colour on both sides. Cool on a rack in a tea towel to keep warm and soft and eat warm on the day they are baked. Serve pancakes with butter and jams. Fill crumpets with butter, lemon juice and sugar or jam or honey or syrup. Roll when cold like a brandy snap. If they crack the mixture has been too stiff.

YEAST BAKING:

Aberdeen Rowies or Butteries

All bakers in the North-East produce their own subtle variations but it is generally accepted that the best are flaky-crisp and well-browned. A 'bready' butterie is not appreciated by local aficionados.

Cook's Tips: The secret of good butteries is to work with the softest dough possible, using plenty of flour to prevent it from becoming sticky. Only if the dough is soft is it possible to achieve the 'misshapen' look.

Bread Dough:
3 teaspoons sugar
25g (1oz) fresh yeast
375-450ml (13-15fl oz) warm water
500g (1lb 2oz) very strong white bread flour, slightly warmed

Fatty Dough:
325g (11oz) solid vegetable fat
1 level tablespoon salt
150g (5oz) very strong white bread flour

Preheat the oven to 425°F/220°C/Gas 7.
Grease baking sheets.
MIXING THE BREAD DOUGH: Dissolve the yeast and sugar in a little of the water and leave for 10 minutes. Add to the warmed flour along with most of the remaining water and knead in to make a soft sticky dough. Knead until smooth and pliable and leave to rest for 10 minutes.

MIXING THE FATTY DOUGH: Cut up the fat and sprinkle with salt and flour. Knead till thoroughly mixed. This can be done in a food processor.

COMBINING THE TWO DOUGHS: Cover the work surface with a thick layer of flour and place bread dough on top. Flour the top of this and spread it out with well-floured hands or a rolling pin till it is rectangular and about 1cm (½ inch) thick. Spread half of the fatty dough on top. Fold down a third to the centre and up a third – as for making puff pastry. Turn and roll out again to 1cm (½ inch). Repeat this procedure with remaining fatty dough. Repeat the procedure one more time using plenty of flour to prevent sticking.

SHAPING: Divide the dough roughly into 50g (2oz) pieces. Flour your hands well. Take up a piece of dough, toss it to coat evenly with flour. Throw it onto the baking tray – this helps to create the misshapen effect. Press down with four well-floured fingers so that it spreads out. Continue with the rest of the dough, leaving a space between each butterie for rising. To finish the shaping, once they are all on the baking trays, flour four fingers outstretched on the left hand and a clenched fist on the right hand. Press out using both floured hands until they are about 5mm (¼ inch) thick.

PROVING: Oil a sheet of clingfilm and cover the rowies. Leave for about 20 minutes in a warm place until they double in size.

BAKING: Bake the rowies for 18-20 minutes in a fairly hot oven until they are crisp and golden. Leave on the tray for about 10 minutes till they have cooled a little then stack them together, on their ends, on the tray. It is important to leave them to cool on the tray as if they are stacked too soon they will have too much moisture and become soggy. Leaving them too long, on the other hand, means they will become too crisp and break easily.

EATING/BUYING: Eat warm with butter. A 'double rowie' is two stuck together with butter. A 'wee rowie' is half sized. A 'cremated rowie' has been well-fired. A 'bag of bitties' is a bag of broken rowies.

Baps

These light, floury breakfast rolls are usually filled with bacon, eggs, or sausages.

Yield: Makes about 10 'man-sized' baps.

500 g (1lb) strong white flour
2 teaspoons salt
25 g (1oz) fresh yeast, 1 tablespoon dried or 1 pkt Fast Action yeast
1 teaspoon sugar
300 ml (10fl oz) water and milk, warmed
50 g (2oz) lard

Pre-heat the oven to 425°F/220°C/Gas 7.
Grease baking tray.

MAKING THE DOUGH: Sift the flour into a bowl, add salt and put aside to warm. Meanwhile cream fresh yeast and sugar together and then mix with the milk and water (add the dried yeast to the milk/water and dissolve it. Mix in the Fast Action yeast to the dry ingredients). Rub the lard into the flour, then add the liquid and knead together till smooth and pliable. Leave to rise till doubled in size — about an hour.

SHAPING AND BAKING: Knock back, knead and then shape into baps. Oval baps are usually about 10cm (4 inch) long by about 7cm (3 inch) wide at this stage before rising. Round ones are about 10cm (4 inch) diameter. Once shaped, brush with milk, dust with flour and cover with oiled clingfilm to prevent drying out and set in a warm place to prove. When they have risen, dust again lightly with flour and bake for 15 minutes. Cool and eat warm.

Oatmeal Bread

This striking loaf is a rich brown on the inside with a light speckled crust, which is caused by lining the tin with rolled oats.

175g (6oz) rolled oats
50g (2oz) lard/butter or 4 tablespoons oil
2-3 teaspoons salt
125g (4oz) molasses or treacle
450ml (16fl oz) lukewarm water
25g (1oz) fresh yeast (1 tablespoon dried or 1 pkt Fast Action yeast)
600g (1½ lb) strong white bread flour
2 eggs
2 tablespoons rolled oats to coat tins

2 x 1lb/500g loaf tins.

Pre-heat the oven to 375°F/190°C/Gas 5.
Grease the tin well with lard or oil and coat the base and sides with rolled oats.

MIXING DOUGH: Put oats, lard, butter or oil and salt into a bowl. Dissolve the molasses in the lukewarm water and pour over the oats. If the yeast is dried, activate it by mixing with a little of the warm molasses water. If fresh, mix the yeast with a teaspoonful of sugar. Add the yeast (you can just stir in the packet of Fast Action yeast) to the oats and stir in half of the flour. Beat well for three or four minutes — this can be done with the mixer. Beat in the eggs and then work in the remaining flour gradually till the dough is soft and sticky but not too dry. Leave for 10 minutes to rest.

KNEADING AND RISING: Turn the dough onto a board and knead till it is smooth and elastic. Cover with greased clingfilm and leave to rise in a warm place for about one and a half hours or until the dough has doubled in size.

SHAPING AND BAKING : Knead the dough for a few minutes and then divide into two. Shape into loaves and put into tins. Cover with greased clingfilm and put back in a warm place till they have risen to double their size again. Brush with milk and sprinkle on top with rolled oats. Bake for 30 minutes to one hour or until they make a hollow sound when tapped on the base. Cool thoroughly.

Scots Cookies

Popular teatime treats which may be made more 'fancy' with cream or icing.

Yield: 25-30

750g (1½ lb) strong plain flour
250ml (8fl oz) milk
50g (1oz) fresh yeast, 1 tablespoon dried yeast or 1 pkt Fast Action yeast
1 teaspoon salt
4 tablespoons sugar
125g (4oz) butter, softened
2 large eggs

Pre-heat the oven to 425°F/220°C/Gas 7.
Grease 2 large baking trays.

MIXING AND KNEADING THE DOUGH: Begin by warming both the milk and flour separately to blood heat (37°C). Yeast will work much more efficiently if everything is warm. If using fresh yeast, blend it with a little of the milk, if using dried yeast, dissolve in some of the milk and leave until it begins to froth up. Make a well in the centre of the flour and add most of the milk, (add the Fast Action yeast now if using), salt, butter and eggs (keeping back some of the egg for glazing). Bring together with your hands till it is a soft, sticky dough, adding more milk if necessary. If it is too wet, add more flour. So many recipes tell you to knead the dough for so many minutes – this is confusing: what you should do is knead it until it is the right consistency, and the time it takes to reach this stage varies. It should be transformed during the kneading process from a soft sticky mess to a smooth, silky, rounded ball which comes away from your fingers easily. If the gluten content of the flour is poor, achieving this result is impossible. Always use a strong flour.

RISING: Cover the bowl with a wet towel (dough likes a damp steamy atmosphere for rising) or oiled clingfilm and leave in a warm place till it has almost doubled in size.

KNOCKING BACK AND SHAPING THE DOUGH: Knock all the air out of the dough, give it another knead to redistribute the yeast and shape the dough into 25–30 small round buns about 5cm (2 inch) in diameter.

PROVING: To prove that the yeast is still working, place in a warm place again, cover with a film of very lightly oiled clingfilm and leave till they have doubled in size. Brush with an egg and milk glaze and bake for 10-15 minutes.

Cream Cookies

Split when cold and fill with whipped cream. Dust on top with icing sugar.

Iced Cookies

Make up a fairly stiff water icing, colour and coat the top of the cookie.

Selkirk Bannock

A burnished golden bannock with all the festive style of an old symbolic sun-worshipper's celebration bannock.

Yield: 1 bannock

500g (1lb 2oz) strong plain flour
125g (4oz) butter
250ml (9fl oz) warm milk
50g (2oz) sugar
15g ($^1/_2$ oz) fresh yeast or 1 x 7g sachet Fast Action yeast
250g (9oz) sultanas
1 egg yolk beaten with a teaspoon water for glazing

MIXING AND RISING: Sift the flour into a bowl and add the sugar (add the Fast Action yeast now if using). If using fresh yeast, dissolve in a little of the warm milk. Melt the butter and add to the warm milk. Cool to lukewarm and add to the flour. Mix to a soft pliable dough and knead until smooth, about five minutes. This can be done in an electric beater with a dough hook or in a bread-making machine. Put into a floured bowl and dust on top with flour. Cover with oiled clingfilm and leave in a warm place until it doubles in size.

SHAPING, PROVING AND BAKING: Knock back to remove air and knead in the sultanas. Shape the dough into a round bannock and place on a greased baking tray. Cover it with oiled clingfilm and leave it in a warm place until it doubles in size. Brush with the egg yolk. Bake for about 45 minutes, reducing the temperature if the bannock is browning too quickly. To test for readiness, tap on the base – it should sound hollow. Remove and cool on a rack. Eat warm, or toasted, with butter.

Petticoat Tails

These were first made by high-class Edinburgh bakers and take their name from the shape of the petticoat hoops worn by women in the nineteenth century. It's thought that they were first made as a delicate shortbread, suitable for ladies' afternoon teas, while men preferred a thicker, crunchier version.

Yield: 1 round

200g (7oz) plain flour
50g (2oz) icing sugar
75g (3oz) butter, softened
25g (1oz) vegetable fat

Dredging: caster sugar

Preheat the oven to 325°F/150°C/Gas 3.
Dust baking tin lightly with flour.

MIXING: Put all the ingredients into the mixing bowl. Put on a slow speed and mix until the dough begins to come together. Then raise the speed a little until it forms a smooth dough. Roll out to a large round – about 5mm (¼ inch) thick. Crimp the edges with your first finger and thumb, and mark all over with a fork. Then cut out a circle from the centre. Divide the rest of the circle into 12 to 18 wedge-shaped biscuits – 'petticoat tails' and place on a baking tray.

BAKING: Bake for 20 minutes then raise the heat to 350°F/180°C/Gas 4 and continue baking till golden brown. Sprinkle with sugar while still warm. Remove from the tin and put to cool on a rack. Store in an airtight container.

Balmoral Shortbread

Queen Victoria is said to have enjoyed this elegant shortbread biscuit regularly with her afternoon tea.

Yield: 25-30

375g (13oz) plain flour
125g (4½oz) caster sugar
250g (9oz) butter, at room temperature

Preheat the oven to 350°F/180°C/Gas 4.
Grease baking trays.

MIXING (traditional method) AND SHAPING: Sift the flour onto the work surface. Put the sugar in a separate pile. Knead the butter into the sugar with both hands. When the sugar is mixed in, begin adding the flour gradually, continuing to knead the mixture lightly. The aim is a firm pliable dough, not too soft yet not too firm, which makes it more difficult to roll out. Do not worry if the mixture does not take all the flour.

MIXING BY MACHINE: Put all the ingredients into the mixing bowl. Put on a slow speed and mix until the dough begins to come together. Then raise the speed a little until it forms a smooth dough. Test the consistency and add more flour if it is too soft.

SHAPING: Dust the work surface with flour and roll out very thinly – about 5mm (¼ inch). Cut into circles about 6.5cm (2½ inch). Prick with a fork three times in the centre, domino style.

BAKING: Place biscuits on the baking tray and bake for about 30 minutes or until they are a light golden brown. Remove from the oven and dust with caster sugar while still hot. Cool on a rack and store in an airtight tin.

Pitcaithly Bannock

This thick golden round of festive shortbread is traditionally flavoured with almonds, caraway, crystallised orange and lemon peel, which decorate the top.

Cook's Tip: It can be made with just almonds on top. Press about eight whole blanched ones onto the top surface before baking in the same style as a Dundee cake.

> 280g (10oz) plain flour, sifted
> 55g (2oz) cornflour, sifted
> 110g (4oz) caster sugar, sifted
> 225g (8oz) unsalted butter, softened and cut into small pieces
> Crystallised orange and lemon peel
> 1 teaspoon caraway seeds
> 50g (2oz) almonds, whole blanched

Preheat the oven to 325°F/150°C/Gas 3. Grease baking tin.

MIXING BY HAND: Sift the flour onto the work surface. Put the sugar in another pile. Begin with the butter and sugar, kneading all the sugar into the butter. Then add a little flour and gradually work into the butter and sugar. Continue adding the flour until the mixture becomes firm and pliable but not too stiff. It should not be difficult to roll out and should not crack.

MIXING BY MACHINE: Put all the ingredients into the mixing bowl. Put on a slow speed and mix until the dough begins to come together. Then raise the speed a little until it forms a smooth dough. Test the consistency and add more flour if it is too soft.

SHAPING INTO LARGE ROUND or RECTANGLE: Roll the dough out into large round or rectangle and place on the prepared baking tray. Or press the mixture into a round or rectangular baking tin and smooth surface with a palate knife. It should be about 2cm (³/₄ inch) thick. If using a baking tray, finish by pinching edge with first finger and thumb to decorate or use the flat side of a fork to mark the edge. Split the almonds, and press the half almonds on top. Press the caraway and crystallised peel into the shortbread to make a centre decoration. Mark all over with a fork to prevent rising. Rest in a cool place for one hour before baking.

BAKING: Bake till evenly golden brown, about 45–50 minutes, and dredge with sugar while still warm. Remove from the tin and put to cool on a rack. Store in airtight container. Break roughly into pieces.

Parkins

A popular Scottish teatime biscuit.

Yield: 12–15 biscuits

100g (3½ oz) plain flour, sifted
125g (4½ oz) oatmeal
40g (1½ oz) soft brown sugar
50g (2oz) soft vegetable cooking fat
1 teaspoon each of ground ginger, ground cinnamon and mixed spice
1 level teaspoon bicarbonate of soda
2 tablespoons golden syrup
1 medium egg, beaten

Topping:
12–15 blanched almonds

Preheat the oven to 350°F/180°C/Gas 4.
Grease baking sheet lightly with oil.

MIXING AND BAKING: Mix all of the ingredients together to make a stiff but pliable dough. Add more egg if necessary. Divide into 12–15 pieces, roll into round balls then leave to rest for five minutes. Place a split almond on top of each piece. Put onto a baking tray, leaving room for spreading, then bake for 10 minutes till golden brown on top. Cool and store in an airtight tin.

Oaties

These are 'flapjack'-style biscuits that became popular after 'rolled oats' were first made by the Quaker Oat Company in 1877.

Yield: 12-15

250g (9oz) butter
250g (9oz) rolled oats
175g (6oz) soft brown sugar
100g (3½oz) desiccated coconut
50g (2oz) walnuts, finely chopped
50g (2oz) dates, stoned and finely chopped

Preheat the oven to 350°F/180°C/Gas 4. Grease a 16 x 26cm (6½ x 10½ inch) baking tin.

MIXING AND BAKING: Melt the butter and add the oats, sugar, coconut, walnuts and dates. Stir well to mix. Pour into a prepared tin and press evenly with a palate knife. Bake for 25-30 minutes till lightly browned. Cut into fingers and leave in the tin till cool.

Abernethy Biscuits

A 'light' shortbread, made with less fat, they are named – not after the town – but after the distinguished Scots surgeon, Dr John Abernethy (1764-1831) who got his local baker to make them as a 'health' biscuit to give to his patients.

Yield: 8 biscuits

100g (3½ oz) plain flour
1 teaspoon baking powder
30g (1oz) soft vegetable cooking fat
30g (1oz) icing sugar
1 tablespoon milk
1 beaten egg

Preheat the oven to 350°F/180°C/Gas 4. Grease baking tin lightly with oil.

MIXING AND BAKING: Put the flour, baking powder, fat and sugar into a bowl. Rub in the fat. Add the milk and egg to make a soft but pliable dough. Divide into 8 pieces, roll into balls, then leave to rest for three to four minutes. Roll out to 5mm (¼ inch), then mark with a fork and place on a baking tray. Bake for 20 minutes until golden brown. Cool on a rack and store in an airtight tin.

Almond Biscuits

These plump little almond-flavoured balls are more of a confection than a biscuit. They are rolled in icing sugar and can be made with other nuts such as walnuts and pecans.

    225g (8oz) plain flour
    125g (4oz) granulated sugar
    $1/2$ teaspoon salt
    225g (8oz) butter
    2 teaspoons vanilla essence
    250g (9oz) finely chopped, flaked almonds

Pre-heat the oven to 350°F/180°C/Gas 4.

MAKING: Mix all of the ingredients in a bowl. Form into a smooth, firm paste and roll into small balls the size of a walnut. Place them on a greased baking sheet about 2.5cm (1 inch) apart and bake for 15 minutes. They should not brown. Roll in icing sugar when almost cool.

Parlies (Ginger Snaps)

A teatime biscuit.

Yield: 25-30 biscuits

150g (5^1/$_2$ oz) plain flour
25g (1oz) self-raising flour
1 teaspoon bicarbonate of soda
2 teaspoons ground ginger
50g (2oz) softened vegetable fat
75g (3oz) demerara sugar
1 tablespoon golden syrup
1 egg

Preheat the oven to 350°F/180°C/Gas 4.
Lightly oil two baking sheets.

MIXING AND BAKING: Sieve flours, soda and ginger into a bowl. Add the fat, sugar and syrup. Beat till smooth. Add the egg and mix till smooth. Let the mixture rest for a couple of minutes, then roll it into a long sausage shape and roll in demerara sugar. Leave it in a cool place to harden. When firm, slice into 25–30 pieces. Place it on a greased baking tin and bake for seven to eight minutes. Cool and store in an airtight tin.

SWEETIE CLASSICS

Edinburgh Rock

Like most shopkeepers in Lowland Scotland in the nineteenth century, Alex Ferguson boils pans of sugar in his Edinburgh back shop to make a range of popular sweeties. It is the heyday of sugar imports from the West Indies and every town has its favourite range of sweeties. Some are also made by street hawkers and travelling packmen. Some get songs written about them:

Ally bally, ally bally bee,
Sittin' on yir mammy's knee,
Greetin' for anither bawbee,
Tae buy some Coolter's Candy.

Sadly, no-one gets the recipe for Robert Coltart's aniseed flavoured candy – sold around the Borders town of Melrose – before he dies, much lamented, in 1890. But not so with Ferguson's sweetie specialities.

Such is his skill at sweetie boiling that he becomes known as 'Sweetie Sandy'. Children, particularly, love his little sticks of variously flavoured, hard, brittle rock which they can hold easily. His sweeties are in such demand that he decides to move to larger premises. But it takes him some time to get the new place organised. And what with one thing and another, a batch of rock is forgotten. Left in the warm atmosphere, the rock crystallises and softens to a powdery texture and at first Sweetie Sandy thinks he will have to throw it out. Until, that is, he has another, more thrifty, idea which is to sell it at a reduced price so all is not lost.

The powdery rock, which melts in the mouth, goes on sale and is a roaring success. 'When are you making some more of that nice soft rock Sandy?' everyone is asking. Well, of course, he doesn't tell them what all the other sweetie sellers in the city think about his 'mistake' rock. Instead, he starts putting aside a batch of rock every day to make it powdery and discovers that if he coats the rock in fine icing sugar and leaves it in the warmth, it will turn powdery in no time at all.

Always an innovator, when it comes to colour and flavour, he thinks up a new range for the powdery rock. Vanilla is plain white. Raspberry and strawberry sticks are pink. Lime sticks are green. Ginger is fawn, and lemon and orange sticks are coloured accordingly.

Sandy's powdery rock soon becomes a city attraction and he is making it in such large quantities and supplying it to so many other small sweetie shops in the city that it needs a new name. So the city which is built on a rock gets its own sweetie rock.

Tablet

For coughs and colds aniseed or cinnamon, rose or horehound are added to the boiling sugar mixture. Then it's set and cut into small rectangular 'tablets of sugar', to be dispensed by doctors. Sucking allows the slow release of the soothing essences and sugar provides a comforting warmth to the patient.

Those who can afford the sugar cure consume large quantities. The English royal household of 1287 uses 300 pounds of violet sugar tablets and 1,900 pounds of rose sugar tablets, some of which are used as a cure for colds, and also as a cure for consumption and melancholy. Delicate children are encouraged to take either rose or violet sugar tablets for their health. Many purchases are made for Henry, son of Edward I (1237–1307), all recorded in the royal household books, but still are not able to prevent his death at the age of six.

The Romans are the first to use sugar as a medicine, finding its warming qualities a welcome winter cure in chilly Northern Europe. For most Britons, however, it is a rare commodity that arrives first with spices from the East and is kept locked up with the equally valuable spices.

By late medieval times, however, sugar has become more available. Still used by doctors as a sweetener for their bitter potions, its medicinal reputation remains important until well into the seventeenth century, though the term 'tablet' is largely dropped and replaced by the more general term 'sugar candy'. Contrary to the rest of Britain, however, the Scots hang on to the word 'taiblet'.

The first recipes appear in a cookery book by Mrs McLintock of Glasgow (1736) and are simple sugar candy recipes with flavourings such as ginger, rose, cinnamon and orange which were all used for medicinal purposes.

'Orange tablets with the Grate: Grate the Oranges, take 2lb of sugar, an a mutchkin of water, then clarify it with the White of 2 eggs, and set it on a slow fire, and boil it till it be almost candyed, then put in the grate of the oranges, and take your white paper, rub it with fresh butter, pour it on your paper, and cut in little pieces.'

At the beginning of the twentieth century, Scots tablet acquires milk, and sometimes butter, distinguishing it from a simple sugar and water sugar candy. It is this improvement in flavour and texture that ensures its long-lasting popularity as it joins the galaxy of other temptations – no longer classed medicinal – to be found in Scottish sweetie shops of the early twentieth century.

'Besides such homely sweets as gundy, glessie, cheugh jeans and black man,' says F M McNeill in *The Scots Kitchen* (1929), 'there were bottles of 'boilings' (Scotch Mixtures) that glittered like rubies, emerals, topazes and all the jewels of the Orient, and tasted of all the fruits of the orchards and spices of the Indies. Striped rock in variegated colours and yellow spiral sticks of barley sugar were always prime favourites, and so was 'taiblet' of various flavours.'

Sweetie traditions:

Almond Cake: a rich buttery toffee mixture, poured into a tin that has a thick layer of flaked almonds on the base. A version of this is made in Orkney.

Barley Sugar: usually made into a twisted stick of hard rock, flavoured with barley water and sometimes liquorice.

Berwick Cockles: peppermint flavoured boilings, white with pink strips and shaped like the cockle shells that used to be fished up near Tweedmouth harbour.

Bon-Bons: strips of candied lemon or orange peel dipped into barley sugar.

Black Man: treacle toffee. Also known as Treacle Candy

Black Striped Balls: black and white striped balls of hard toffee with a strong peppermint flavour.

Butterscotch: a hard boiling with a buttery flavour. Made as a quality sweetie by Keiller's in Dundee up to the 1950s, shaped rectangular and wrapped in silver foil with a dent in the middle where it broke into two pieces. Packaged in cigarette sized packets.

Cheugh Jeans: chewy (cheugh) toffee made in different flavours – clove, cinnamon, peppermint, ginger or chocolate.

Coltart's Candy: pronounced 'coolter' and made famous by the song that the sweetie man sang as he travelled round the country selling his candy. The candy was aniseed flavoured but the recipe and the custom were lost when Coltart died, greatly lamented, in 1890.

Claggum or Clack: made with treacle and water, boiled till soft ball stage and then pulled into long sticks of rock.

Curly Andra: a white coral-like sweet with a coriander seed in the centre. The name comes from the Scots' corruption of coriander which is 'curryander'.

Curlie Murlies also known as **Curly Doddies**: were a specialised Angus delicacy. In F M McNeill, *The Scots Kitchen*, they are described as: 'mixed sweets of various shapes and sizes, the texture of pandrops although the Curly Murlie proper had a rather knarled exterior. They were formed on a seed or other foundation such as a carvie, clove or almond. The nucleus of the Curlie Murlie proper was probably aniseed. It was about the size of a large pea. These sweets were popular on feeding-market days when Jock was expected to give Jenny her 'market' in the form of a pockie (poke) of market sweeties or Curlie Murlies.' (Murl means a crumb or fragment).

Edinburgh Rock: not the customary solid stick with letters down the centre, but a light pastel-coloured sugary confection, delicately flavoured. It was discovered by accident when Alexander Ferguson, popularly known as 'Sweetie Sandy', came across a piece of confectionery that he had overlooked and left lying for several months. He became one of Edinburgh's most successful confectioners in the nineteenth century and the rock is now exported worldwide.

Glessie: 'But the glessy! Who that ever tasted it can forget the stick of sheeny, golden rock, which stretched while you were eating it to gossamer threads of silver glistening like cobwebs in the sun.' *Scots Magazine*, 1925.

Gundy: an aniseed or cinnamon flavoured hard boiling.

Hawick Balls: cinnamon flavoured hard toffee with a subtle hint of mint.

Helensburgh Toffee: more a tablet than a toffee, it has a rich creamy flavour that comes from the use of condensed milk.

Horehound Boilings: well-loved by Dundonian jute workers who sucked them to relieve their dry throats from jute dust in the factories. Still a useful sore-throat boiling.

Jeddart Snails: dark brown toffees, mildly peppermint flavoured. The name and shape were given to them by a French prisoner-of-war from Napoleon's army who made them for a Jedburgh baker.

Lettered Rock: long sticks of hard rock with a strong peppermint flavour, bright pink on the outside, white in the middle with red letters down the middle of the sweetie shop's appropriate town.

Mealie Candy: a hard boiling flavoured with treacle and ginger and with oatmeal added.

Moffat Toffee: a hard toffee, amber and gold striped with a sherbert-like tangy centre. It is now made commercially by a local Moffat family who have been making toffee for generations. One of its early names was Moffat Whirlies. The Moffat Toffee shop in the town is Mecca for sweetie lovers.

Oddfellows: soft lozenges made in delicate colours and aromatic flavours such as cinnamon, clove and rose geranium.

Pan Drops: mint imperials, or Granny sookers. The sweetie your granny slipped you in church for the minister's sermon.

Soor Plooms: originated in the Borders where they were made to celebrate an incident in local history when a band of English marauders were surprised and overcome while eating unripe plums. They are round, bright green balls with an acidic astringent tang.

Starrie Rock: still made in the Star Rock shop in the narrow (car-less) wynd known as The Roods in Kirriemuir, Angus. It was made originally by a stone mason who was blinded in 1833. The sticks are short and thin, slightly chewy, and with a delectable buttery flavour (the Rock Shop also makes excellent Horehound Boilings).

Sugar-ally-water: liquorice water. Hard block liquorice is mixed with water in a lemonade bottle and shaken until it dissolves.

Sugar-bools: small, round sugar plums like marbles.

Sugar-hearts: pink, heart-shaped fondants.

Basic Sugar Boiling Process

Cook's Tips: This can easily be done without professional equipment, such as a sugar thermometer, since the practical test of putting a few drops of the boiling sugar into a cup of cold water will tell you exactly what stage the sugar is at. If the result is a little past the desired stage, remove the pan from the heat, add a little warm water to lower the temperature and continue.

500g (1lb 2oz) granulated sugar
300ml (10fl oz) water
Pinch of cream of tartar to prevent granulation

Dissolve the sugar over a low heat in the liquid and stir with a wooden spoon until no particles of sugar are left. To test – examine the back of the spoon for any sugar crystals. Brush the sides of the pan with water to remove any crystals. When all is dissolved, bring gradually to the boil and simmer gently till the required stage is reached.

Stages in Sugar Boiling:

Smooth/Transparent Icing: (108°C) for crystallising purposes and fondant. The mixture begins to look syrupy. To test, dip finger in water and then very quickly into the syrup, the thumb will slide smoothly over the fingers, but the sugar will cling.

Soft ball: (115°C) for soft caramel, candy, fudge and tablet. To test, drop a little syrup into cold water and leave for a few minutes. Pick up between the finger and thumb when it should roll into a small soft ball.

Firm or hard ball: (121°C) for caramels, marshmallows, nougat, Edinburgh Rock and soft toffee. Test as above when the syrup should roll into a hard ball.

Small crack: (138°C) for toffees and rock. Test as above, when the thread of syrup should break lightly.

Hard crack: (154°C) for hard toffees, boiled sweeties and drops, pulled sugar and rock. Test as above, when the thread of syrup should break sharply.

Caramel: (160°C upwards) when the syrup begins to discolour, turning a darker brown colour, caramel stage is reached. If allowed to become too dark, the taste will be bitter.

Tablet

(SEE SWEETIE CLASSICS P166)

Cook's Tip: Slightly harder than fudge, but not chewy like toffee, tablet should have a slight 'bite' to it.

Basic Recipe:
175ml (6fl oz) milk
175g (6oz) unsalted butter
800g (1lb 12oz) caster sugar
1 tin condensed milk

Use a large 3L (5–6pt) thick-based aluminium pot to make tablet. Line a tray, 18 x 27cm (7 x 10½ inch), with a layer of tinfoil covered with a layer of clingfilm. Place prepared baking tray in the freezer overnight.

TO MAKE: Put milk and butter, cut into cubes, into the pan and melt. Add the sugar and stir to dissolve. When dissolved and beginning to simmer, add the condensed milk. Stirring all the time to prevent burning, simmer for about 9–10 minutes or until the mixture turns light amber in colour. To test for readiness: put a little of the mixture in a cup of cold water and it should form a soft ball (115°C on sugar thermometer see p170). Take off of the heat, place on a wet cloth and beat until the mixture lightens a little in colour and begins to thicken and 'grain'. Do not allow it to become too thick or it will not pour well and will develop a fudge texture with no 'bite' to it.

FINISHING Pour the mixture into the chilled tray. Leave for 30 minutes to set. Cover with clingfilm and put it in the freezer for one and a half hours. Take out. Remove from the tin and turn onto a cutting board. Leave for 10 minutes. Score the tablet into 4 squares with the heel of a sharp knife. Break into 4. Then score each square into 3 lengths. Break off each length. Score into cubes. Finally, break into small cubes and store in an airtight container.

Tablet variations

Orange – Add 175ml (6fl oz) fresh orange juice instead of milk. Before pouring, mix in the orange zest.

Vanilla and Walnut – Mix in 1 teaspoon of vanilla extract and 50g (2oz) finely chopped walnuts when the sugar is removed from the heat.
Coffee and Walnut – Add 1 tablespoon instant coffee powder and 50g (2oz) finely chopped walnuts before pouring.

Cinnamon – Add 1 teaspoon cinnamon oil.

Ginger – Add 50g (2oz) chopped preserved ginger before pouring.

Peppermint – Add 2-3 drops of peppermint oil before pouring.

Fruit and Nut – Add 50g (2oz) finely chopped nuts and 50g (2oz) seedless raisins before pouring.

Treacle Toffy for Coughs

An eighteenth-century medicinal sweetie from Lady Clark's extensive collection.

125 g (4½ oz) butter
125g (4½ oz) black treacle
500g (1lb 2oz) granulated sugar
1 teaspoon ground ginger
1 teaspoon grated lemon zest

Use a large 3L (5–6pt) thick-based aluminium or stainless steel pot. Line a tray, approximately 18 x 27cm (7 x 10½ inch), with tin foil covered with a layer of clingfilm – place in the freezer for a few hours or overnight.

MAKING: Melt the butter and treacle together in a pan, stir and add the sugar. Increase the heat gradually until it bubbles. Keep stirring all the time to dissolve the sugar. Test in a cup of cold water. When it forms a firm ball (121°C see p170), remove from the heat and add the lemon and ginger. Pour out very thinly into a prepared baking tin. Crack into pieces when cold and store in an airtight tin.

Glessie

Cook's Tips for handling hot sugar: The final shaping is best done with a partner because there is only a short time (perhaps two to three minutes) when the hot sugar is cool enough to handle and is still flexible. It will suddenly cool and stiffen, which can leave you caught out with a piece of sugar totally the wrong size and shape. If an extra pair of hands are not available and you get caught, reheat the sugar gently in a warm oven with the door open, checking frequently. The other hazard of working with hot sugar is its inner heat. While the outside feels cool enough to handle, the inside may be hot enough to burn your hands.

> 250g (9oz) soft brown sugar
> 25g (1oz) butter
> 1 tablespoon water
> ½ teaspoon cream of tartar
> 700g (1½ lb) golden syrup

Use a large 3L (5–6pt) thick-based aluminium or stainless steel pot. Line a tray, approximately 18 x 27cm (7 x 10½ inch), with tin foil covered with a layer of clingfilm – place in the freezer for a few hours or overnight.

BOILING: Boil the sugar, butter and water for five minutes to dissolve the sugar. Add the cream of tartar and golden syrup. Bring up to a gentle simmer and continue to simmer without stirring until it reaches hard crack (154°C, see p170). Pour out onto an oiled laminated or marble surface.

FINISHING: Leave the sugar to cool for a few minutes. Then, scrape into the centre with a palette knife or plastic scraper. When cool enough to handle, oil hands and push the mixture into a thick, short, tubular shape. Roll out between the fingers to double its size. Fold over and roll out again. It will begin to stiffen up. Before this happens, roll out and cut into strips with oiled scissors. Roll each strip out to about the thickness of a finger. Place on trays. Store in an airtight tin.

Gundy

An aniseed or cinnamon flavoured hard boiling.

500g (1lb 2oz) Demerara sugar
1 tablespoon black treacle or golden syrup
50g (2oz) butter
300ml (10fl oz) water
Aniseed or cinnamon oil

Use a large 3L (5–6pt) thick-based aluminium or stainless steel pot. Line a tray, approximately 18 x 27cm (7 x 10½ inch), with tin foil covered with a layer of clingfilm – place in the freezer for a few hours or overnight.

BASIC SUGAR BOILING: Dissolve the sugar treacle or golden syrup, butter and water over a low heat in the liquid, stirring with a wooden spoon until no particles of sugar are left. To test – examine the back of the spoon for any sugar crystals. Brush the sides of the pan with water to remove any crystals. When all is dissolved, bring gradually to the boil and continue to simmer gently testing a few drops regularly in a cup of cold water. When it reaches hard crack (154°C, see p170) remove from the heat and pour into well-greased tins. Mark into squares just before setting. When set, break up into pieces and store in an airtight tin.

Edinburgh Rock

Cook's Tips for handling hot sugar: the final shaping of the rock is best done with a partner because there is only a short time (perhaps two to three minutes) when the hot sugar is cool enough to handle and is still flexible. It will suddenly cool and stiffen, which can leave you caught out with a piece of sugar totally the wrong size and shape. If this happens, reheat gently in a warm oven with the door open, checking frequently. The other hazard of working with sugar is its inner heat. While the outside feels cool enough to handle, the inside may be hot enough to burn your hands. So go cannily to begin with.

500g (1lb 2oz) granulated sugar
300ml (10fl oz) water
½ teaspoon cream of tartar
Icing sugar
Flavourings/colourings to taste: use either a few drops of peppermint oil or a teaspoon vanilla extract (white), or a teaspoon ground ginger (fawn), or a few drops of raspberry or rose essence (pink), or a few drops lemon essence (yellow)

Use a large 3L (5–6pt) thick-based aluminium or stainless steel pot. Line 2 trays, approximately 18 x 27cm (7 x 10½ inch), with tin foil covered with a layer of clingfilm.

BASIC SUGAR BOILING: Dissolve the sugar over a low heat in the liquid stirring with a wooden spoon until no particles of sugar are left. To test – examine the back of the spoon for any sugar crystals. Brush the sides of the pan with water to remove any crystals. When all is dissolved, bring gradually to the boil and simmer gently till it reaches hard ball (121°C, see p170). Remove from the heat and add a flavouring and colouring.

FINISHING: Leave the sugar to cool for a few minutes. Dust the work surface lightly with icing sugar. Pour out the hot sugar, scraping it into the centre with a palette knife or plastic scraper. When cool enough to handle, oil hands and push the mixture into a thick, short, tubular shape. Roll out between the fingers to double its size. Fold over and roll out again. It will become opaque with working and begin to stiffen up. Before this happens, roll out and cut into strips with oiled scissors. Roll each strip out to about the thickness of a finger. Place on trays and leave, uncovered, in a warm atmosphere overnight, or until the texture softens and becomes powdery. Store in an airtight tin.

Barley Sugar

Cook's Tips for handling hot sugar: the final shaping of the rock is best done with a partner because there is only a short time (perhaps two to three minutes) when the hot sugar is cool enough to handle and is still flexible. It will suddenly cool and stiffen, which can leave you caught out with a piece of sugar totally the wrong size and shape. If this happens, reheat gently in a warm oven with the door open, checking frequently. The other hazard of working with sugar is its inner heat. While the outside feels cool enough to handle, the inside may be hot enough to burn your hands. So go cannily to begin with.

50g (2oz) pearl barley
600ml (1pt) water
500g (1lb 2oz) granulated sugar
25g (1oz) butter

Use a large 3L (5–6pt) thick-based aluminium or stainless steel pot. Line 2 trays, approximately 18 x 27cm (7 x 10½ inch), with tin foil covered with a layer of clingfilm.

MAKING BARLEY WATER: Put the barley and water into a pan and bring to the boil. Cover and simmer for about an hour. Strain into a bowl and leave to settle, allowing the starchy particles to settle to the bottom. Add more water to make up barley water to 600ml (1pt) – some will have evaporated.

BASIC SUGAR BOILING: Dissolve the sugar over a low heat in the barley water, stirring with a wooden spoon until no particles of sugar are left. To test – examine the back of the spoon for any sugar crystals. Brush the sides of the pan with water to remove any crystals. When all is dissolved, add the butter and bring gradually to the boil, testing a few drops frequently in cold water until it reaches hard crack (154°C, see p170). Remove from the heat.

FINISHING: Leave for a few minutes before pouring onto an oiled laminate work surface (not wood) or marble slab. Begin by turning the sugar into the centre with a scraper or palate knife. When cool enough to handle, oil hands and push the mixture into a thick, short, tubular shape. Roll out between the fingers to double its size. Fold over and roll out again. Continue rolling and folding. It will quickly become opaque with working and begin to stiffen up. But before this happens, roll out and cut into thick strips with oiled scissors. Roll each strip out to about the thickness of a finger give it a twist and cut with scissors into shorter lengths. Store in an airtight tin.

Butterscotch

These were originally shaped into small half-ounce bars, indented in the middle so each piece could be broken in two.

125g (4½ oz) butter
500g (1lb 2oz) light brown sugar
600ml (1pt) water
1 tablespoon treacle (optional)

Use a large 3L (5–6pt) thick-based aluminium or stainless steel pot. Line a tray, approximately 18 x 27cm (7 x 10½ inch), with clingfilm – place in the freezer for a few hours or overnight.

BASIC SUGAR BOILING: Dissolve the butter and sugar over a low heat in the liquid stirring with a wooden spoon until no particles of sugar are left. To test – examine the back of the spoon for any sugar crystals. Brush the sides of the pan with water to remove any crystals. When all is dissolved, add treacle (if using), bring gradually to the boil and simmer gently. Test by putting a few drops into cold water until it reaches hard crack (154°C, see p170).

FINISHING: Remove from the heat and pour into the prepared tin. Leave to cool. When almost set, mark the surface into rectangle bars. Break up when set and store in an airtight tin.

Whisky Fudge

Whisky is optional, but for the most subtle flavouring avoid the strongly peaty island malts.

Yield: 45–50 pieces

300ml (10fl oz) double cream
250g (9oz) unsalted butter
250g (9oz) glucose
1kg (2lb 4oz) granulated sugar
2 – 3 tablespoon Lowland malt whisky (optional)

Use a large 3L (5–6pt) thick-based aluminium or stainless steel pot. Line a tray, approximately 18 x 27cm (7 x 10½ inch), with tin foil covered with a layer of clingfilm – place in the freezer for a few hours or overnight.

TO MAKE: Put cream and butter into the pan and bring to a simmer. Add the glucose. Continue simmering and add sugar. Stir well to dissolve sugar. Simmer for about 9–10 minutes, stirring frequently, when it should turn a light amber in colour. Test for readiness: put a little in a cup of cold water and it should form a soft ball. (115°C, see p170). Take off the heat. Add the whisky. Place pan on a wet cloth and beat until it begins to turn creamy and 'grains'. This is beaten for longer than tablet.

FINISHING: Pour into the chilled trays. Leave for 30 minutes to set. Then put in the freezer for 1½ hours. Take out. Remove from the trays and turn onto a cutting board. Leave for 10–12 minutes. Score with the heel of a sharp knife into four squares. Then score each square into three lengths and then into cubes. Break into pieces.

Rum Truffles

This name comes from the similarity to the earthy fungus: dark, intense and a rare treat.

Yield: 20–28

200g (7oz) best quality plain chocolate
75ml (3fl oz) double cream
25g (1oz) unsalted butter, softened
1–2 tablespoons rum

TO MAKE: Break the chocolate up finely (this can be done in the food processor). Put into a bowl. Heat the cream to boiling point and add the butter and rum and mix through. Pour over chocolate and blend till smooth and all the chocolate is melted. Pour onto a large flat plate and chill in the fridge until it is set and firm enough to shape.

TO SHAPE:

Method 1: With a teaspoon, scrape across the chocolate to form a truffle 'curl' in the same style of a butter 'curl'. Roll in cocoa powder.

Method 2: As soon as the mixture sets and before it hardens, put it into a piping bag with a 1cm (½ inch) nozzle. Line the baking tin with clingfilm. Pipe into small rounds. Refrigerate for about an hour.

Method 3: When the mixture is firm, use 2 teaspoons to shape into roughly oval bite-sized portions. Leave in rough shape or roll by hand into round balls, using cocoa powder to prevent sticking. Finish by rolling in either cocoa powder or ground toasted hazelnuts or almonds.

PRESERVING CLASSICS

Marmalade

It's a cold, blustery January day in the late 1700s when a storm-bound ship from the south of Spain docks in Dundee harbour. The town does not normally trade with Spain, so the cargo of 'Seville sours' (bitter oranges) on board is especially intriguing. Retired tailor, John Keiller, has taken a wander down to the harbour, as he does most days, to join in the quayside chat whilst keeping an eye out for the odd package of fruits or spices that might be a useful ingredient for his wife's bakery business. No one is very interested in the inedible bitter oranges, so he decides to buy some and, unknowingly, founds a dynasty which will last a hundred years and become bigger in confectionery, during the nineteenth century, than either Cadburys or Frys.

John's wife, Janet Keiller, has her shop on the south side of the Seagate where she has spent the best part of her life making preserves, jellies, biscuits, sweeties and cakes. She has always believed in diversifying into unique lines and it has certainly paid off. Now she is almost 60 and is ready to retire. She is keen, however, to use the modest assets she has accumulated over the years to help her son, James, develop the business. Of all her seven children, he is the only son who has shown an interest in her enterprise and has developed her innovative flair. He is just 22 when she hands over the business to him in 1797.

Though the Keillers were not marmalade's inventors (recipes exist in English cookery books dating back to the seventeenth century), they were the first to perfect the recipe and make it on a large scale. While his mother provided the financial support, it was James who was the marmalade innovator. One local writer of the day refers to his 'remarkable success in experiments with oranges'.

Once the process was perfected, the Keillers developed strong links with the growers in Spain where they bought the best Seville oranges, aiming to beat their competitors on quality, as they did in all their other products. Despite their early success, however, the Keiller family lost control of the business in the closing years of the nineteenth century, though the name and their marmalade survived into the 1980s, when it eventually became a victim of take-over and asset-stripping by multinational confectioners. The Albert Museum in Dundee has a rich archive of Keiller memorabilia and the history of the family has been researched by W M Mathew in *Keiller's of Dundee and the Rise of the Marmalade Dynasty* (Dundee 1998).

Scottish Soft Fruit preserves

The Northern climate in Scotland (long hours of summer daylight and little scorching summer sun) is particularly suited to growing soft, delicate berries. They ripen slowly to an exceptional sweetness and have grown wild for centuries. In the Tayside area, in particular, large scale commercial growing began in the early twentieth century – strawberries to begin with, later raspberries. This led to the tradition of preserving the fruit in jams and jellies mostly in Dundee, which for a time, was known as the 'jam capital' of Scotland.

General Cook's Tips for Preserves: It's best to use a large, wide, stainless steel, brass or lined aluminium preserving pan or large wide, heavy-based pot to allow maximum evaporation. The faster the evaporation, the sooner the preserve will set and therefore the better the finished flavour.

Never fill above halfway. If making jellies, use either a jelly bag or a square of muslin. Never squeeze the bag since it will make the jelly cloudy.

Pectin is the setting agent in fruit – the less ripe the fruit, the higher the pectin content. Naturally high-pectin fruits are: Seville oranges, gooseberries, cooking apples, lemons and damsons. Naturally low-pectin fruits are: cherries, grapes, peaches, rhubarb and strawberries. All others have a medium content. To improve the setting qualities, high-pectin fruits may be added, such as lemons, or commercially bottled liquid pectin, or preserving sugar with pectin added. Using these will speed up the boiling time necessary to achieve a set and improve the finished flavour.

TO TEST FOR A SET WITH A SUGAR THERMOMETER: the preserve is ready when the temperature reaches 105°C/221°F.

TO TEST FOR A SET WITH SAUCERS: put two saucers into the freezer to chill before beginning the boiling. Put a little of the preserve onto the cold saucer. Push the preserve with a finger across the saucer and if the surface wrinkles it has reached setting point. If not, continue to boil and test again in five minutes with the second saucer.

POTTING, COVERING AND STORING: pots should be thoroughly cleaned and heated before potting the preserve. The surface should be covered with a wax disc as soon as they are filled. Allow them to cool before covering with a lid or cellophane cover. If covered before they have cooled they are more likely to mould. Label and store in a cool, dry place.

Seville Orange Marmalade (thick-cut)

This is an old-fashioned thick, bitter marmalade using lemon for added sharpness. All the bitter white pith can be used.

Cook's Tips: The pips are the main source of pectin (gelling material) in oranges and should be put in a bag and boiled with the rest of the oranges and sugar. For best results make up in small quantities since it is then easier to control the setting point.

> Yield: 5-6 jars
>
> 1kg (2lb 4oz) Seville oranges
> Water to cover
> 500g (1lb) sugar to every 600ml (1pt) juice
> 2 lemons

Heat jars.

PREPARING THE FRUIT: Wash the oranges well and put them in the preserving pan. Pour over boiling water to cover. Simmer until the fruit softens. It should take between one and two hours. When cool, cut in half, remove the pulp with a spoon and put into a bowl. Cut up the skins into chips. Size is a personal taste. Put the pulp through a sieve. It goes through easily and you can decide at this point whether you want to put all the bitter pith through or not. Extract the pips, put into a muslin bag and tie up.

FINISHING THE MARMALADE: Put the chips and pulp into the water that the fruit was boiled in. Measure and add 500g (1lb 2oz) preserving sugar for every 300ml (1pt) liquid. Put into the pan with the zest and juice of the lemons. Bring to the boil and simmer till set. Test by putting a teaspoonful on a chilled saucer and placing it in the deep freeze compartment for a few minutes to chill and give you a quick result. The surface should set and crinkle when pushed with a finger. Do not boil too vigorously while the test is being done otherwise the setting point may be missed. Remove from the heat, skim with a slotted spoon and leave for 10 minutes to cool before potting – this prevents the chips sinking. Pour into clean, hot jars. Seal with waxed disk and cover. Label and store in a cool, dry place.

ADDING OTHER FLAVOURS: Spirits or liqueurs can be added to marmalade at this point before it is set. Leave a space at the top of the jar and add a tablespoonful. Cover and seal. Use whisky, brandy or rum.

Seville Orange Marmalade (thin-cut)

This is a sweeter and less time-consuming recipe than the previous one since a processor is used to cut the skins and pulp.

Cook's Tip: It is important to extract as much of the pectin from the pips since they provide the main setting agent in marmalade.

Yield: 6-7 jars

1kg (2lb 4oz) Seville oranges
2 lemons, juice of
2L (3pt 10fl oz) water
2kg (4lb 8oz) preserving sugar

Heat jars.

PREPARATION: The day before: halve the oranges and squeeze out the juice. Soak the pips in 600ml (1pt) water. Remove the pith. Shred the orange skins in a food processor and soak overnight in the remainder of the water.

MAKING THE MARMALADE: Strain the liquid from the pips into the preserving pan. Tie the pips up in a muslin and add to the pan. Add the shredded peel soaked in the water. Bring to the boil, stirring occasionally, till the peel is soft (one to two hours) and the liquid has reduced by about half. Add the sugar, orange and lemon juice. Stir to dissolve sugar. Boil to 221°F/105°C and test for a set (see p181). Remove scum with a slotted spoon and leave to stand for 15 minutes. Stir to distribute the peel. Pot and seal surface with a waxed disc as soon as they are filled. Then, allow to cool before covering with a lid or cellophane cover. Label and store in a cool, dry place.

Fresh Raspberry Conserve

(ALSO SUITABLE FOR TAYBERRIES AND BRAMBLES)

The full, fresh tang of raspberries is preserved in this non-cooked jam, which is thickened with liquid pectin then deep frozen. It can be stored in the refrigerator for several weeks.

Yield: 3 jars or several small plastic tubs

450g (1lb) fruit
600g (1lb 5oz) caster sugar
2 tablespoons lemon juice
125ml (4fl oz) commercial liquid pectin (Certo)

MAKING: Put the fruit into a bowl with the sugar and lemon juice and stir till the sugar is dissolved. Leave to stand for at least an hour or overnight. Stir. Add the pectin and mix in well. Ladle into jars, cover with lids or put into small plastic tubs with lids and store in the fridge where it will keep for two to three weeks. Alternatively, put into the freezing compartment if you want to store for longer.

Raspberry Jam

Cook's Tips: For the best flavour in a cooked jam, it should be boiled briefly which will not, in this case, produce a firm jam, but one that can be used as a sauce with puddings, pancakes, ices and meringues.

Yield: 3-4 jars

1kg (2lb 4oz) raspberries
1kg (2lb 4oz) sugar
Knob of butter

Heat jars.

PREPARING: Pick over the fruit and place in layers in a large bowl with the sugar. Cover and leave in a cool place for about 24 hours to allow the juice to run. Stir to dissolve the sugar.

MAKING AND POTTING: Turn the raspberries and sugar into a preserving pan, add the butter and bring gently to the boil. Boil for three minutes. Leave to cool. Pot and seal surface with a waxed disc as soon as they are filled. Then allow to cool before covering with a lid or cellophane cover. Label and store in a cool, dry place.

Strawberry Conserve

This is a runny syrup with whole berries and not a spreading jam. It can be served with hot pancakes or crumpets (see p151) from the girdle, or with ice cream or other sweets.

Cook's Tips: Not suitable for very ripe fruit.

Yield: 3 jars

500g (1lb 2oz) small firm strawberries
1 lemon, juice of
500g (1lb 2oz) granulated sugar

Heat jars.

MAKING: Wash and drain the strawberries, remove stalks and put them into a wide, shallow pan (a large, deep frying pan) with the lemon juice. Put the sugar on a plate in a warm oven to dry out for about an hour. Cook the berries on the lowest heat until soft and the juices are running. Add sugar and stir to dissolve. Bring to the boil. Remove the berries with a slotted spoon and place in a sieve over a bowl. Continue to simmer the sugar syrup to reduce it by about half. Add the liquid which has drained from the berries. Bring up to simmering point and reduce again. Return strawberries to the syrup. Pot in heated jars and seal surface with a waxed disc as soon as they are filled. Then allow to cool before covering with a lid or cellophane cover. Label and store in a cool, dry place.

Strawberry Jam

A spreading jam which is best made with firm small berries.

Yield: 5-6 jars

900g (2lb) small strawberries, hulled
1kg (2lb 4oz) preserving sugar with pectin
2 tablespoon lemon juice

Heat jars.

MAKING: Put the strawberries in a preserving pan with the sugar and lemon juice. Heat gently, stirring until the sugar has dissolved. Bring to the boil and boil until setting point is reached (see p181 for test). Remove the pan from the heat and remove any scum with a slotted spoon. Leave to stand for 15 minutes. Stir to distribute the fruit. Pot in heated jars and seal surface with a waxed disc as soon as they are filled. Then allow to cool before covering with a lid or cellophane cover. Label and store in a cool, dry place.

Rum Preserved Berries

Start with the first local strawberries, adding a variety of berries as they ripen during the summer. This pot can be stored – and consumed – throughout the winter.

250g (9oz) strawberries, washed and hulled
250g (9oz) granulated sugar
1 bottle, dark rum

Use a large-lidded stoneware pot about 4-5L (8-10pt) capacity. Smaller will do, but this gives less scope for adding.

STARTING THE POT: Put the strawberries into the pot, cover with sugar, stir well and leave for half an hour. Add enough rum to just cover. Stir the fruit. Stir regularly every two to three days, for about a week.

TO CONTINUE ADDING: Add about 250g (9oz) of fruit at a time. Suitable soft fruit includes: cherries, redcurrants, blackcurrants, brambles, blueberries, blaeberries, raspberries, plums or apricots. Add about 2 tablespoons of sugar each time a new batch of fruit is added and enough rum to keep the fruit well covered. While new fruit is being added, stir every two to three days for a week. When no fruit is being added, give it a stir every two to three weeks.

AT THE END OF OCTOBER: It is better to leave the fruit to mature, at least till the end of October, though it can be used sooner. Serve with ice cream, whipped cream, with sponge cakes, with meringues, instead of jam in a trifle or on its own in a tall chilled glass.

Bramble Jam

Cook's Tip: Best results are with fruit that is slightly under-ripe. Over-ripe fruit has less pectin and will not set so well.

Yield: 4-5 jars
1kg (2lb 4oz) brambles
2 tablespoons lemon juice
2 tablespoons water
Knob of butter
1kg (2lb 4oz) preserving sugar with pectin

Heat jars.

MAKING: Put the brambles in a preserving pan with the lemon juice and water. Bring to a slow simmer and cook until the berries are soft and slightly reduced, stirring occasionally. Add the butter and sugar and stir until dissolved. Bring to the boil and simmer until setting point is reached. (see p181 for test). Remove scum with a slotted spoon. Pot heated jars and seal surface with a waxed disc as soon as they are filled. Then allow to cool before covering with a lid or cellophane cover. Label and store in a cool, dry place.

Bramble Jelly

Cook's Tip: Best results are with fruit that is slightly under-ripe. Over-ripe fruit has less pectin and will not set so well.

Yield: 3-4 jars
1.8kg (4lb) brambles, slightly under-ripe
2 lemons, juice of
425ml (15fl oz) water
350g (12oz) preserving sugar with pectin to every 600ml (1pt) juice

Heat jars.

PREPARING JUICE: Place the brambles, lemon juice and water into a preserving pan and bring to the boil. Simmer gently for about 15 minutes till the fruit is very soft. Put the pulp into a jelly bag and leave to drip for at least 12 hours.

MAKING JELLY: Measure the extracted juice and add sugar required for every 600ml (1pt) juice. Put into a preserving pan and bring to the boil, stirring until the sugar is dissolved. Boil rapidly until setting point is reached (see p181 for test). When set, take off the pan and remove any scum with a slotted spoon. Pot in heated jars and seal surface with a waxed disc as soon as they are filled. Then allow to cool before covering with a lid or cellophane cover. Label and store in a cool, dry place.

Blackcurrant and Apple Jam

Yield: 7 jars

1kg (2lb 4oz) blackcurrants
450g (1lb) cooking apples
Water
1.6kg (3lb 8oz) sugar

Heat jars.

MAKING: De-stalk currants by pulling the stems through the prongs of a fork. Pick over. Put in a preserving pan with just enough water to cover. Heat gently and simmer until the fruit is soft. Peel, core and slice the apples and place them in another pan. Add enough water to prevent burning and cook until soft, stirring occasionally. The blackcurrants will take longer to cook. When both are soft, mix them together. Add the sugar and stir to dissolve over a medium heat. Bring to the boil, and simmer until setting point is reached (see p181 for test). Remove from the heat and leave to cool for 10 minutes. Stir. Pot in heated jars and seal surface with a waxed disc as soon as they are filled. Then allow to cool before covering with a lid or cellophane cover. Label and store in a cool, dry place.

Blackcurrant Jam

Yield: 6-7 jars

1kg (2lb 4oz) blackcurrants
800ml (1pt 7fl oz) water
1.5kg (3lb 5oz) sugar

Heat jars.

MAKING: Remove the currants from their stems. This can be done by pulling the stem through the prongs of a fork. Pick over and wash, then place berries in the pan. Add water and bring to the boil. Reduce the heat and simmer until the berries are soft. Add the sugar and stir to dissolve. Bring to the boil and boil until setting point (see p181 for test). Remove from the heat and leave to settle for 10 minutes. Stir. Pot in heated jars and seal surface with a waxed disc as soon as they are filled. Then allow to cool before covering with a lid or cellophane cover. Label and store in a cool, dry place.

Plum Jam

Cook's Tip: Cracking open plum stones may sound like a bit of a fiddle, but the kernels inside do give the jam a special flavour.

Yield: 3 jars

1kg (2lb 4oz) under-ripe plums, preferably Victoria plums
900g (2lb) sugar

Heat jars.

PREPARING: Wash the plums, cut them in half and remove the stones. Tie half of the stones in a muslin bag and crack open the remainder to extract the kernels. This can be done by wrapping in a teatowel and cracking open with a hammer. Put the plums and sugar into a bowl in layers. Leave overnight.

MAKING: Put the plums and sugar into a preserving pan, add the muslin bag of stones and bring up to the boil stirring well to dissolve the sugar. Boil until a set is obtained. Add kernels and remove the bag of stones. Pot in heated jars and seal surface with a waxed disc as soon as they are filled. Then allow to cool before covering with a lid or cellophane cover. Label and store in a cool, dry place.

Rhubarb and Ginger Jam

Cook's Tip: The amount of ginger can be doubled.

Yield: 4-5 jars

1.3kg (3lb) mature rhubarb
1kg (2lb 4oz) sugar
175g (6oz) preserved ginger, finely chopped
2 lemons, grated zest and juice of

Heat jars.

PREPARING FRUIT: Wash rhubarb and cut into 2cm (1 inch) pieces. Put into a bowl in layers with sugar and leave for 24 hours. Stir occasionally. The sugar will have mostly dissolved into a syrup.

MAKING THE JAM: Pour the liquid from the bowl into a preserving pan and add the ginger and sugar. Bring to the boil. Dissolve the sugar and boil for about half an hour, stirring occasionally. Add the rhubarb, lemon juice and zest and return to the boil. Simmer until it sets. Remove from the heat and leave to stand for 10 -15 minutes. Stir. Pot in heated jars and seal surface with a waxed disc as soon as they are filled. Then allow to cool before covering with a lid or cellophane cover. Label and store in a cool, dry place.

Gooseberry and Elderberry Jam

Flowery aromas of the elderberry provide an intriguing combination with gooseberries.

Yield: 6 jars

1kg (2lb 4oz) gooseberries
450ml (16fl oz) water
1.3kg (3lb) sugar
Knob of butter
6 large elderflower heads, fully opened

Heat jars.

MAKING: Wash, top and tail the gooseberries. Put the gooseberries in the pan with the water and bring to the boil. Simmer until soft , stirring and mashing the fruit to a pulp. Add the sugar and butter, stir well to dissolve and bring to the boil. Using a rubber glove to protect your hand from popping jam, hold the elderflowers in a bunch with the heads down and swirl them in the jam for a few minutes. Some small flowers may come off but this adds character to the jam. Continue to boil to setting point (see p181 for test). Remove from the heat and leave to settle for 10-15 minutes. Pot in heated jars and seal surface with a waxed disc as soon as they are filled. Then allow to cool before covering with a lid or cellophane cover. Label and store in a cool, dry place.

Rowan Jelly

With its sharp, astringent tang this is an indispensable accompaniment to roasts of venison and game birds. For a more intense flavour, substitute some of the apples for more rowans.

Yield: 3-4 pots

1kg (2lb) slightly under-ripe rowan berries
1kg (2lb) unpeeled cooking apples

Heat jars.

MAKING JUICE: Chop apples roughly and remove stalks from berries. Put both into a pan with just enough water to cover and bring to the boil. Simmer the fruit till soft and put into a preserving bag or muslin to drip overnight.

MAKING JELLY: Measure the juice and add 500g (1lb 2oz) of sugar to every 600ml (1pt) liquid. Put it into the pan and bring to the boil, simmer till set (see p181 for test). Pot in heated jars and seal surface with a waxed disc as soon as they are filled. Then allow to cool before covering with a lid or cellophane cover. Label and store in a cool, dry place.

Redcurrant Jelly

Yield: 5-6 jars

1.4kg (3lb) redcurrants
600g (1pt) water
500g (1lb 2oz) sugar to every 600ml (1pt) juice
45ml (3 tablespoons) port

Heat jars.

MAKING JUICE: Place the currants in a preserving pan with the water and simmer gently until the fruit is soft and pulpy, stirring from time to time. Put into a jelly bag or into a muslin square and leave to drip overnight. Discard pulp.

MAKING JELLY: Measure juice and add 500g (1lb 2oz) of sugar to every 600ml (1pt) in the preserving pan. Boil up juice and sugar, stirring to dissolve and continue to boil rapidly until setting point is reached (see p181 for test). Remove from the heat and leave to settle for 10-15 minutes. Add port. Pot in heated jars and seal surface with a waxed disc as soon as they are filled. Then allow to cool before covering with a lid or cellophane cover. Label and store in a cool, dry place.

Mint and Apple Jelly with Cinnamon

Yield: 4-5 jars

1.5kg (3lb 5oz) cooking apples, peeled and cored
Water to cover
500g (1lb 2oz) sugar to every 600ml (1pt) juice
125g (4oz) mint, roughly chopped and tied in a muslin bag
2 sticks cinnamon

Heat jars.

MAKING JUICE: Chop cooking apples and put them in a pan. Just cover with water and cook till soft and pulpy. Pour into a jelly bag or muslin and drip overnight without squeezing.

MAKING JELLY: Measure juice and weigh out 500g (1lb 2oz) of sugar to every 600ml (1pt) liquid. Put both into the pan and stir over a low heat till the sugar is dissolved. Add mint tied in a muslin bag. Bring to the boil and simmer till set. Remove from the heat and allow to stand for about five minutes. Add 1 or 2 whole mint leaves and/or a small piece of cinnamon to each of the pots once they have cooled. Seal surface with a waxed disc as soon as they are filled. Then allow to cool before covering with a lid or cellophane cover. Label and store in a cool, dry place.

Lemon Curd

As well as being a piquant spread for scones, pancakes and crumpets, this is a useful filling for small and large tarts. Mixed with some double cream it is also a good filling for a Vanilla Butter Sponge (see p138).

Yield: To fill a 25cm (9½ inch) baked pastry flan ring or 2 jars.
6 lemons, zest and juice
225g (8oz) caster sugar
8 eggs, beaten
175g (6oz) unsalted butter

TO MAKE IN A DOUBLE BOILER: Put the lemons, sugar and eggs into a double boiler or in a large heatproof bowl over a pan of simmering water. Whisk well to mix thoroughly and dissolve the sugar. Add the butter. Cook, stirring occasionally until it thickens and coats the back of the spoon. Remove from the heat.

TO MAKE IN THE MICROWAVE: Put the butter and sugar in a bowl in the microwave and cook uncovered until the butter has melted. Add the lemon juice and zest and stir to dissolve the sugar. Add the eggs and whisk everything together. Return to the microwave and continue to cook, taking it out every 60 seconds to give it a whisk and check on its thickness. It should coat the back of a spoon when ready.

STORING: Strain, pot and cover when cold. Store in a cool place. Use as required. Will keep for two to three weeks.

Candied Fruit or Peel

This is a lengthy process but not an arduous one.

Cook's Tip: Only use fruit or peel of the best quality and therefore the best flavour.

> 500g (1lb 2oz) ripe fruit (plums, apples, pears, cherries) or orange and lemon peel
> 300ml (10fl oz) cooking liquid
> 600g (1lb 5oz) granulated sugar

PREPARING FRUIT: Plums should be pricked all over, cherries stoned and apples and pears peeled and halved or cut into quarters. Orange and lemon peel should be cut into quarters. Place fruit or peel in a pan and just cover with water. Cook gently till tender. Drain. Measure 300ml (10fl oz) of the cooking liquid and add 175g (6oz) of the granulated sugar. Put into the pan and bring to the boil, dissolving the sugar and boiling for a few minutes. Pour the syrup over the fruit/peel and leave covered for 24 hours.

CANDYING PROCESS: Drain off the syrup and add 50g (2oz) sugar. Put into a pan and bring to the boil, dissolving the sugar. Pour over the fruit and leave for another 24 hours. Repeat this process 6 times. On the seventh day, add 75g (3oz) sugar and leave to soak for 48 hours. Repeat again with 75g (3oz) pour over fruit/peel and leave for four days.

FINISHING: Remove fruit/peel from the syrup and put in a warm place for two to three days, turning occasionally to dry off the fruit. Pack in an airtight container between layers of greaseproof paper. For a sugary finish, dip quickly into boiling water, drain and roll in caster sugar.

Cooks Tips: All fresh fruit and vegetables must be free from mould and blemishes. If any vinegar is included in the recipe it is important not to use metal lids which will corrode.

Green Tomato Chutney

650g (1½ lb) cooking apples, peeled, cored and grated
1.4kg (3lb) green tomatoes, thinly sliced
500g (1lb 2oz) onions, peeled and grated
500g (1lb 2oz) sultanas
1 head of celery, diced
2 teaspoon sea or rock salt
350g (12oz) Demerara sugar
2 teaspoons mustard powder
1 teaspoon ground ginger
½ teaspoon cayenne pepper
700ml (1pt 3fl oz) apple cider vinegar

Heat jars.

MAKING: Put all of the ingredients into the pan and bring to the boil, then lower the heat. Simmer gently for about two hours until the mixture is reduced to a thick consistency with no excess liquid. Stir regularly to check for burning.

POTTING: Spoon the chutney into sterilised jars and seal surface with a waxed disc as soon as the pots are filled. Then allow to cool before covering with a lid or cellophane cover. Label and store in a cool, dry place.

Red Tomato Chutney

This kind of chutney was the precursor of commercial tomato ketchup – essential lubrication for fish and chips.

Yield: 10-12 jars

1.5kg (3lb) red tomatoes, peeled and roughly chopped
1.5kg (3lb) cooking apples, peeled and chopped
225g (8oz) onions, chopped
25g (1oz) pickling spice, tied in muslin bag
25g (1oz) mustard powder
25g (1oz) sea or rock salt
300ml (10fl oz) cider vinegar
250g (9oz) sultanas
350g (12oz) light brown sugar

Heat jars.

MAKING: Put all of the ingredients into the pan and bring to the boil, then lower the heat. Simmer gently for about two hours until the mixture is reduced to a thick consistency with no excess liquid. Stir regularly to check for burning.

POTTING: Spoon the chutney into sterilised jars and seal surface with a waxed disc as soon as the pots are filled. Then allow to cool before covering with a lid or cellophane cover. Label and store in a cool, dry place.

Apple Chutney

Yield: 12-15 jars

1.5kg (3lb 5oz) cooking apples, peeled, cored and grated
1kg (2lb 4oz) onions, peeled and blended in blender till fine
1.5kg (3lb 5oz) red or green tomatoes, chopped
1kg (2lb 4oz) sultanas
1kg (2lb 4oz) dates, chopped or raisins
1kg (2lb 4oz) soft dark brown sugar
200g (7oz) fresh ginger, grated
1 teaspoon ground allspice
$\frac{1}{2}$ teaspoon sea or rock salt
50g (2oz) pickling spice, tied in muslin bag
700ml (1pt 3fl oz) apple cider vinegar

Heat jars.

MAKING: Put all of the ingredients into the pan and bring to the boil, then lower the heat. Simmer gently for about two hours until the mixture is reduced to a thick consistency with no excess liquid. Stir regularly to check for burning.

POTTING: Remove the bag of pickling spice, spoon the chutney into sterilised jars and seal surface with a waxed disc as soon as the pots are filled. Then allow to cool before covering with a lid or cellophane cover. Label and store in a cool, dry place.

Plum Chutney

A highly-spiced chutney, best stored for at least six months to allow the flavours to mature. After two years the flavours grow and mellow with unique results.

Yield: 6-8 jars

1½ kg (3lb) stoned plums
2 medium onions, chopped
2 medium apples, chopped
4 tablespoons ground ginger
4 tablespoons cinnamon
4 tablespoons allspice
1½ tablespoons salt
600ml (1pt) cider vinegar
375g (13oz) sugar

Heat jars.

MAKING: Put the plums, onions, apples, ginger, cinnamon, allspice, salt and vinegar into a pan and cook gently, stirring regularly, for half an hour. Add the sugar and simmer to the consistency of thick jam. Stir regularly to check for burning.

POTTING: Spoon the chutney into sterilised jars and seal surface with a waxed disc as soon as the pots are filled. Then allow to cool before covering with a lid or cellophane cover. Label and store in a cool, dry place.

Raisin Chutney

Plump raisins are cooked slowly in tomatoes blended with cinnamon and cloves. Good with cold meats and game as well as mature hard cheeses.

Yield: 5-6 jars

50g (2oz) butter
500g (1lb 2oz) seedless raisins
2 X 200g tin chopped tomatoes
300ml (10fl oz) water
4 whole cloves
2 sticks cinnamon bark
2 teaspoon salt
1-2 teaspoon ground black pepper or to taste
150g (5½ oz) brown sugar
100ml (3½ fl oz) cider vinegar

MAKING: Melt the butter in a large, wide pan and add the raisins. Toss the raisins in the butter for a few minutes, then add tomatoes, water, cloves, cinnamon, salt and black pepper. Cook uncovered for about one hour, stirring occasionally, till very thick. Add the sugar and cider vinegar, mix through and simmer for a few minutes. Taste for flavour. Remove cinnamon.

POTTING: Spoon the chutney into sterilised jars and seal surface with a waxed disc as soon as the pots are filled. Then allow to cool before covering with a lid or cellophane cover. Label and store in a cool, dry place.

Creamy Mustard

This recipe makes a creamy mustard – rich and glossy with a faint sweetness – which also keeps very well.

Cook's Tip: Use either a non-brewed condiment or acetic acid from the chemist. Vinegar is too sharp.

Yield: 2 pots
1 x 125g (4½ oz) tin Coleman's mustard
250g (9oz) caster sugar
225ml (8fl oz) double cream
2 eggs
½ teaspoon potato flour
1 tablespoon non-brewed condiment or acetic acid

MAKING: Empty the contents of the mustard tin into a pan. Then fill up the tin with sugar (250g), empty into pan and then fill with cream (225ml) and add to pan. Add the eggs, mix in the potato flour and cook gently till it thickens. This can be done in a double boiler. When cold, stir in non-brewed condiment or acetic acid and pour into pots. Cover and seal. Store in a cool place.

Wholegrain Mustard

Yield: 2 pots
125g (4½ oz) mixture of black and white mustard seeds
Water
Cider vinegar
Salt
Flavourings – green peppercorns, chillies, tarragon, horseradish, honey, sesame seeds

MAKING: Grind the mustard in a coffee grinder or in a pestle and mortar according to the coarseness required. Put into a stoneware crock with a lid and add half water half cider vinegar to just cover. Add salt and flavourings. Stir well, cover and leave for a week at room temperature stirring regularly. Drain off excess liquid and pack into sterilised jars. Seal and store for at least six months before use.

Horseradish Sauce

This is often made with vinegar, but toning down the fiery root with bland cream or crème fraiche makes for a less harsh result.

Cook's Tip: Horseradish, like onions, makes eyes water. It can be soaked in cold water before grating which reduces the effect a little.

Yield: 1-2 pots
75g (3oz) piece of fresh horseradish root, peeled
$\frac{1}{2}$ lemon, juice of
300ml (10fl oz) crème fraiche
Sea salt and ground pepper

MAKING: Grate the horseradish finely. Sprinkle with lemon juice to prevent discolouring. Mix with crème fraiche and season to taste. Store in a jar in the fridge and use as required.

Green Herb Relish

This lively relish (packed with vitamins) goes with almost anything, from cold meats to cooked vegetables or hard boiled eggs. It can also be thinned down with olive oil and used to dress a salad.

Cook's Tip: If using a food processor to blend, it's important to leave some texture and avoid puréeing to a pulp.

Yield: 1-2 pots
125g (4oz) flat leafed parsley
125g (4oz) tender leaves of curly kail (English spelling: kale)
50g (2oz) fresh mint, chopped
2 tablespoons capers
4-6 cloves garlic, crushed
300ml (10fl oz) extra virgin olive oil
Sea salt and ground black pepper

MAKING: Wash and chop the parsley, kail and mint very finely. Add capers and garlic and put into a bowl with olive oil. Mix well and season. Or put everything into a food processor and blend until finely chopped. Serve with all meats, roasted, boiled or cold as well as vegetables and fish. Store in a jar in the fridge. It will keep for about two weeks.

Raspberry Vinegar

An old recipe that has now found its way into the modern chef's repertoire. A useful sharp partner for fatty meats such as duck and goose. It's also used in salad dressings though it was originally added to water as a refreshing drink.

Cook's Tip: Do not squeeze the jelly bag or the vinegar will go cloudy.

Yield: 600ml (1pt)

500g (1lb) raspberries
600ml (1pt) white wine vinegar
350g (12oz) granulated sugar to every 600ml (1pt) juice

MAKING: Put the raspberries into a bowl and cover with vinegar. Cover and leave for 48 hours. Strain the liquid through a jelly bag or muslin. Measure the juice and add sugar accordingly. Place in a pan and boil for about 10 minutes till the sugar is dissolved. Cool. Pour into bottles, seal and store in a cool, dark place. It is ready to use immediately and will keep for up to a year.

Spiced Vinegar

The flavour of this vinegar is entirely dependent on the slow mellowing of the many spices and flavourings, preferably in the summer sun.

4L (7pt) white wine vinegar
150g (5oz) black mustard seeds
50g (2oz) fresh ginger root
75g (3oz) whole allspice
15g (1/2 oz) cloves
50g (2oz) black peppercorns
15g (1/2 oz) celery seeds
750g (1 1/2 lb) brown sugar
40g (1 1/2 oz) grated horseradish
1 head garlic
1 1/2 lemon, sliced

MAKING: Combine all of the ingredients in a large glass jar and leave in the sun all summer or for at least four months. Strain and use with vegetables or in salad dressings.

Pickled Onions

Classic accompaniment to fish 'n' chips, though equally good with an extra mature cheddar.

Cook's Tips: To avoid streaming eyes, drop the onions into boiling water for a minute. Remove, drain and put into a basin of cold water. Remove skins under cold water with a sharp vegetable knife. Take as little from the base and crown as possible.

> 1kg (2lb 4oz) pickling onions
> 50g (2oz) sea salt (for crisp pickle onions)
> Or
> 100g (4oz) sea salt to 1L (1pt 15fl oz) water (for softer pickled onions)
>
> Spiced vinegar:
> 1.2L (2pt) white wine vinegar
> A few blades of mace
> 1 teaspoon whole cloves
> 1 tablespoon whole allspice
> 1 tablespoon whole black peppercorns
> 2 cinnamon sticks
> 1 teaspoon whole cloves
> 25g (1oz) sugar
> Bay leaves
> Whole red chillies

SALTING ONIONS: For a crisp pickle put the onions into a bowl in layers with the sea salt. Cover and leave overnight. For a softer onion, make a brine solution by dissolving the salt in water. Add the onions and leave overnight.

POTTING: Remove the onions from the salt. Wash and dry thoroughly. Pack firmly into sterile jars with non-metal lids. Make the vinegar by boiling with the mace, cloves, allspice, peppercorns and cinnamon for a few minutes. Add the sugar and dissolve. For a stronger flavour leave the spices in the vinegar. Alternatively, leave the vinegar to cool, infusing with the spices and then strain. Use hot vinegar for a softer finished onion, or leave to cool for a crisper onion. Add bay leaves and chillies to the jars. Cover with non-metal lids and store for at least a month before using.

Pickled Eggs

Another classic accompaniment to fish 'n' chips.

16 hardboiled eggs
Whole red chillies

Spiced vinegar:
1.2L (2pt) white wine vinegar
A few blades of mace
1 teaspoon cloves
25g (1oz) sugar

MAKING: Remove the shells from the eggs and place in a wide-necked jar with chillies to taste. Boil the vinegar, mace and cloves for about five minutes, add sugar and dissolve. Leave to cool and infuse for two hours. Strain and pour over the eggs. Cover with a non-metal lid and store for three weeks before use. Use within one to two months.

Spiced Damsons

There are overtones of mulled wine in this deep crimson preserve that enlivens both cold meats and roasts, particularly game.

600ml (1pt) full-bodied red wine
150g (5oz) sugar
2 X 10cm (4 inch) sticks cinnamon
1kg (2lb 4oz) ripe damsons

MAKING: Dissolve the sugar in the wine, add the cinnamon and bring to the boil for one minute. Add damsons and simmer for two to three minutes or until they are just soft. Pack into jars and pour over syrup.

CHAPTER TEN: HOGMANAY, HALLOWEEN AND CHRISTMAS

HOGMANAY CLASSICS

Hot Toddy/Het Pint

An hour or so before 'the chappin' o twal', the toddy-kettle is filled up with water. It simmers over the fire in the open hearth for several hours. Just before 'the bells' it must be livened up into a sustaining hot drink. At the turn of the nineteenth century, every Scot has their own idea about the best toddy recipe to see out the Old and bring in the New, but whisky is becoming a more popular choice.

The 'rascally Highland gill', as Burns calls it, is now being distilled, illicitly, in Lowland towns and cities. Soon, the whole country will be claiming it as their national drink. But for the moment, some like to mix it with hot water and sweeten it with a little sugar for a winter warming toddy. Some spice it up with a grated nutmeg, strengthen it with some ale and thicken it with eggs. Then they pour the mixture from one kettle to another to get a good frothy 'head' on it.

And when the brew is piping hot, the men set off for the city streets, carrying their bright copper toddy-kettles accompanied by a cup-bearer.

'Het pint!' they cry, as the streets fill up with Hogmanay revellers. And cups of the steaming beverage are poured out as everyone toasts: 'A gude New Year to ane an' a.'

Sir Walter Scott was a New Year hot pint enthusiast according to his son-in-law, J G Lockhart. 'He [Scott] would certainly have felt it very uncomfortable, not to welcome the New Year in the midst of family, and a few old friends, with the immemorial libation of a 'het' pint.'

For Scott and his generation, these revels at Hogmanay had developed as an alternative to Christmas. The anti-Catholic establishment, post-Reformation, had banned the Christ's mass on 25 December. And so, unlike the rest of Britain, the Scots moved their feasting to the 'hinner end o' Yule'. Though pagan in origin, Yule had the advantage of being untainted by the Church of Rome. The curious word 'Hogmanay' is thought to have come from a Franco-Scottish street cry, 'aguillaneuf', meaning a New Year's day gift, which was shouted by beggars and children as they went round knocking on doors for their goodies.

Get up guid wife and shake your feathers,
And dinna think that we are beggars,
For we are bairns come out to play
Get up and gie us our Hogmanay.

This generous giving was a remnant of the pre-Reformation 'Daft Days' which began with the Christ's mass of thanksgiving in church on 25 December and was followed by secular revels, satirical plays and community gatherings in the streets followed by feasting. It ended on 6 January with the great court festival of Epiphany, or Twelfth Night, when there was much pageantry and more drinking of many 'het' pints.

Atholl Brose

Water mixed with oatmeal was at one time as common a drink as whisky mixed with honey. It was a Duke of Atholl, however, during a Highland rebellion in 1475, who joined the two drinks and foiled his enemies when he filled the well they normally drank from with the ambrosial mixture. It so intoxicated them that they were easily taken and the legend of the special drink was born.

Black Bun

Dense and black with spices, dried fruit and treacle, it's so rich it must be held together in a pastry casing. That's today's version of Scotland's answer to Christmas Cake. Popular Hogmanay sustenance – with a dram of course – but quite a different bun to its original version.

First recipes are for large, enriched yeasted breads, or buns, made for all festive occasions. A recipe appears in the first Scottish cookery book, written by Mrs McLintock (Glasgow 1736), which is made with a rich bread dough, including butter, eggs, and a pint of brandy. It's mixed with a large amount of currants, lemon peel, orange peel, blanched almonds, cinnamon, nutmeg, cloves and caraway seed. So rich with fruit now that it cannot hold together on its own. Another piece of dough is rolled out thinly and wrapped round the whole bun for a 'cover'.

Another early sighting of a rich Scotch yeasted bun is in Lady Grisell Ballie's household books (1692-1733). There is no recipe as such, but she notes the quantities as 'five pounds of flour, one of butter, two of raisins, one of currants, four ounces of caraway seed, four ounces of sugar and yeast'.

And so it seems to have remained in this form throughout the remainder of the eighteenth century. Certainly until Mrs Fraser provides another similar version in her *Practice of Cookery and Pastry* (1791). Meanwhile, of course, a more extravagant festive cake, creamed with sugar, butter and eggs for a raising agent is becoming popular in England, but in Scotland it is still a rarity.

It is not until the growing fraternity of nineteenth-century Scottish bakers decide to make their own version of the old bun that it begins its transformation.

They discover an eager market for quality Scottish baking in the rest of Britain. Scotch Christmas bun – as it is now described – is particularly popular with the spice-loving English who regard it as an essential item of their Christmas festivities. It's their Christmas pudding in a crust, which they can go on eating throughout the 12 festive days.

'These buns,' says Meg Dods (1826) in *The Cook and Housewife's Manual*, 'weighing from four to eight, ten, twelve and sixteen or more pounds are still sent from Edinburgh... to many parts of the three kingdoms.'

Their subsequent history is unclear and many questions remain unanswered. Did an Edinburgh baker decide to outdo his rivals and make a denser and blacker bun without yeast? Who made the change from bread dough crust to pastry? And did the bun get its 'black' tag when Robert Louis Stevenson (1850-1894) described it as: 'a black substance inimical to life'?

HALLOWEEN CLASSICS

Dookin' for apples and catching treacly scones

Hold breath: face into water. Teeth grasping for a floating apple. No hands are allowed. Eventual success. Face dried. Then move on to the next game which also depends on good teethwork and no hands. But this time it's a scone, coated in treacle, hanging from the ceiling. Not as easy as the apple, it's a lot more messy as blobs of black treacle drip relentlessly onto upturned face.

Of course it's Halloween. And everyone is having a fun night of spooky merriment as summer fades into winter and old rites and customs of guising and symbolic sun-worshipping bonfires surface once again. They are a link back to the days before the first Christian missionaries arrived in 300AD and superstitious nature-lovers were converted to Christianity which superimposed many of its religious trappings on their old traditions. The name for the old Celtic New Year, 'Samhuinn' meaning summer's end was changed to All Hallows Eve (Halloween). The Norse Yule was changed into a mass for Christ's birthday. Yet despite the changes, the old rites of myth, magic, superstition and folklore carried on. Which is where the apple and the treacle scone, and everything else related to Halloween, comes from.

The apple was a talisman for the early pre-Christian Celts, admitting them to the Otherworld: a Land of Immortals which had the power to foretell the future. The two main Apple rites were the Ordeal by Water and the Ordeal by Fire. The act of going through water to obtain the apple-key to the Otherworld (as in dooking for apples) is thought to have originated with the Druids and is described in one of the Border Ballads when Thomas the Rhymer meets the Queen of the Faeries.

On they rode on, and further on,
And they waded thro' rivers abune the knee.
Syne they cam to a gairden green,
And she pu'd an aipple frae a tree;
Tak this for thy wage, True Thomas, she said,
It will gi'e thee tongue that ne'er can lee.

Another way to reach the Otherworld involved passing through fire to get to the apple. A small rod of wood was suspended horizontally from the ceiling by a cord, and an apple and a candle were balanced on either end. The 'ordeal', once the rod had been set spinning, was to get hold of the apple with your teeth without burning your hair. A habit subsequently abandoned as mothers – for safety's sake – decided to hang a scone dipped in black treacle instead.

Halloween Stapag (gathering of friends for eating or drinking)

This Highland tradition is described by M M Banks in *British Calendar Customs, Scotland Vol III* (1941): 'Good thick cream was put in a basin and well beaten up. While the cream was being stirred round and round, oatmeal was gradually added till the whole got as thick as porridge. Then all the members of the household gathered round, each armed with spoon and partook of the stapag. On Halloween, stapag was always made, and, as milk would be beginning to get scarce then a considerable amount of saving up used to be gone thro' in connection with the cream. Into this stapag a ring, a thimble and a button along with some silver coins used to be added. Each had to dip his or her spoon to the very bottom of the dish but no scraping was allowed. People did not always keep their Sunday manners about them on Halloween, and tho' only one spoon was supposed to be in the dish at one time, yet by some means a dozen or so might be seen scraping about.'

CHRISTMAS CLASSICS

Post-Reformation Scotland largely abandoned the Christ's mass and everything connected with the Roman church, though there were several areas that remained faithful to the Catholic church. It was not until the middle of the twentieth century that Christmas, both secular and sacred, was fully revived in Scotland. Until the 1960s, most people in the Highlands went to work on Christmas Day. Now Scotland has the best of both worlds with a two-week, mid-winter festive holiday stretching from Christmas through to Hogmanay.

Though roast goose was the popular pre-Reformation Christmas bird in Scotland, today Christmas eating traditions have been largely copied from the rest of Britain and mostly revolve round the festive turkey, a spicy pudding known as a Clootie Dumpling, mincemeat and Christmas cake.

HOGMANAY:

Hot Toddy/Het Pint

Entirely a matter of individual taste.

> Boiling water
> Whisky
> Honey or sugar
> 1 whisky tumbler

MAKING: Place a teaspoon in the tumbler and half fill it with boiling water. Leave for a few minutes to heat the glass. Pour out. Put sugar or honey into the glass and add about an inch of boiling water. Stir to dissolve sugar/honey. Add about the same amount of whisky. Sip immediately.

Atholl Brose

Some traditional recipes leave in the oatmeal, but this one – reputed to have come from the Duke of Atholl himself – uses only the strained liquid from steeping the oatmeal in water.

175g (6oz) medium oatmeal
400ml (14fl oz) water
4 tablespoons heather honey
800ml (1pt 7fl oz) malt whisky

MAKING: Put the oatmeal into a bowl and add the water. Leave for about an hour. Put into a fine sieve and press all the liquid through (use the remaining oatmeal for putting into bread/bannocks or making porridge see p92). Add honey to the sieved liquid and mix well. Pour into a large bottle and fill up with the whisky. Shake well before use.

USES: May be drunk as a liqueur which is the most usual form for festive celebrations such as Hogmanay, or may be mixed with stiffly whipped cream and served with shortbread as a sweet.

Trifle

Cook's Tip: This popular pudding comes after Steak and Kidney Pie (see p73) for New Year's day dinner and is usually made with a Victoria or egg sponge, but a festive Italian yeast cake (panettone) adds its special light texture and aromatic flavours.

Yield: 8–10

125g (4oz) ratafia biscuits or macaroons
250g (8oz) Victoria, egg-batter Cream Sponge (see p141), or panettone
4–5 tablespoons medium dry sherry or Madeira
3–4 tablespoons strawberry conserve, or raspberry jam,
    or rum preserved berries

Custard:
6 egg yolks
40g (1½ oz) caster sugar (1)
500ml (18fl oz) milk
75g (3oz) caster sugar (2)

Cream: 300ml (10fl oz) whipping cream, whipped

Finishing:
2 tablespoons toasted flaked almonds
And/or 6-8 small meringues

Glass bowl: 1.5L (3pt).

MAKING THE BASE: Crumble the biscuits into the base and cover with the sponge or panettone. Sprinkle with brandy or Madeira and leave to soak for a few hours or overnight. Cover with conserve, jam or Rum Preserved Berries (see p186) and spread evenly.

TO MAKE THE CUSTARD: Put the egg yolks into a bowl and beat with sugar (1) till the mixture forms a white ribbon. Put the milk and sugar (2) into a pan and bring to almost boiling point stirring all the time to dissolve the sugar. Pour onto the egg mixture, stirring well. Return to the pan and cook very gently over a low heat, stirring all the time, until the mixture thickens and coats the back of the spoon. Remove from the heat. When almost cool, pour over sponge base.

FINISHING: When custard is set, pour over cream and decorate with toasted flaked almonds or meringues.

Clootie Dumpling

Lighter and less rich than a Christmas pudding, this is made in a cloth (cloot) for first foots throughout the night. It's also fried up for a sustaining breakfast with bacon and eggs. For other festive occasions such as birthdays, it's made with 'surprises'. The traditional cloth method makes the 'skin': a vital part of the eating experience. Alternatively it can be made in a pudding bowl.

450g (1lb) plain flour
175g (6oz) fine white breadcrumbs
225g (8oz) beef suet from the butcher, or prepared beef, or vegetarian suet
1 teaspoon baking powder
2 teaspoon ground cinnamon
2 teaspoon ground ginger
2 teaspoon mixed spice
225g (8oz) sultanas
225g (8oz) California raisins
125g (4½ oz) currants
225g (8oz) soft brown sugar
225g (8oz) black treacle
2 eggs
2 large cooking apples, grated
2 large carrots, grated
1 orange or lemon, zest and juice

Dusting: plain flour

PREPARING CLOOT AND SURPRISES: Prepare cloth (cloot): 55cm (22 inch) square white cotton or linen. Fill a pan with boiling water and add the cloth. Boil the cloth for a few minutes. Lift out with tongs and spread out on work surface. While still hot, sprinkle evenly with a thick dusting of flour. Shake to disperse evenly over all the cloth, then shake off excess. Prepare 'surprises' or 'charms'. The most commonly used are: the coin, foretelling wealth; the button, bachelordom; the thimble, spinsterhood; the horseshoe, good luck. It's also common to use just a few silver coins. They are all wrapped in greaseproof paper before adding.

TO MAKE THE DUMPLING: Place a grid or upturned saucer in the base of a very large pot to prevent the dumpling sticking. Put all of the ingredients into a bowl and mix to a soft dropping consistency using more orange juice to mix if necessary. The mixture should be neither too soft (when it will crack on turning out) or too stiff (when it will be too heavy a texture). Add the 'surprises' and mix through. Pour into the centre of the cloth. Bring up the sides, making sure all the edges of the cloth are caught up. Tie with a string, leaving space for expansion. Hold up the tied ends and pat the dumpling into a good round shape. Lower into the pot of boiling water. The water should come about halfway up the dumpling. Tie the ends of the string to the pot handle (if there are two handles on either side of the pot, tie the two ends of string to either side so the pudding hangs in the middle) which will prevent the dumpling rolling over and water getting in at the top. This also helps to keep it a good round shape. Cover tightly with a lid and simmer gently for 4 hours, checking the water level regularly.

TO TURN OUT AND SERVE: Fill the sink, or a large basin, with cold water and lift out the dumpling, holding it by the string. Submerge in the water and leave for a minute. This releases the cloth from the dumpling skin. Move to a bowl about the same size as the dumpling. Cut the string, open out the cloth, hanging edges over the bowl edge. Invert a serving plate onto the dumpling and turn over. Remove the cloth carefully. It should come away cleanly. Put into a warm oven to dry off when the skin will turn a dark, shiny brown or leave for a day in a warm room (this is preferred by some who like a softer skin). Serve with a bowl of soft brown sugar and/or whipped cream or custard.

Black Bun

This is the traditional Scottish Hogmanay Bun, always accompanied by a 'dram' of whisky. It is very rich and 'black' and improves with keeping.

1kg (2lb 4oz) currants and raisins
1 tablespoon freshly ground cinnamon
1 tablespoon freshly ground ginger
2 grated nutmegs
$\frac{1}{2}$ teaspoon ground cloves
$\frac{1}{2}$ bottle brandy
125g (4oz) ground almonds
2 tablespoons black treacle
175g (6oz) blanched almonds
2 cooking apples, grated
150g (5$\frac{1}{2}$ oz) plain flour

Savoury shortcrust pastry:
200g (7oz) unsalted butter
400g (14oz) plain flour
150ml (5fl oz water)
Pinch of salt

SOAKING THE FRUIT: Put the currants and raisins in a pan with the spices and pour over the brandy. Mix well and place over a low heat. Heat gently till the aromas are released. Remove from the heat, cover and keep in a cool place overnight, or longer (up to a week), stirring occasionally.

Preheat the oven to 325°F/170°C/Gas 3.
Line 2 x 1.5L loaf tins or 1 x 23cm (9 inch) deep cake tin with baking parchment or silicone.

TO MAKE THE PASTRY: Put the butter into the mixer bowl (or blend in a food processor) and add half the flour. Beat on a slow speed until this has combined into a soft paste. Add the remaining flour, salt and water and mix at a slow speed till it becomes a smooth paste. Do not overmix. The mixture should be firm but pliable. Wrap in clingfilm and leave to rest in a cool place for at least an hour before use.

TO MAKE THE BUN: Add the ground almonds, treacle, blanched almonds, grated apple and flour to the steeped fruit and spices. Mix thoroughly. Divide pastry into a $^2/_3$ and $^1/_3$ piece. Using the $^2/_3$ piece roll out to about 8mm ($^3/_8$ inch) thick and use to line the tin(s). Overlap the top edges a little.

Leave this to rest in a cool place till the pastry hardens, about 30 minutes. Fill the tin(s) with bun mixture and smooth on top. Turn in the top edges of the pastry over the bun mixture and brush with water. Roll out lid(s) to fit the tins exactly, trimming edges to fit. Place on top. Press down to seal edges. Brush lightly with beaten egg. Prick all over with a skewer, through to the base of the tin. Leave to rest for 30 minutes.

BAKING: Bake for two to three hours, depending on size (the larger size will take three hours). Remove bun (buns) from their tins after two hours and continue baking, upside down, to ensure base is completely cooked. Cool completely. Wrap in clingfilm and foil and store for at least a week (or up to a year) – the longer the better. Serve in thin slices with whisky at New Year.

Halloween Cake with Charms

Fruit and nuts in this cake make their own earthy connections with birth and death as Halloween revellers celebrate the old Celtic New year.

250g (9oz) caster sugar
250g (9oz) fine self-raising cake flour
250g (9oz) butter, softened
4 medium eggs
3 tablespoons milk
700g (1lb 7oz) fresh ripe autumn fruits peeled and chopped
    into even-sized chunks (apples, pears, plums)
1 heaped tablespoon ground cinnamon
50g (2oz) hazelnuts or walnuts
50g (2oz) undyed glacé cherries

Topping:
2 egg yolks
50g (2oz) softened butter
2 dessertspoons honey

Preheat the oven to 350°F/180°C/Gas 4.
Line a 25cm (9 inch) round or square cake tin. Wrap charms: button, thimble, coins and horseshoe tightly in greaseproof paper.

MAKING: To aerate the flour and sugar, sift both into a bowl and beat with an electric beater for about a minute. Add the butter. Whisk the eggs and milk together and add three-quarters to the bowl. Beat for a minute to aerate and build up the structure of the cake. It should lighten in colour slightly. Add the remainder of the egg/milk and continue to beat for another minute.

ASSEMBLING CAKE: Put a layer of the mixture in the base of the cake tin. Put charms on top. Cover with the fruit. Sprinkle over the cinnamon. Cover with the remainder of the cake mixture. Spread evenly. Cover with nuts and cherries. Bake for about one and a half hours. Test with a skewer which should come out clean.

TO FINISH: About half an hour before the cake is ready, mix the butter, yolks and honey to a runny paste. Remove the cake from the oven and spread over evenly. Return to the oven to set the crust. Best served warm with cream or custard.

CHRISTMAS:

Christmas Pudding

Yield: 6–8

100g (3½ oz) breadcrumbs
100g (3½ oz) beef suet, finely chopped
or Atora brand, beef or vegetarian
150g (5½ oz) currants
150g (5½ oz) raisins
100g (3½ oz) soft brown sugar
50g (2oz) ground almonds
50g (2oz) mixed peel
50g (2oz) crystallised ginger, chopped finely
1 lemon, zest
1 orange, zest
100g (3½ oz) glacé cherries, chopped finely
3 large eggs, beaten
2 tablespoons whisky
125ml (4fl oz) stout

Size of pudding bowl: 850ml (1½ pt) with lid, well greased

MIXING AND STEAMING: Put all of the dry ingredients into a large mixing bowl and mix well. Whisk the eggs, whisky and stout together and pour on top of the dry ingredients. Mix well. The mixture should be a soft dropping consistency. Pour into the pudding bowl and smooth on top. Clip on the lid. Place in a pan of boiling water which should reach three quarters of the way up the side of the bowl. Steam gently for four to six hours. The longer it is steamed, the better the flavour. Serve immediately or leave to cool and reheat as required. Will keep for at least a year, well wrapped in greaseproof paper and foil, in a cool place. Serve with Brandy Butter.

Christmas Cake

800g (1lb 12oz) currants
375g (13oz) sultanas
375g (13oz) raisins
150ml (5fl oz) brandy or rum
8 large eggs
500g (1lb 2oz) unsalted butter, softened
500g (1lb 2oz) soft brown sugar
550g (1lb 4oz) plain flour
2 teaspoons cinnamon
2 teaspoons mixed spice
$^1/_2$ grated nutmeg
1 lemon, zest
1 orange, zest
2 tablespoons black treacle
2 tablespoons milk
150ml (4fl oz) rum or brandy for 'maturing' the cake

SOAKING FRUIT: Soak the currants and sultanas in the brandy or rum, cover and leave overnight or up to a week in a cool place, turning occasionally.

Preheat the oven to 350°F/180°C/Gas 4.
Line a 25cm (10 inch) round cake tin or 23cm (9 inch square), or for half quantity of mixture use 1 x 22cm (8½ inch) round cake tin. Tie a double band of brown paper round the outside of the tin to protect the cake during the lengthy baking.

HEATING THE EGGS: Put the eggs, still in their shells, into a bowl of very hot, but not boiling water, leave for two minutes to heat the eggs without cooking.

MIXING: Put the butter and sugar into a bowl and beat till white and fluffy. Add the eggs gradually, beating between each addition. Sift the flour and spices together. Stir in the flour gently. Add the dried fruit, orange and lemon zest and treacle which has been mixed through the milk and mix in by hand. Pour into the tin. Level the surface and bake for about three to four hours (22cm or 8½ inch tin will take two to two and a half hours). Cover top with double layer of foil, or several layers of greaseproof paper, if top surface is browning too much and turn down oven to 325F/170C/Gas 3. Test, after two hours, with a skewer when it should come out clean if it is ready. Leave in the tin to cool. Do not remove lining paper. When cool, make holes in the cake with a skewer and pour over rum or brandy. Wrap in clingfilm and foil and store till required.

Christmas Cake Marzipan and Icing

Marzipan for 1 large size cake:

500g (1lb 2oz) ground almonds
125g (4oz) caster sugar
125g (4oz) icing sugar
2 large eggs
2 teaspoons lemon juice
1 teaspoons dry sherry
Vanilla extract, few drops

Ready to roll fondant icing:

For large cake 1kg (2¼ lb)
For small cake 700g (1½ lb)

TO MAKE: Put the ground almonds, caster sugar and icing sugar into a mixing bowl and blend together. In a separate bowl, beat the eggs with the lemon juice, sherry and vanilla. Add to the almond mixture in three lots, beating on slow speed between additions (or mix by hand: make a well in the almond mixture and add the egg mixture. Knead in the liquid till the mixture comes together). Dust a working surface with icing sugar and knead till smooth. Cover and leave to rest before use.

For one small cake: use half quantity marzipan.

APRICOT GLAZE: 125g (4oz) apricot jam; 2 tablespoon water.
Place the jam and water in a pan and bring to the boil, stirring occasionally. Simmer for about a minute. Remove from the heat. Strain, cover and store.

TO FINISH CAKE: Brush apricot glaze liberally over the top and the sides of the cake. Roll out marzipan to fit and cover sides and top of cake. Roll out fondant icing to fit and cover sides and top of cake. Decorate as desired.

Mincemeat

This is easy to make – once you collect the ingredients. It also improves with age. So is worth waiting for a year-old vintage.

175g (6oz) beef or vegetarian suet, finely chopped
750g (1lb 10oz) raisins, sultanas, currants
125g (4oz) mixed peel
125g (4oz) soft brown sugar
125g (4oz) strawberry jam
1 teaspoon salt
1 tablespoon ground cinnamon
1 tablespoon ground allspice
1 tablespoon ground mace
1 grated nutmeg
$1/2$ teaspoon ground cloves
2 lemons, zest and juice
$1/2$ bottle Amontillado sherry
$1/4$ bottle brandy

TO MAKE: Combine all the ingredients in a large container (pot, bowl, earthenware crock, plastic container) which has a lid, or cover, and mix well. Cover well and leave in the container to mature for at least one month, preferably longer. Turn occasionally, and add more sherry and brandy as required. Pot and store. Use as required.

Mince Pies

200g (7oz) pre-prepared puff pastry
Mincemeat (see above)
1 beaten egg

Preheat the oven to 450°F/230°C/Gas 8. Grease baking tray.

TO MAKE: Roll out Puff Pastry to 5mm ($1/4$ inch) thick and cut into rounds. Rest in fridge.

FINISHING AND BAKING: Remove from the fridge and place a spoonful of mincemeat in the centre of half the rounds. Wet the edges, put the remaining puff pastry rounds on top and press down round the edges to seal. Brush with beaten egg. Put to rest for half and hour. Brush with egg again and bake for 15–20 minutes till golden brown on top. Dust with sugar and serve hot or cold.

Mincemeat Cake

A lighter alternative to a rich fruit cake, a Victoria sponge mixture forms the base of the cake which has a layer of mincemeat on top covered with a crunchy topping.

250g (9oz) self-raising cake flour
250g (9oz) caster sugar
250g (9oz) butter, softened
1 teaspoon vanilla extract
4 eggs, beaten with 3 tablespoons milk
500g (1lb) jar mincemeat (see p220)
1 tablespoon brandy

Crunchy Topping

50g (2oz) plain flour
75g (3oz) soft brown sugar
50g (2oz) butter
3 teaspoons ground cinnamon
125g (4oz) crunchy oat cereal

Preheat the oven to 350°F/180°C/Gas 4.
Grease or line cake tin, 23cm (9 inch) round cake tin, with removable base.

MIXING THE SPONGE CAKE: Sift the flour into a bowl and add the sugar. Beat with an electric beater for about 30 seconds. Add butter and about three quarters of the egg and milk mixture. Beat for about a minute till the mixture becomes light and creamy. Add the remainder of the egg mixture and vanilla and beat for another 30 seconds. Pour into prepared tin.

MINCEMEAT/CRUNCHY TOPPING: Remove the mincemeat from the jar, add brandy, then spoon on top of cake mixture, spreading evenly. Put the ingredients for the crunchy topping in a blender and pulse for a few minutes till they form fine crumbs. Sprinkle evenly over the mincemeat.

BAKING: Bake for 60 minutes or until a skewer inserted into the centre comes out clean. Cool in the tin for 10 minutes, then turn out onto a rack. Dust with icing sugar.

MEASURING

ALWAYS USE EITHER METRIC OR IMPERIAL
– DO NOT MIX THE TWO.

Weight:

15g (½ oz)
25g (1oz)
40g (1½ oz)
50g (2oz approx. or 1¾ oz exact)
75g (3oz approx. or 2¾ oz exact)
100g (4oz approx. or 3½ oz exact)
125g (4oz approx. or 4½ oz exact)
150g (5oz approx. or 5½ oz exact)
175g (6oz)
200g (7oz)
225g (8oz)
250g (8oz approx. or 9oz exact)
275g (9oz approx. or 9½ oz exact)
300g (10oz approx. or 10½ oz exact)
325g (11oz approx. or 11½ oz exact)
350g (12oz)
375g (13oz)
400g (14oz)
425g (15oz)
450g (16oz)
500g (16oz approx. or 1lb 2oz exact)
600g (1lb 5oz)
750g (1lb 10oz)
1kg (2lb approx. or 2lb 4oz exact)
2.25kg (5lb)

Volume:

15ml (½ fl oz)
25ml (1fl oz)
50ml (2fl oz)
75ml (3fl oz approx. or 2½ fl oz exact)
100ml (3fl oz approx. or 3½ fl oz exact)
125ml (4fl oz)
150ml (5fl oz, ¼ pt)
175ml (6fl oz)
200ml (7fl oz, ⅓ pt)
250ml (8fl oz approx. or 9fl oz exact)
300ml (10fl oz, ½ pt)
325ml (11fl oz)
350ml (12fl oz)
400ml (14fl oz)
425ml (15fl oz, ¾ pt)
450ml (16fl oz)
475ml (17fl oz)
500ml (20fl oz approx. or 18fl oz exact)
600ml (20fl oz, 1pt)
1L (2pt approx. or 1¾ pt exact)
1.2L (2pt)
2L (3½ pt)
3L (5¼ pt)

BIBLIOGRAPHY

Anderson, W. *The Poor of Edinburgh and Their Homes*, Menzies, 1867

Baillie, Lady Grisell, *The Household Book of Lady Grisell Baillie 1692-1733*, edited by R Scott-Moncrieff, 1911

British Deer Society (Scotland), *Venison Recipes*

Boyd, Lizzie (Ed.), *British Cookery*, Croom Helm, 1976

Brown, Catherine, *Scottish Regional Recipes*, Molendinar, 1981, Penguin 1983

Brown, Catherine, *Scottish Cookery*, Richard Drew, 1985, Mercat Press, revised 1999

Brown, Catherine, *Broths to Bannocks: a history of cooking in Scotland from 1690 to the present day*, John Murray, 1990

Brown, Catherine, *A Scottish Feast*, Argyll, 1995, co-author poet Hamish Whyte

Brown, Catherine, *A Year in a Scots Kitchen*, Neil Wilson Publishing, Glasgow, 1996, revised 2002

Brown, Catherine, *Traditional Foods of Britain*, Prospect Books, 1999, co-author Laura Mason

Brown, Catherine, *Arran Taste Trail*, Argyll and the Islands Enterprise, 2002

Brown, Catherine, *The Baker's Tale*, Neil Wilson Publishing, Glasgow, 2002

Brown, P. Hume (Ed.), *Early Travellers in Scotland*, Edinburgh, 1891

Burt, Edward, *Letters from the North of Scotland*, 5th ed., London, 1822

Clark, Lady of Tillypronie, *The Cookery Book of Lady Clark of Tillypronie*, edited by Catherine F Frere, London, 1909

Chambers, Robert, *Walks in Edinburgh*, Edinburgh, 1825

Chambers, Robert, *Traditions of Edinburgh*, 2nd ed., Edinburgh, 1868

Chambers, Robert, *Domestic Annals of Scotland*, Edinburgh, 1859

Chapman, R.W. (Ed.), *Johnson's Journey to the Western Islands of Scotland and Boswell's Journal of a Tour to the Hebrides with Samuel Johnson*, Oxford University Press, 1961

Cleland, Elizabeth, *The Practice of Cookery*, Edinburgh, 1759

Craig, Elizabeth, *The Scottish Cookery Book*, Deutsch, 1956

Cutting, Charles L, *Fish Saving*, Leonard Hill, 1955

Dalgairns, Mrs, *The Practice of Cookery*, Edinburgh, 1829

David, Elizabeth, *English Bread and Yeast Cookery*, Allen Lane, 1977

Davidson, Alan, *North Atlantic Seafood*, Macmillan, 1979

Dods, Mistress Margaret, *The Cook and Housewife's Manual*, Edinburgh, 1826

Drysdale, Julia, *The Game Cookery Book*, Collins, 1975

Eden, Ronald, *The Sporting Epicure*, Kyle Cathie, 1991

Edmonston, Elizabeth, *Sketches and Tales of Shetland*, Edinburgh, 1856

Faujas de Saint-Fond, B, *Travels in England, Scotland and the Hebrides etc.*, London, 1799

Fenton, Alexander, *Scottish Country Life*, John Donald, 1976

Fitzgibbon, Theodora, *A Taste of Scotland*, Dent, 1970

Foulis, Sir John, *Foulis of Ravelston's Account Book, 1671-1707*, Scottish History Society, 1894

Fraser, Margaret, *Highland Cookery Book*, 1930

Fraser, Mrs, *The Practice of Cookery and Pastry*, Edinburgh, 1791

Fulton, Willie, *The Hebridean Kitchen*, Buidheannfoillseachaidh nan Eilean an Iar, 1978

Fulton, Willie, *The Glasgow Cookery Book: Queens College Glasgow*, John Smith, Revised Edition, 1962

Fyfe, J G, *Scottish Diaries and Memoirs*, Volume I (1550-1746), Volume II (1746-1843), Maclean, 1928

Grant, Elizabeth, *Memoirs of a Highland Lady*, London, 1898

Grigson, Jane, *Good Things*, M. Joseph, 1971

Grigson, Jane, *Fish Cookery*, Penguin, 1975

Grigson, Jane, *Jane Grigson's Vegetable Book*, M. Joseph, 1978

Grigson, Jane, *Jane Grigson's Fruit Book*, M. Joseph, 1982

Heptinstall, William, *Gourmet Recipes from a Highland Hotel*, Faber, 1967

Hodgson, W C, *The Herring and its Fishery*, Routledge, 1957

Hope, Annette, *A Caledonian Feast*, Mainstream, 1987

Jamieson, John, *Etymological Dictionary of the Scottish Language*, new ed., 1879-82

Jamieson, J H, *The Edinburgh Street Traders and their Cries*, in *Book of the Old Edinburgh Club*, Volume II, Constable, 1909

Johnston, Mrs, *Receipts for all sorts of pastry, cream puddings etc.*, Edinburgh, 1740

Kinchin, P, *Tea and Taste: The Glasgow Tea Rooms 1875-1975*, White Cockade, 1991

King, A and Dunnet, F, *The Home Book of Scottish Cookery*, Faber, 1967

Kitchen, A H, *The Scotsman's Food*, Livingston, 1949

Lawrence, Sue, *Scots Cooking*, Headline, 2000

Lawrence, Sue, *Sue Lawrence's Scottish Kitchen*, Headline, 2002

Lochhead, Marion, *The Scots Household in the Eighteenth Century*, Moray Press, 1948

Lockhart, G W, *The Scot and His Oats*, Luath Press, 1983

Mabey, Richard, *Food For Free: A guide to the edible wild plants of Britain*, Collins, 1972

Mabey, David and Rose, *The Penguin Book of Jams, Pickles and Chutneys*, Penguin, 1975

MacClure, Victor, *Scotland's Inner Man*, Routledge, 1935

MacClure, Victor, *Good Appetite, My Companion*, Odhams Press, 1955

MacIver, Susanna, *Cookery and Pastry*, Edinburgh, 1773

Martin, Martin A, *Description of the Western Islands of Scotland, etc. 1703*, Stirling, 1934

Mathew, W M, *Keiller's of Dundee and the Rise of the Marmalade Industry*, Abertay History Society, 1998

McNeill, F Marian, *The Scots Kitchen, Its Traditions and Lore*, Blackie, 1929

McLintock, Mrs, *Receipts for Cookery, Glasgow, 1736*, Facsimile Aberdeen University Press, 1986, edited by Iseabail Macleod

Menhinick, Gladys, *Grampian Cookbook*, Aberdeen University Press, 1984

Mitchison, Rosalind, *Life of Scotland*, Batsford, 1978

Murray, Janet, *Wartime Cookery Book*, Fraser, 1944

Murray, Janet, *Janet Murray's Cookery Book*, London, 1950

Murray, Janet, *Traditional Recipes from Scotland*, BBC, 1964

Murray, Janet, *With a Fine Feeling for Food*, Impulse, 1972

Nelson, Janet M (Ed.), *A Mull Companion*, Mull, 1977

Nice, Jill, *Home-Made Preserves*, Collins, 1982

Ochtertyre, *The Ochtertyre House Book 1737 – 1739*, Scottish History Society, Ed. James Colville, 1907

Olney, Richard, *Simple French Food*, Penguin, 1983

Penant, Thomas, *Tour in Scotland*, 1771

Phillips, Roger, *Wild Food*, Pan, 1983

Plant, Marjorie, *The Domestic Life of Scotland in the Eighteenth Century*, Edinburgh University Press, 1952

Pococke, Richard, *Tours in Scotland, 1747, 1750, 1760*, Scottish History Society, 1887

Pollard, H B C, *The Sportsman's Cookery Book*, 1926

Reid, Nancy (Ed.), *Highland Housewives' Cook Book*, Highland Printers, 1971

Reid, Nancy (Ed.), *Scottish Women's Rural Institutes Traditional Scottish Recipes Cookery Book*, 6th Edition, 1946

Salaman, Redcliffe N, *The History and Social Influence of the Potato*, Cambridge University Press, 1970

Samuel, A M, *The Herring: Its Effect on the History of Britain*, Murray, 1918

Sibbald, Sir R, *What the Poor might eat; Provision for the Poor in time of Dearth and Scarcity*, Edinburgh, 1707

Simmons, Jenni, *A Shetland Cook Book*, Thuleprint, 1978

Sinclair, Sir John (Ed.), *The Statistical Account of Scotland*, Edinburgh, 1791-99

Sinclair, Sir John (Ed.), *General View of the Agriculture of the Northern Counties and Islands of Scotland*, Edinburgh, 1795

Southey, Robert, *Journal of a Tour in Scotland in 1819*, The Mercat Press, 1972

Steven, Maisie, *The Good Scots Diet*, Aberdeen University Press, 1985

Stout, Margaret B, *The Shetland Cookery Book*, Manson, 1968, first published in 1925 as *Cookery for Northern Wives*

Stuart, Marie W, *Old Edinburgh Taverns*, Hale, 1952

Tannahill, Reay, *Food in History*, Stein and Day, 1973

Victoria, Queen, *Leaves From a Journal of Our Life in the Highlands*, 1846-1861

Whyte, Hamish, *Lady Castehill's Receipt Book, A Selection of Eighteenth Century Scottish Fare*, Molendinar, 1976

Wilson, C Anne, *The Book of Marmalade*, Constable, 1987

Wilson, C Anne, *Food and Drink in Britain*, Constable, 1973

Wilson, John (Christopher North), *Noctes Ambrosianae 1822-1835*, Blackwoods Magazine

Wolfe, Eileen, *Recipes from the Orkney Islands*, Gordon Wright, 1978

Youngson, A J, *Beyond the Highland Line, Three Journals of Travel in Eighteenth Century Scotland*, Collins, 1974

INDEX